FEDERAL TAXATION OF INCOME, ESTATES AND GIFTS

SECOND EDITION

BORIS I. BITTKER

Sterling Professor of Law Emeritus, Yale University

LAWRENCE LOKKEN

Professor of Law, New York University

**Volume 5
Tables & Index**

WARREN, GORHAM & LAMONT
Boston • New York

How to Use the Tables and Index

This Tables and Index pamphlet contains master tables listing all references in the second edition of Volume 5 to sections of the Internal Revenue Code, regulations, rulings, other IRS releases, and judicial decisions. At the end of this pamphlet, a topical index lists all points covered in the second edition of Volume 5. Use of these reference aids will ensure your receiving the most up-to-date information on any particular point. This pamphlet may be discarded upon receipt of the Tables and Index Volume for the 1993 Cumulative Supplement No. 1 to *Federal Taxation of Income, Estates and Gifts,* wherein these references will be fully incorporated.

Table of Contents

Volume 5 Tables & Index

Tables

Table of Cases

[*References are to paragraphs (¶) and notes (n.).*]

A

Abely's Est. v. CIR 129.3.3 n.23
Abrams v. US 126.4.2 n.33
Abruzzino's Est. v. CIR 129.3.3 n.38
Acme Mills, Inc. v. CIR 135.1.2 n.24
Acord's Est. v. CIR 129.2.2 n.14
Adams v. CIR 131.3.2 n.12
Adam's Est. v. CIR 129.4.3 n.60
Adee v. US 129.5.2 n.6
Adriance v. Higgins 126.5.4 n.72
Aetna Ins. Co. v. US 137.7.3 n.25
Agnew's Est. v. CIR 131.3.2 n.12
Ahlstrom's Est. v. CIR 129.2.3 n.28
Ahmanson Found. v. US ... 129.2.3 n.33,
    135.2.3 n.25, 135.3.4 ns. 30, 31, 40,
    43, 50
Akers v. CIR 135.5.2 n.20
Albright's Est., CIR v. 126.8.2 n.16,
    126.8.5 ns. 76, 94
Aldrich's Est. v. CIR 135.1.2 n.54,
    135.7.3 n.48
Alexander v. US 121.3.2 n.18
Alexander's Est. v. CIR (4th Cir.)
    .... 129.4.3 & ns. 80, 82
Alexander's Est. v. CIR (TC 1983)
    .... 126.5.5 n.88, 126.6.3 ns. 55, 65
Alexander's Est. v. CIR (TC 1955)
    .... 135.4.10 n.113
All v. McCobb ... 126.8.2 n.38, 126.8.4 &
    n.68
Allen, CIR v. 122.2 n.8
Allen v. Henggeler 120.1.2 n.6, 125.9
    n.3
Allen, Shukert v. 126.3.7 n.71
Allen v. Trust Co. of Ga. 126.3.5 n.58
Allen v. US (2d Cir.) ..... 129.3.3 & n.33
Allen v. US (EDNY) 129.3.3 n.33

Allen, US v. .... 126.3.5 & ns. 62, 63,
    126.4.4 ns. 68, 69, 126.6.6 n.105
Allen's Est. v. CIR (TC) 126.8.2 n.19,
    129.2.3 n.18, 129.3.3 n.45
Allen's Est. v. CIR (TCM) ... 129.2.3 n.31
Alperstein's Est. v. CIR 128.3.2 n.7
Alston v. US 130.6 n.8
Alvary v. US .... 135.5.1 ns. 3, 17
Ambassador Apartments, Inc. v. CIR
    ..... 135.2.1 n.3, 135.2.3 ns. 25, 32, 35,
    135.2.4 n.45, 135.3.8 n.70
Amerada Hess Corp. v. CIR 135.1.2
    n.20, 135.3.3 n.21, 135.4.2 n.11
American Nat'l Bank v. US 129.5.2
    n.12
American Nat'l Bank & Trust Co. v.
    CIR 126.3.1 n.7, 127.7 n.1
American Nat'l Bank & Trust Co. v.
    US (7th Cir. 1987) 127.4.7 n.47
American Nat'l Bank & Trust Co. v.
    US (7th Cir. 1979) 135.1.2 n.43
American Nurseryman Publ. Co. v.
    CIR 125.2 n.2
Anderson v. CIR 135.5.2 n.21
Anderson, Untermyer v. 120.1.2 n.20
Anderson's Est. v. CIR ..... 121.4.5 & ns.
    44, 45
Andrews v. CIR (2d Cir.) 135.1.2 n.22
Andrews v. CIR (TCM) 135.4.3 n.30,
    135.5.2 & ns. 18, 26
Andrews' Est. v. CIR ... 135.3.2 ns. 8, 11,
    135.3.4 ns. 26, 35, 37, 135.4.3 n.28
Anglim, Rosenblum v. 134.2.3 n.44
Anselmo v. CIR 135.1.1 n.11, 135.1.2
    n.51
Anthony, Fidelity Union Trust Co. v.
    .... 137.4.1 n.11

[References are to paragraphs (¶) and notes (n.).]

Arbury's Est. v. CIR 121.3.4 n.37
Archbold v. CIR 121.3.2 n.15
Arents' Est., CIR v. 126.6.4 n.70,
                 126.6.6 n.102
Arnaud's Est. v. CIR 134.2.7 n.90
Aronauer v. US 132.4 n.17
Atkins' Est. v. CIR 131.4.1 n.9
Atlee v. CIR .... 135.4.6 ns. 72, 73
Audenried's Est. v. CIR 131.2 n.3,
                131.6.1 n.2
Awrey's Est. v. CIR 125.11.4 n.49
Awtry's Est. v. CIR 129.3.3 n.40

B

Babbitt's Est. v. CIR 124.3.1 n.11
Bach v. McGinnes 130.3.2 n.17
Bacon, Manly v. ..... 135.5.1 ns. 9, 11, 12
Bader v. US 135.3.2 n.12
Bagley's Est. v. US 128.3.2 n.7
Bahen's Est. v. US ...... 126.8.2 & ns. 20,
            33, 38, 126.8.3 n.61
Bahr's Est. v. CIR 131.3.2 n.36
Bailey v. Ratterre 126.3.2 n.28
Bailly's Est. v. CIR 131.3.2 n.37
Baker, US v. .... 124.4.1 ns. 5, 6
Baldwin's Est. v. CIR (TC) 131.3.2
                n.19
Baldwin's Est. v. CIR (TCM 1961)
                    135.1.1 n.18
Baldwin's Est. v. CIR (TCM 1959)
           131.3.2 n.25, 131.4.1 n.6
Ballard v. CIR 135.4.6 n.76
Ballard's Est. v. CIR 132.7.1 n.4,
                132.7.4 n.46
Baltimore Nat'l Bank v. US 135.3.10
               ns. 112, 113
B&B Auto Supply, Southern Rock,
  Inc. v. 137.6.2 n.9
Bank of Cal. v. US 135.4.10 n.112
Bank of New York v. US ..... 131.4.3 ns.
                38, 47
Bankers Trust Co. v. Higgins 126.5.1
                n.2
Bankers Trust Co. v. US
  (2d Cir. 1971) 137.9 n.7
Bankers Trust Co. v. US
  (2d Cir. 1960) 135.1.2 n.54, 135.4.6
                n.79
Bankers Trust Co. v. US (Ct. Cl.)
  .... 135.2.5 n.47, 135.3.3 n.18
Barlow's Est. v. CIR 126.6.2 n.36

Bar L Ranch, Inc. v. Phinney 135.4.6
                n.72
Barnette, Board of Education v.
  .... 126.4.4 n.59
Barret's Est., In re 137.8 n.12
Barrett v. CIR 135.4.8 n.90
Barrett's Est. v. CIR (TC 1971) .. 123.6.1
           n.19, 131.4.3 n.71
Barrett's Est. v. CIR (TC 1954) .. 129.2.3
                n.32
Barritt v. Tomlinson 128.2.2 n.32
Barr's Est. v. CIR 125.6 n.7, 126.8.2
                n.20
Bartlett v. CIR 129.3.3 n.39
Bartlett's Est. v. CIR 127.4.2 n.10,
             127.4.7 n.47
Bartman's Est. v. CIR 121.3.2 n.10,
             121.4.2 n.19
Bartram v. US ... 131.2 n.10, 135.7.2 n.22
Bary's Est. v. CIR 125.7 n.9
BASF Wyandotte Corp. v. CIR ... 135.2.4
                n.45
Bath's Est. v. CIR 131.6.1 n.12
Batterton v. US 129.3.3 n.38
Bauersfeld's Est. v. CIR 129.6.4 n.20
Baumer v. US .... 135.4.7 & ns. 81, 84
Baur v. CIR ... 137.4.1 n.11, 137.6.3 n.25,
             137.7.2 n.4
Bayliss v. US 126.6.6 n.100
Beachy's Est. v. CIR 126.5.1 n.23
Beal's Est. v. CIR ..... 126.8.2 ns. 13, 20
Beaty v. US 137.6.2 n.8
Beauregard's Est. v. CIR 127.4.2 n.9,
     127.4.3 ns. 18, 22, 127.4.7 n.46
Beavers v. CIR 125.10 n.5
Becklenberg's Est. v. CIR ... 126.6.2 n.48
Beck's Est., CIR v. 121.4.1 n.3
Beckwith's Est. v. CIR 126.6.5 n.82
Bedford v. CIR 121.2 n.5
Begg's Est. v. CIR 126.3.2 n.24
Belcher's Est. v. CIR 125.2 n.4
Bell's Est. v. CIR (9th Cir.) 137.5.3
                n.45
Bell's Est. v. CIR (TC 1989) 137.5.1
                n.6
Bell's Est. v. CIR (TC 1976) 126.5.3
                n.65
Belzer's Est. v. CIR 131.4.1 n.9
Bender's Est. v. CIR 125.7 n.11
Bendet's Est. v. CIR 125.11.4 n.54
Benjamin's Est. v. CIR 129.4.3 n.55
Bensel, CIR v. 135.3.10 n.116

TABLE OF CASES

[References are to paragraphs (¶) and notes (n.).]

Benton v. CIR 124.4.1 n.7
Berg v. US 128.2.2 n.32
Bergan's Est. v. CIR 125.5 n.8
Berger, CIR v. 122.3.6 n.29
Berger v. US 122.3.1 n.9
Bergh v. Warner 121.4.3 n.31
Berg's Est. v. US 137.4.2 n.25
Berkman's Est. v. CIR 131.2 n.2
Berkowitz v. CIR 125.11.4 n.47
Berzon v. CIR 124.3.2 n.36, 135.3.10
n.112
Bettin's Est. v. CIR 122.2 n.3, 122.3.2
n.15
Beveridge v. CIR .... 121.4.5 & n.50
Bickford-Smith v. US 134.2.3 n.56
Bingham's Est. v. CIR 126.5.1 n.24
Binney v. Long 120.1.2 n.20
Bintliff v. US 127.3 n.3
Bischoff's Est. v. CIR ..... 126.3.1 ns. 14,
15, 135.3.4 n.50, 135.3.10 n.117
Bishop v. US 121.7.4 n.38, 125.11.2
n.21
Bixby v. CIR 126.6.2 n.47
Black v. CIR 125.11.2 n.27
Blackburn v. CIR 135.4.6 n.75
Blackburn v. US 131.2 n.13
Blackford's Est. v. CIR 130.5.5 n.42
Blaine's Est. v. CIR 121.9 n.7
Bland, Free v. 125.11.2 n.19
Bland v. US 129.4.2 n.19
Blasdel v. CIR 124.3.1 n.7, 124.3.2
n.23, 124.3.3 n.39
Blass' Est. v. CIR 121.3.6 n.49
Bloch's Est. v. CIR .... 127.4.6 ns. 38, 44
Blodgett v. Holden 120.1.2 n.20
Blodgett v. Silberman 134.2.3 n.30
Bloise's Est. v. CIR .... 125.2 ns. 3, 7
Blumenthal, Pingree's Est. v. 137.4.2
ns. 18, 25
Blumenthal, Watson's Est. v. 137.4.2
n.25
Blunt v. Kelly ... 126.5.1 n.2, 126.5.3 n.53
Board of Education v. Barnette .. 126.4.4
n.59
Boardman's Est. v. CIR 126.6.4 n.72
Boatmen's First Nat'l Bank v. US
.... 132.3 n.5
Bob Jones Univ. v. US 130.2 n.5
Boeshore's Est. v. CIR 130.5.3 n.32
Boeving v. US 128.3.2 n.7
Bogley's Est. v. US 125.6 n.7
Bolles v. CIR 135.3.7 n.66

Bolton v. CIR 122.3.6 n.29
Bomash's Est. v. CIR 125.10 n.9
Booher v. US 130.4 n.10
Borax v. CIR .... 129.2.2 & n.9
Borg Warner Corp. v. CIR 135.4.3
n.30, 135.4.5 n.64
Borland's Est. v. CIR 125.4 n.4, 131.5
n.8
Borough Operating Corp. v. CIR
.... 135.5.1 n.14
Bosch's Est., CIR v. ... 125.2 n.6, 129.2.3
& n.34, 129.4.3 n.30
Boston Safe Deposit & Trust Co. v.
CIR 129.5.2 n.6
Bouchard v. CIR 123.4 n.1
Bowers, Bowring v. ...... 134.2.1 ns. 5, 7
Bowers, Corliss v. .... 122.3.1 & n.3
Bowers, Sanchez v. 134.2.3 n.54
Bowers, Schuette v. 125.9 n.2
Bowers, Wilson v. 135.3.10 n.107
Bowers' Est. v. CIR 127.4.2 n.16,
127.4.7 n.46
Bowling's Est. v. CIR .... 129.4.5 ns. 121,
123
Bowring v. Bowers .... 134.2.1 ns. 5, 7
Boyce's Est. v. CIR 131.4.3 n.44
Boyd's Est. v. CIR ... 129.2.3 n.39, 129.5.2
n.6
Bradford v. CIR 121.3.2 n.11, 121.4.1
n.4
Bradley's Est. v. CIR 135.7.6 n.68
Brandon's Est. v. CIR ..... 129.2.3 ns. 33,
35
Brannen v. CIR 135.1.2 n.33, 135.4.8
n.88
Breidert v. CIR 131.3.2 n.10
Bremer v. Luff 125.11.4 n.66
Briar Homes Corp. v. US 135.2.1 n.3
Briggs v. CIR .... 124.4.1 ns. 4, 5
Bright's Est. v. US ... 135.3.3 n.23, 135.3.4
& ns. 35, 36, 39, 44
Bristol, CIR v. .... 121.4.2 & n.16
Britenstool's Est. v. CIR 130.6 n.8
Brockman v. CIR 135.6.2 n.21
Brock's Est. v. CIR 130.5.5 n.43
Brodrick v. Moore 129.2.3 n.27
Bromley v. McCaughn 120.1.2 n.13
Bronson, CIR v. 131.3.2 n.5, 131.6.1
n.3
Brooks, Burnet v. 134.2.3 n.24
Brooks v. Willcuts 135.1.2 n.24
Brooks' Est. v. CIR 126.8.5 n.89

T-3

[References are to paragraphs (¶) and notes (n.).]

Brown v. Routzahn .... 121.7.1 & n.3
Brown's Est. v. CIR 135.3.4 n.50
Bruning's Est. v. CIR 129.6.4 n.21
Brush's Est. v. CIR 135.3.3 n.16,
                   135.3.4 n.44
Bryan's Est. v. CIR 131.8 n.3
Bryant v. CIR 135.1.2 n.45
Buchanan v. US 130.6 n.3
Buchholtz's Est. v. CIR (TC) 137.4.2
                   n.21
Buchholtz's Est. v. CIR (TCM) ... 122.3.2
                n.14, 125.11.1 n.8
Bucholz v. CIR 122.2 n.12
Buckley v. CIR 125.11.2 n.20
Buckwalter's Est. v. CIR 125.5 n.12
Budd's Est. v. CIR 126.5.3 n.62,
                 126.6.4 n.71
Buddy Schoellkopf Prods. v. CIR
    .... 135.4.5 n.64
Buder's Est. v. CIR 124.2 n.5
Budlong's Est. v. CIR ..... 126.5.2 ns. 52,
                 53, 57
Buffalo Tool & Die Mfg. v. CIR
    .... 135.5.2 n.27
Bull v. Smith 135.3.3 n.18
Bull v. US .... 125.8 & ns. 8, 9
Bullard, Helvering v. 126.6.8 n.120
Bullock's Est. v. CIR 125.11.4 n.51,
                 131.3.2 n.17
Bunn's Est. v. US 121.7.1 n.8
Burdick v. CIR 130.2 n.16
Burdick's Est. v. CIR 130.5.6 n.47
Burghardt's Est. v. CIR .... 134.2.7 & ns.
                 88, 90
Burnet v. Brooks 134.2.3 n.24
Burnet v. Guggenheim 121.3.3 n.25,
   122.2 n.7, 122.3.1 & ns. 1, 2, 122.4.1
    & n.2, 122.5 & n.7, 124.3.3 n.43
Burnet v. Logan .... 125.7 & ns. 4, 5,
   135.1.1 & ns. 16, 18, 135.4.7 n.84
Burnet v. Northern Trust Co. (US)
    .... 126.6.8 n.119
Burnet v. Northern Trust Co.
   (7th Cir.) 125.5 n.5
Burnett v. US 129.4.3 n.62
Burns v. CIR 126.4.4 n.66
Burns v. US 132.5 n.13
Burrow Trust v. CIR 131.3.2 n.14,
     131.3.3 & ns. 49, 51, 55, 56
Bush's Est. v. US .... 130.6 ns. 2, 5, 131.7
                 n.5
Bushman v. US 125.11.4 n.49

Butler's Est. v. CIR 130.3.1 n.7
Butscher's Est. v. CIR 135.2.3 n.31
Byram's Est. v. CIR 125.9 n.10
Byran v. CIR 121.4.5 n.44
Byrum, US v. ... 126.3.3 & ns. 36, 37, 40,
   41, 126.5.2 n.49, 126.5.5 & n.90,
     126.6.5 & ns. 82, 83, 86

C

Cadden v. Welch 131.3.2 n.17
Cain v. CIR 126.6.2 n.50
Calcagno's Est. v. CIR 131.2 n.2
Calder v. CIR .... 124.3.2 ns. 15, 36,
                 135.3.3 n.23
Callaghan's Est. v. CIR 130.3.1 n.5
Callahan's Est. v. CIR 137.7.3 n.17
Camp v. CIR .... 122.3.1 n.7, 122.5 & ns.
                 4, 6
Campanari's Est. v. CIR 135.3.4 n.51
Campbell, Grossman v. .... 126.3.2 ns. 28,
                 29
Campbell v. US (657 F2d 1174
   (Ct. Cl. 1981)) 137.4.2 n.25
Campbell v. US (661 F2d 209
   (Ct. Cl. 1981)) 135.1.2 n.43, 135.3.2
                 n.12
Canfield's Est. v. CIR 122.4.1 n.8
Canfield's Est., CIR v. 126.6.8 n.129
Cardeza's Est. v. CIR 131.2 n.12
Cardeza's Est., CIR v. 125.7 n.6
Cardeza's Est. v. US 126.7.4 n.45,
              135.4.10 n.115
Carey's Est. v. CIR 130.3.2 n.13
Carli's Est. v. CIR 131.4.3 n.64
Carlstrom's Est. v. CIR 127.4.7 n.47,
                 127.4.8 n.59
Carpenter v. US 121.3.3 n.24
Carpenter's Est. v. US 126.5.3 n.68
Carpousis' Est. v. CIR 125.11.4 n.48,
                 135.7.6 n.68
Carson v. CIR 121.9 n.4
Carson's Est. v. CIR ... 131.3.2 ns. 41, 46
Carter v. US .... 131.2 & n.7
Carter's Est. v. US ..... 132.6.3 ns. 24, 25,
              135.4.10 n.112
Cartwright, US v. 135.1.2 n.22, 135.4.2
               ns. 19, 20
Cary's Est. v. CIR 135.4.1 n.5
Casey's Est. v. CIR 126.5.1 n.7
Cassidy Co. v. CIR 135.1.2 n.27
Catalano v. US 131.6.2 n.31

TABLE OF CASES

[References are to paragraphs (¶) and notes (n.).]

Cathcart v. Schwaner 131.4.3 n.61
Centerre Trust Co. v. US 126.3.2 n.27
Central Trust Co. v. US (6th Cir.)
.... 126.5.2 n.46
Central Trust Co. v. US (Ct. Cl.)
..... 135.2.3 ns. 25, 27, 28, 135.3.2 n.10
Central Trust Co. v. Welch ... 131.3.3 n.60
Ceppi's Est. v. CIR 126.4.2 n.34
Cerf v. CIR 121.3.5 n.42, 122.5 n.3,
126.3.2 n.20
Cervi v. US 122.2 n.1
C.G. Meaker Co. v. CIR 135.1.2 n.39
Chambers v. CIR 122.4.1 n.17
Champion v. CIR 135.3.3 n.13
Chandler, US v. 122.2 n.12, 125.11.2
n.19
Chanin v. US 124.2 n.4, 124.3.1 n.8
Chapman's Est. v. CIR 132.5 n.13
Chase Manhattan Bank, CIR v. .. 122.3.6
n.32, 127.5 ns. 3, 6
Chase Nat'l Bank v. CIR 121.4.5 n.49
Chase Nat'l Bank v. US 126.5.1 n.1
Chenoweth's Est. v. CIR 135.3.4 n.43
Chertkof v. CIR .... 135.5.1 ns. 11, 14
Chesterton's Est. v. US .... 131.4.2 ns. 31,
32
Cheveron, U.S.A., Inc. v. US 137.6.2
n.9
Chew's Est. v. CIR 127.2 n.3
Chicago Stock Yards Co. v. CIR
.... 126.4.4 n.61
Child v. US 130.2 n.10
Childs' Est., CIR v. 125.5 n.7
Chiles v. US 129.5.2 n.14
Chotin's Est. v. US 126.4.4 n.49
Christiernin v. Manning 126.8.3 n.56
Christie's Est. v. CIR .. 135.3.3 ns. 14, 16
Christmas's Est. v. CIR .... 129.6.4 ns. 19,
20
Christ's Est. v. CIR 126.3.4 n.51,
135.4.10 ns. 100, 101, 108
Chrysler's Est. v. CIR 125.2 n.2,
125.11.2 n.20, 126.6.4 n.73
Churchill v. US 130.4 n.4
Church's Est., CIR v. .... 126.1 & n.8,
126.2 n.5, 126.6.8 & ns. 126, 127,
126.7.2 n.18, 126.7.4 n.33
Citizens & S. Nat'l Bank, King v.
.... 129.7.2 n.18
Citizens & S. Nat'l Bank v. US ... 129.2.3
ns. 28, 29

Citizens Bank & Trust Co. v. CIR
.... 135.3.4 n.39
City Bank Farmers Trust Co. v. CIR
.... 125.11.4 n.42
City Bank Farmers Trust Co.,
Helvering v. ... 126.5.5 & n.81, 126.6.3
n.62, 127.4.5 n.33
City Bank Farmers Trust Co. v. Hoey
.... 121.3.2 n.18, 122.2 n.6
City Bank Farmers Trust Co. v.
McGowan 122.2 n.6
City Bank Farmers Trust Co. v.
Schnader 134.2.3 n.34
City Nat'l Bank v. US 125.2 n.5
Claflin v. CIR 135.3.7 n.60
Clapp's Est. v. CIR 135.3.4 n.51
Clark v. CIR (TC 1975) 123.5.3 n.24
Clark v. CIR (TC 1943) 131.3.3 n.49
Clark v. US (D. Colo.) 125.2 n.5
Clark v. US (EDNC) 135.2.3 n.37
Clauson, National Bank of
Commerce v. 126.3.2 n.28
Clauson v. Vaughan 128.1 n.19
Clay's Est. v. CIR .... 127.8 ns. 10, 14
Clayton v. CIR 135.4.6 n.73
Clayton's Est. v. CIR .... 129.4.5 & ns.
124, 125
Cleavenger, US v. 137.6.2 n.9
Clement v. Smith 122.5 n.9
Clifford, Helvering v. .... 121.3.5 & n.40,
125.3 & ns. 2, 3, 8
Clinard v. CIR 124.4.2 n.25
Clinard's Est. v. CIR 135.6.3 n.38
Cline's Est. v. CIR 129.3.3 n.34,
129.4.3 n.29
Clinton Cotton Mills v. CIR 135.2.4
n.43
Clise, CIR v. 126.8.1 n.7
Cloud's Est. v. US 129.2.3 n.19
Cockrill v. O'Hara 127.4.7 n.47
Cohan v. CIR 126.8.3 n.57
Cohen's Est. v. CIR 126.6.5 n.82
Colley's Est. v. CIR 131.4.1 n.4
Collins v. CIR 121.3.5 n.38
Collins v. US .... 135.6.6 ns. 86, 88
Collins, US v. 131.2 n.15
Colonial-Am. Nat'l Bank v. US ... 126.6.2
n.24
Colonial Fabrics, Inc. v. CIR ... 135.5.2 &
n.22
Colwell v. US .. 129.5.2 n.13, 129.7.1 n.12

[References are to paragraphs (¶) and notes (n.).]

Commerce Union Bank v. US 126.8.5 n.89

Commercial Nat'l Bank v. US 131.6.1 n.7

Commonwealth Trust Co. v. Driscoll 132.4 n.17

Computing & Software, Inc. v. CIR 135.4.5 n.66

Concord Control, Inc. v. CIR 135.2.3 n.36, 135.4.5 n.67

Condon Nat'l Bank v. US .... 128.2.1 ns. 12, 18

Connecticut Bank & Trust Co. v. US .... 125.6 & ns. 2, 3, 128.2.1 n.23

Connelly's Est. v. US 127.4.2 n.15

Conrad v. CIR 135.3.8 n.75

Continental Illinois Nat'l Bank & Trust Co. v. US (7th Cir.) ... 132.6.3 & n.21

Continental Ill. Nat'l Bank & Trust Co. v. US (Ct. Cl.) .... 130.2 ns. 1, 17, 19

Cook's Est. v. CIR 128.2.1 n.20

Coolidge, Nichols v. ...... 120.1.2 & n.19

Coon's Est. v. CIR 135.6.5 n.52

Cooper's Est. v. CIR .... 126.6.2 & ns. 41, 43

Copley's Est., CIR v. 121.3.2 n.15

Corliss v. Bowers .... 122.3.1 & n.3

Corwin, Dimock v. ... 125.6 n.10, 125.11.4 n.54

Costin v. Cripe 126.7.3 n.28

Cotchett's Est. v. CIR 135.3.8 n.71, 135.3.10 n.106, 135.5.2 n.27

Council v. US 126.3.4 n.45

Courtney's Est. v. CIR 131.4.1 n.8

Couzens v. CIR 135.1.2 n.36

Cowles v. US 127.3 n.3

Cowser's Est. v. CIR 135.6.2 n.14

Cox v. US 129.3.3 n.27

Coyle, Lake Shore Nat'l Bank v. .... 129.3.3 ns. 14, 48

Craft's Est. v. CIR ... 126.5.1 n.26, 131.3.2 n.8

Crafts' Est. v. CIR 130.5.7 n.62

Craig, Randolph v. .... 125.9 ns. 2, 12

Crail's Est. v. CIR 122.2 n.12, 125.7 n.16

Cripe, Costin v. 126.7.3 n.28

Cristofani's Est. v. CIR .... 124.3.3 ns. 46–48

Critchfield's Est. v. CIR 129.2.3 n.19

Crocker Nat'l Bank v. US ... 135.4.8 n.89

Crown v. CIR 121.3.4 n.30

Cruikshank's Est. v. CIR 135.3.8 n.72

Crummey v. CIR ... 124.3.3 & ns. 39, 41, 42, 50, 124.4.2 & n.21, 128.3.4 n.19

Cuddihy's Est. v. CIR 126.6.6 n.104

Cullers v. CIR 135.5.2 n.17

Cupler v. CIR 135.2.2 n.18, 135.4.5 n.49

Curie's Est. v. CIR 126.6.8 n.128

Curry's Est. v. CIR .... 125.7 & ns. 5, 15, 16

Curry's Est. v. US ..... 135.3.4 ns. 31, 40, 50, 135.3.10 ns. 109, 120

Cury, US v. 137.4.3 n.32

Cutcheon's Est. v. CIR 126.5.1 n.15, 126.5.6 n.94

Cutter's Est. v. CIR 126.6.4 n.76

D

Dallman, Second Nat'l Bank v. ... 128.2.1 n.9, 128.4 n.8

Daly v. US 127.5 n.6

Damon's Est. v. CIR 132.4 n.17

Dancy's Est. v. CIR .... 121.7.4 n.38, 125.12 ns. 2, 3

Daniels v. CIR .... 124.4.1 ns. 2, 8

Darlington's Est. v. CIR 131.7 n.7

Daubert v. US 127.5 n.7

Dauer's Est. v. CIR 131.4.3 n.45

David v. CIR 135.5.1 n.12

Davis v. CIR 124.4.2 n.11

Davis, CIR v. 131.3.3 n.49, 131.5 n.12

Davis v. US 122.2 n.1

Davis, US v. .... 123.6.1 ns. 2, 13, 135.2.5 n.47

Davis, YMCA v. 125.6, 137.8 n.7

Davis' Est. v. CIR (TC 1986) .... 129.4.3 ns. 36, 53, 135.6.3 n.37

Davis' Est. v. CIR (TC 1972) .... 131.4.3 & ns. 52, 81, 83, 131.5 n.10, 132.3 n.11

Dawson's Est. v. CIR 127.4.3 n.24

Dean, US v. .... 130.4 & ns. 2, 6

DeBie's Est. v. CIR 135.1.2 n.24, 135.5.1 n.6

Dees v. CIR 135.1.2 n.30

De Foucaucourt's Est. v. CIR 131.3.2 n.15

Degroft, US v. 137.7.1 n.2

DeGuebriant v. CIR 135.3.7 n.60

TABLE OF CASES

[References are to paragraphs (¶) and notes (n.).]

Delaney v. Gardner 130.2 n.15
Delaney v. Murchie ..... 134.2.3 & ns. 31, 32
DeLappe v. CIR 127.5 n.6
Delbridge v. US 130.2 n.15
Del Drago, Riggs v. ..... 137.8 & ns. 4, 8
Dempsey v. First Nat'l Bank 125.11.2 n.20
Denzer's Est. v. CIR 126.3.2 n.22
de Perigny's Est. v. CIR 134.2.3 n.28
Detroit Bank v. US ... 137.6.1 n.2, 137.6.2 n.17
Detroit Bank & Trust Co. v. IRS
.... 130.3.3 n.22
Detroit Bank & Trust Co. v. US 127.8 n.9
De Vos' Est. v. CIR 131.4.3 n.67
DeWitt, Marcus v. 131.3.2 n.45
Dewitt's Est. v. CIR 131.6.1 n.14
Dickinson's Est. v. CIR 135.3.10 n.121
Dickman v. CIR .... 121.3.4 & ns. 30, 32–35
Diedrich v. CIR 132.5 n.8
Dillingham's Est. v. CIR 121.3.2 n.11
DiMarco's Est. v. CIR 121.2 n.8
Dimen's Est. v. CIR 127.4.8 n.58
Dime Trust & Safe Deposit Co.,
  Phillips v. 125.11.1 n.4
Dimock v. Corwin ... 125.6 n.10, 125.11.4 n.54
Dinell's Est. v. CIR 126.4.4 n.54
Disston, CIR v. .. 124.3.2 & n.24, 131.2.2 n.9
Dixon's Est. v. CIR 129.5.1 n.1
Doctors' Bldg. Hosp. v. US 135.2.5 n.47
Dodd v. US 129.5.2 n.8, 137.8 n.11
Dodge v. Gagne 131.4.3 n.54
Doelle's Est. v. US 135.3.9 n.82, 135.5.1 n.9
Doerr v. US 121.1 n.19, 121.2 n.3
Doetsch v. Doetsch 137.8 n.10
Doetsch, Doetsch v. 137.8 n.10
Doherty's Est. v. CIR ..... 135.6.6 ns. 79, 88
Donnan, Heiner v. .... 120.1.2 n.6, 126.4.2 n.12, 126.4.4 & n.60
Dooley v. US 126.8.5 n.79
Doriss v. CIR 137.3 n.16
Dorn v. US 135.3.10 n.114
Downer v. CIR 135.1.2 n.30
Downe's Est. v. CIR 135.7.6 n.67

Downs' Est. v. US 128.1 n.23
Doyle v. US 128.3.2 n.7
Drake's Est. v. CIR .... 128.4 ns. 3, 17
Draper's Est. v. CIR 125.5 n.2, 127.3 n.4
Drazen v. CIR 125.11.4 n.45
Drescher, US v. .... 135.1.2 ns. 52, 54, 135.4.9 n.94
Dresser Indus., US v. ..... 135.2.3 & n.22
Dreyer's Est. v. CIR 125.12 n.2
Driscoll, Commonwealth Trust Co. v.
.... 132.4 n.17
Drummond's Est. v. Paschal 125.11.4 n.68
Drybrough v. US 121.1 n.20, 135.3.4 n.51
Du Charme's Est. v. CIR ... 126.5.5 n.83, 128.2.3 n.35
Dudley, Eggleston v. ..... 129.4.2 & n.21, 129.4.4 n.101
Duffield v. US 125.7 n.15
Duggan, W.T. Grant Co. v. ... 135.1.2 n.35
Dulles v. Johnson 130.2 n.1, 131.3.2 n.25
Dumont's Est. v. CIR ..... 130.3.2 & n.11
Duncan v. US 125.10 n.10
Duncan Indus. v. CIR ...... 135.1.2 n.24, 135.2.3 n.38, 135.4.3 ns. 28, 31
Dunn v. US 129.4.2 n.17
Du Pont v. CIR 121.1 n.15, 121.4.3 n.35, 123.6.2 n.28, 135.3.3 n.20
Du Pont, In re 122.2 n.5, 126.4.3 n.38
Du Pont v. US 121.9 n.7
Du Pont's Est. v. CIR 126.6.2 n.36, 127.7 n.3
Dutcher's Est. v. CIR 131.3.2 n.25
Dwight's Est., CIR v. ..... 126.6.2 ns. 21, 22, 30

E

Eager v. US 130.5.2 n.18
Earle's Est. v. CIR 131.4.3 n.81
Eastern Serv. Corp. v. CIR 135.3.7 n.69
Eccles v. CIR 129.2.2 n.5
Edelman's Est. v. CIR 128.2.1 n.13
Edens' Est. v. CIR 125.2 n.5
Edmond's Est. v. CIR 126.5.1 n.26, 132.6.3 n.20
Edmonds' Est. v. CIR (TC 1979)
.... 129.3.3 & ns. 31, 32

[*References are to paragraphs (¶) and notes (n.).*]

Edmonds' Est. v. CIR (TC 1951) ... 127.2 n.7

Edwards v. CIR 124.3.2 n.16

Edwards, CIR v. 135.4.9 n.93

Edwards v. Slocum .... 130.6 & n.2

Eggleston v. Dudley ..... 129.4.2 & n.21, 129.4.4 n.101

Ehret's Est. v. CIR 125.11.4 n.50

Ehrman v. CIR ... 122.2 n.14, 124.4.1 n.2

Eichheim v. US 137.5.4 n.50

Eichstedt v. US 126.5.1 n.6, 126.6.2 n.29, 126.8.2 n.29

Eisner, New York Trust Co. v. .... 120.1.2 & ns. 10, 12, 14, 125.5 ns. 1, 3

Ekins' Est. v. CIR ... 120.1.2 n.23, 126.4.2 n.12

Elkins' Est. v. US 131.4.1 n.6

Ellingson's Est. v. CIR 129.4.5 n.117

Ellis v. CIR 121.4.2 n.19, 121.4.3 n.25, 122.4.1 n.14

Ellis v. US 125.5 n.7, 128.4 n.17

Ellis' Est., CIR v. 129.4.7 n.159

Ellman's Est. v. CIR ... 131.4.3 ns. 62, 75

Emmet v. CIR 135.4.1 n.5

Endicott Trust Co. v. US ... 125.11.4 n.62

Englert v. CIR 137.7.3 n.14

English v. US 125.11.4 n.64

Ensley's Est. v. CIR ... 125.11.4 ns. 49, 62

Epstein v. CIR 121.1 n.5, 123.5.3 n.23

Equitable Life Assurance Soc'y v. CIR 137.7.3 n.14

Equitable Trust Co. v. CIR 137.7.3 n.16

Erickson, Smyth v. 131.3.2 n.25

Essex v. US 131.4.1 n.3

Evans v. US .... 129.4.3 ns. 58, 60

Ewing v. Rountree 128.1 n.23

Exchange Bank & Trust Co. v. US 126.3.1 n.14, 126.6.2 n.29, 126.6.7 n.113

F

Fabric's Est. v. CIR 126.3.4 n.45, 135.4.10 n.110

Fahs, Merrill v. ..... 121.4.2 & ns. 19, 21, 121.4.3 & n.27, 121.4.4 & n.40, 121.4.5, 123.6.1 & ns. 1, 6, 10, 123.6.2, 125.9 ns. 3, 9

Fair v. CIR 134.2.3 n.28

Fairchild's Est. v. CIR 134.3 n.3

Falk v. CIR 123.5.2 n.15

Farber v. CIR 135.4.8 n.89, 135.5.1 n.11, 135.5.2 n.27

Farid-es-Sultaneh v. CIR ...... 121.4.2 & n.22

Farley v. US 129.2.3 n.32

Farmers' Loan & Trust Co. v. US 134.2.1 n.5

Farmers Trust Co. v. US 130.3.3 n.26, 130.6 n.3

Farrel's Est. v. US ... 126.6.3 n.65, 126.6.4 & ns. 68, 69, 126.6.6 n.103, 126.6.7 n.114

Fatter v. Usry 126.4.4 n.57

Faulkner v. CIR ... 121.9 n.7, 124.4.2 n.10

Fawcett's Est. v. CIR .... 131.4.2 n.20, 131.5 n.7, 135.2.2 & n.11, 135.2.2 n.16, 135.5.1 n.4

Fedders Corp. v. CIR 135.2.4 n.43, 135.4.3 n.30, 135.4.5 n.64

Feder's Est. v. CIR 131.4.2 n.28

Fehrs v. US 121.4.5 n.52, 135.2.3 n.25

Fein v. US (8th Cir.) 120.1.2 n.23

Fein v. US (ED Mo.) 126.4.2 n.11

Feinberg's Est. v. CIR 131.5 n.10

Fenton's Est. v. CIR ... 131.4.3 ns. 71, 76

Fernandez v. Wiener .... 120.1.2 & ns. 16–18, 120.2.3 & n.16, 123.2.1 n.1, 125.5 n.2, 125.10 & ns. 5, 6, 126.6.2 n.44, 129.1 & ns. 5, 6

Fidelity-Philadelphia Trust Co. v. Smith .... 126.6.2 & ns. 39, 40, 46, 126.7.1 n.2, 127.2 & ns. 11, 12, 129.3.5 n.51

Fidelity-Philadelphia Trust Co. v. US 131.3.1 n.1, 131.6.1 n.13

Fidelity Trust Co. v. CIR 137.7.2 n.8

Fidelity Union Trust Co. v. Anthony 137.4.1 n.11

Fidelity Union Trust Co. v. US ... 126.5.2 n.48

Fiedler's Est. v. CIR .... 129.4.4 ns. 102–104

Field, US v. .... 125.3 n.7, 128.1 & ns. 12–14

Field's Est. v. CIR 129.4.3 n.60

Field's Est. v. US 126.5.4 n.75

Fifth Ave. Bank v. CIR 134.2.1 n.7

Fillman v. US 134.2.2 n.13, 134.2.3 n.37

Fine's Est. v. CIR 129.5.2 n.10

Finlay v. US 128.3.2 n.7

TABLE OF CASES

[References are to paragraphs (¶) and notes (n.).]

First Kentucky Trust Co. v. US 127.3 n.4

First Nat'l Bank, Dempsey v. 125.11.2 n.20

First Nat'l Bank v. US (5th Cir.) 129.5.2 n.10

First Nat'l Bank v. US (D. Nev.) 131.3.2 n.17

First Nat'l Bank v. US (D. Or.) 127.8 n.9

First Nat'l Bank v. US (WD Pa.) ... 131.5 n.6

First Nat'l Bank v. US (ND Tex.) 131.6.1 n.11

First Nat'l Bank, US v. 127.3 n.1

First Nat'l Bank & Trust Co. v. US .... 132.4 & ns. 10–12

First Nat'l Bank of Kansas City v. US 125.11.4 n.59

First Nat'l Bank of Kenosha v. US 135.1.2 n.36

First Nat'l Bank of Omaha v. US ... 130.2 ns. 6, 10

First Nat'l Bank of Ore. v. US 127.8 n.13

First Nat'l Bank of Topeka v. US 131.3.2 n.19

First Northwest Indus. v. CIR 135.4.5 n.51

First Trust Co. v. US (D. Minn.) 126.8.5 n.89

First Trust Co. v. US (D. Mont.) .... 129.3.3 ns. 14, 48

First Trust Co. of St. Paul v. US 129.5.2 n.8

First Va. Bank v. US 128.2.2 n.28

First Western Bank & Trust Co. v. CIR 137.7.3 n.14, 137.7.4 n.30

First Wis. Trust Co. v. US .. 122.3.2 n.13, 123.4 n.1

Fisher v. CIR (9th Cir.) 124.3.2 n.12

Fisher v. CIR (BTA) 135.2.3 n.40

Fitts' Est. v. CIR 135.2.2 n.15, 135.5.2 n.24

Fitzpatrick, Whittemore v. .. 135.1.2 n.39, 135.3.4 n.33

Flanagan v. US ...... 130.3.2 & ns. 19, 20

Flanders v. US ...... 135.7.2 & ns. 29, 30

Fleming's Est. v. CIR (TCM 1989) 121.7.4 n.33

Fleming's Est. v. CIR (TCM 1974) 135.7.2 n.22

Fletcher Trust Co. v. CIR 137.7.2 n.8

Flora v. US 137.5.3 n.46

Florida v. Mellon 132.4 n.2

Florida Bank v. US 129.5.1 n.1

Florida Nat'l Bank v. US ... 126.6.8 n.130

Folks' Est. v. CIR ... 135.1.2 n.46, 135.3.3 ns. 15, 16, 135.5.1 ns. 6, 9

Fondren v. CIR ... 124.3.1 n.5, 124.3.2 & n.13, 124.4.1 & n.1

Ford, US v. 129.3.3 n.40

Ford's Est. v. CIR ... 126.4.4 n.51, 126.6.4 ns. 71, 75, 77

Forster v. Sauber 126.8.1 n.7

Fort Worth Nat'l Bank v. US 130.4 n.10

Foss v. US 135.6.6 n.82

Foster's Est. v. CIR 129.4.3 n.60

Fourth Nat'l Bank, US v. 130.4 n.4

Francis v. CIR 123.2.1 n.1, 125.10 n.5

Frazee v. CIR .... 135.4.6 & n.77.1

Free v. Bland 125.11.2 n.19

Freedman v. US 127.3 n.1

Freeman's Est. v. CIR 128.3.2 n.7

French v. CIR 121.3.2 n.11

Freshman v. CIR 135.1.2 n.31

Frick, Lewellyn v. 120.1.2 n.24

Fried's Est. v. CIR 129.4.2 n.19, 131.4.1 n.2, 137.4.2 n.23

Frieders' Est. v. CIR 135.1.2 n.41

Friedman's Est. v. CIR .... 121.4.5 ns. 49, 50

Fruehauf's Est. v. CIR 127.4.6 n.36

Fry's Est. v. CIR 126.6.2 n.48, 126.6.6 n.98, 131.4.3 n.45

Fuchs' Est. v. CIR 127.4.7 n.47

Fuller v. CIR 121.7.1 n.5

Funkhouser v. CIR 124.3.2 n.30

Furstenberg v. US ... 135.4.8 n.89, 135.5.1 n.14

Fusz' Est. v. CIR .... 126.8.2 & ns. 29, 47

FX Sys. Corp. v. CIR 135.2.5 n.47

G

Gagliardi's Est. v. CIR 125.2 n.4

Gagne, Dodge v. 131.4.3 n.54

Gall v. US 124.4.2 n.27

Galluzzo v. CIR 121.4.5 n.47

Galt v. CIR 121.3.2 n.16, 121.3.5 n.43

Gamble's Est. v. CIR ... 125.7 n.11, 132.4 n.7

Gannon's Est. v. CIR 125.5 n.10

[References are to paragraphs (¶) and notes (n.).]

Gardner, Delaney v. 130.2 n.15

Gardner's Est. v. CIR 137.3 n.12

Garner's Est. v. CIR 126.3.3 n.41, 126.6.2 n.36

Garstin v. US 135.5.1 n.7

Gartland's Est. v. CIR ..... 128.4 & n.15

Gaskill v. US 128.2.1 n.18

Gawne's Est. v. CIR 132.3 n.15

Gay, Wells v. 132.4 n.3

Geiger's Est. v. CIR 135.6.4 n.40

Gelb v. CIR ... 124.3.2 n.34, 129.4.3 n.68

German's Est. v. US 126.6.2 n.17, 126.6.4 n.73

Gesner v. US 127.4.5 n.32

Giacopuzzi's Est. v. CIR 125.11.4 n.51

Giannini v. CIR .... 126.3.4 & ns. 48, 49, 135.3.10 ns. 105, 120

Giardina v. US 126.8.5 n.86

Gidwitz' Est., CIR v. 126.4.4 n.66

Gilbert's Est. v. CIR 130.3.2 n.14

Gilchrist's Est. v. CIR ...... 126.6.3 n.65, 128.3.2 ns. 7, 8

Gilespie's Est. v. CIR 130.5.1 n.3

Gilford's Est. v. CIR 135.1.2 n.36, 135.3.7 n.64

Gillespie's Est. v. CIR 131.2 n.3

Gillette Rubber Co. v. CIR 135.2.2 n.14

Gillette's Est. v. CIR 122.5 n.5

Gill's Est. v. CIR 126.4.4 n.45

Gilman's Est. v. CIR 126.3.3 n.41, 126.6.5 n.82

Giselman's Est. v. CIR 126.3.2 n.27

Gist v. US 126.3.4 n.51

Glaser v. US 125.11.2 n.27, 126.4.4 n.68

Glenn, Hanner v. 125.6 n.12

Glenny's Est., US v. 137.4.2 n.25

Glen's Est. v. CIR ... 123.6.1 & ns. 9, 11, 12, 14, 131.4.3 ns. 77, 79

Gnichtel, Phillips v. 126.3.4 n.47

Goelet's Est. v. CIR .. 121.1 n.15, 122.4.1 n.16, 123.5.3 n.21

Goetchius' Est. v. CIR 121.4.2 n.14, 126.3.4 n.45, 131.4.3 n.53

Gokey's Est. v. CIR 126.6.2 n.21

Goldman v. CIR 135.1.2 n.48

Goldsborough's Est. v. CIR 125.11.4 n.59

Goldschmidt-Rothschild v. CIR ... 134.2.2 n.13

Goldstein's Est. v. CIR (10th Cir.) 129.2.3 n.28

Goldstein's Est. v. CIR (Ct. Cl.) 127.4.5 n.31

Goldstone v. US 126.7.2 n.18

Goldwater's Est. v. CIR 129.2.2 n.11

Goodall's Est. v. CIR 131.6.2 n.27

Goodman v. CIR 122.3.6 n.31, 127.5 n.3

Goodman v. Granger .... 125.5 n.1, 125.6 & ns. 8, 9

Goodrich's Est. v. CIR 135.2.2 n.19

Good's Est., In re 132.4 n.3

Goodwyn's Est. v. CIR 126.3.3 n.40

Goodyear, US v. 131.4.5 n.97

Goodyear's Est. v. CIR 126.7.4 n.35

Gooel's Est. v. CIR ...... 130.4 ns. 6, 10, 135.4.10 n.101

Gordon's Est. v. CIR 129.2.2 n.14

Gosch's Est. v. CIR 131.4.2 n.27

Gottlieb v. CIR ..... 135.2.2 n.16, 135.2.3 ns. 25, 32, 35, 135.3.8 n.70

Gould's Est. v. CIR .... 135.1.2 ns. 55, 57, 135.3.8 n.76

Gowetz v. CIR 131.4.2 n.33

Grace Bros. v. CIR 135.4.5 n.54

Grace's Est., US v. .... 126.3.1 & n.13

Gradow v. US 126.3.4 n.51

Graham's Est. v. CIR 125.7 n.6

Gramm's Est. v. CIR 122.5 n.11

Granger, Goodman v. .... 125.5 n.1, 125.6 & ns. 8, 9

Granquist, Murphy v. 135.3.4 n.50

Graves' Est. v. CIR 126.6.8 n.129

Gray, Piatt v. 129.4.3 n.59

Gray v. US (3d Cir.) ... 126.8.2 ns. 38, 41

Gray v. US (9th Cir.) 131.4.3 n.71

Great Northern Nekoosa Corp. v. US .... 135.3.7 ns. 60, 61

Green v. CIR 135.4.10 n.106

Greenberg v. US 130.2 n.13

Greenberg's Est. v. CIR 131.4.2 n.26

Greene, CIR v. 121.4.3 n.26

Greene v. US (7th Cir.) 126.6.2 n.47

Greene v. US (Ct. Cl.) 121.3.1 n.2

Greene v. US (ND Ill.) 130.6 n.3, 131.4.2 n.20

Green's Est. v. US .... 129.3.3 & n.23

Gregory's Est. v. CIR 135.3.4 n.51

Gresham v. CIR 135.3.7 n.64

Grill v. US 135.2.1 n.10

Grimes v. CIR 121.3.3 n.27

TABLE OF CASES

[References are to paragraphs (¶) and notes (n.).]

Grimes' Est. v. CIR .... 135.6.6 ns. 82, 83
Grinnell, Helvering v. 128.1 n.16
Griswold v. CIR 121.7.1 n.8
Gross v. CIR .... 121.4.5 & n.53
Grossinger's Est. v. CIR 122.2 n.1, 124.3.1 n.7
Grossman v. Campbell .... 126.3.2 ns. 28, 29
Grossman v. CIR .... 135.1.2 n.46, 135.2.1 ns. 5, 7
Grossman's Est. v. CIR 126.5.5 n.83
Guaranty Trust Co. v. CIR ... 121.3.2 n.11
Guest v. CIR ... 135.3.8 n.75, 135.5.1 n.9
Guggenheim, Burnet v. ..... 121.3.3 n.25, 122.2 n.7, 122.3.1 & ns. 1, 2, 122.4.1 & n.2, 122.5 & n.7, 124.3.3 n.43
Guggenheim v. Rasquin .... 135.2.1 & ns. 1, 2, 7
Gulf, Mobile & O. RR v. US 135.1.2 n.31, 135.4.3 n.30
Gunland's Est. v. CIR 135.6.6 n.83
Gunther v. US 126.8.5 n.84
Gutchess' Est. v. CIR 126.6.2 n.34
Guynn v. US 126.6.2 n.36
Guzy v. CIR 123.4 n.1

H

Hagar's Est., CIR v. 126.5.2 n.51
Haggart's Est. v. CIR 131.3.3 n.49
Haggett's Est. v. CIR 126.3.1 n.7
Hagmann's Est. v. CIR 131.4.2 n.23
Halbach's Est. v. CIR 126.4.4 n.58
Hall v. US 126.7.4 n.41
Hall's Est. v. CIR (TC) ..... 130.5.6 & ns. 48, 52
Hall's Est. v. CIR (TCM) 135.4.3 n.29
Hallock, CIR v. 131.6.3 n.43
Hallock, Helvering v. .... 126.1, 126.7.7 & n.59
Halsted v. CIR 129.4.3 n.43
Hambleton v. CIR 121.3.3 n.27, 122.5 n.14
Hamelsky's Est. v. CIR 129.7.2 n.20
Hamilton v. US 124.3.2 n.37
Hamilton Nat'l Bank v. US 129.3.3 n.23
Hance's Est. v. CIR 135.7.4 n.53
Hanley v. US 135.4.10 n.100
Hanner v. Glenn 125.6 n.12
Hansen v. Vinal 129.4.2 n.17
Hardenbergh v. CIR 121.7.2 n.23

Harmon, CIR v. 123.2.1 n.4
Harms' Est. v. CIR 135.2.3 n.37
Harrell, US v. 137.6.2 n.9
Harriet M. Bryant Trust v. CIR ... 135.3.9 ns. 82, 83
Harris v. CIR (US) ..... 123.6.1 & ns. 15, 16, 123.6.2 & n.33, 131.4.3 & ns. 51, 66
Harris v. CIR (2d Cir.) 121.3.2 n.15
Harris v. CIR (5th Cir.) 124.4.2 n.11
Harrison's Est. v. CIR ...... 135.4.4 n.38, 136.3.1 & ns. 1, 2
Harris Trust & Sav. Bank v. US .. 130.5.7 n.62
Hart, CIR v. 123.4 n.2
Harter's Est. v. CIR 129.2.3 n.27, 129.5.3 n.15
Hartford Nat'l Bank & Trust Co. v. US 126.5.3 n.62
Harvey v. US .. 125.11.2 n.18, 125.11.4 & ns. 56, 57
Harwood v. CIR 121.3.3 n.29, 121.4.5 n.56
Haskell's Est. v. CIR 129.5.2 n.8
Hassett v. Welch 120.1.2 n.24, 126.6.8 n.125
Hawaiian Trust Co. v. US 129.3.3 n.26
Hayes' Est. v. CIR 135.3.2 n.9
Hays' Est. v. CIR 126.6.2 n.18
Hazeltine Corp. v. CIR 135.2.2 n.12
Headrick's Est. v. CIR 126.4.2 n.22, 127.8 n.10
Heasty, US v. 125.11.2 n.27
Heath v. CIR 124.4.2 n.25
Heath v. US 125.2 n.5
Heckscher's Est. v. CIR 131.3.3 n.62, 135.5.2 n.27
Heffley's Est. v. CIR ... 135.6.2 ns. 21, 24
Heidrich v. CIR ..... 124.4.2 & ns. 14, 20
Heim's Est. v. CIR 129.4.2 n.17
Heiner v. Donnan .... 120.1.2 n.6, 126.4.2 n.12, 126.4.4 & n.60
Heiner, May v. ... 125.5 & n.5, 126.6.8 & n.118
Heitsch v. Kavanagh 120.1.2 n.10
Helis' Est. v. CIR 131.4.5 n.96
Hellé, US v. 134.2.1 n.9
Heller v. CIR 122.2 n.14, 124.4.1 n.2
Helmholz, Helvering v. ..... 126.5.5 & ns. 80, 84, 85, 127.4.5 n.34
Hemme, US v. ..... 120.1.2 & ns. 20, 21, 23, 132.3 n.15

[References are to paragraphs (¶) and notes (n.).]

Hendry's Est. v. CIR 126.6.2 n.34

Henggeler, Allen v. 120.1.2 n.6, 125.9 n.3

Henritze v. CIR 135.1.2 n.43

Henry Finck Co. v. CIR 135.3.3 n.15

Henry's Est. v. CIR 125.7 n.6

Henslee, May v. 131.8 n.1

Henslee, National Bank of Commerce v. 126.6.6 n.97

Henslee v. Union Planters Nat'l Bank & Trust Co. 130.4 n.9

Heringer v. CIR ... 121.4.5 n.51, 124.2 n.4

Herr v. CIR .... 124.4.2 & n.32

Herr, CIR v. 124.4.2 n.29

Herrmann's Est. v. CIR 124.3.2 n.27

Herson v. Mills 129.5.2 n.11

Hertsche v. US 135.7.3 n.40

Herzog v. CIR ...... 122.5 ns. 13, 14, 17

Hessenbruch v. CIR 124.3.2 n.21

Heyen v. US 124.2 n.11

Hibernia Bank v. US ... 131.1 n.1, 131.3.2 ns. 12, 32, 131.6.1 ns. 14, 21

Higgins, Adriance v. 126.5.4 n.72

Higgins, Bankers Trust Co. v. 126.5.1 n.2

Higgins v. CIR 122.5 n.17

Higgins, Maass v. ..... 135.7.1 n.1, 135.7.2 ns. 16–18

Higgins, Marks v. 126.6.4 n.70, 126.6.6 n.102

Higgins' Est. v. CIR 129.4.5 n.127

Higgs' Est. v. CIR 126.8.1 n.8

Hill v. CIR 121.4.3 n.31

Hill's Est. v. CIR ...... 126.5.1 ns. 14, 22

Hill's Est., In re .. 125.7 ns. 4, 6, 135.4.10 n.118

Hinds' Est. v. CIR 125.9 n.7

Hipp v. US .. 124.3.2 n.34, 135.4.10 n.106

Hitchon's Est. v. CIR 121.4.5 n.51

Hite's Est. v. CIR 126.4.4 n.53

Hlefrich's Est. v. CIR 126.6.2 n.21

Hockman v. US 124.3.2 n.30

Hodgdon's Est. v. CIR 131.4.3 n.44

Hoelzel v. CIR 129.7.2 n.18

Hoey, City Bank Farmers Trust Co. v. 121.3.2 n.18, 122.2 n.6

Hoey, Lyeth v. ...... 126.3.2 n.27, 129.2.3 n.29, 130.3.2 & n.12

Hoffman v. CIR .... 135.3.10 ns. 105, 120

Hoffman's Est. v. CIR 126.3.2 n.20

Hofford's Est. v. CIR 126.6.2 n.49

Hogan's Est. v. CIR 135.4.3 n.31

Hogle v. CIR 121.3.6 n.48

Hogle, CIR v. .... 121.3.6 & ns. 47, 49

Hohensee's Est. v. CIR 130.6 n.7

Holbrook v. US 132.6.3 n.27

Holden, Blodgett v. 120.1.2 n.20

Holland's Est. v. CIR (TC) 129.4.3 n.62

Holland's Est. v. CIR (BTA) 126.6.2 n.49

Hollander v. US 126.5.4 n.75

Hollingshead's Est. v. CIR ... 129.4.3 n.73

Hollingsworth v. CIR 124.3.1 n.8

Holl's Est. v. CIR 135.7.2 n.25

Holmes' Est., CIR v. .... 126.5.1 n.16, 126.5.2 & ns. 36, 37, 45, 126.5.6 & n.91

Holtz' Est. v. CIR 122.5 n.11

Honickman's Est. v. CIR 131.4.1 n.4

Hooker v. CIR 123.6.1 n.18

Hooper v. CIR 127.3 n.3

Hope v. US 126.3.1 n.4, 127.8 n.10

Horne's Est. v. CIR 130.6 n.8

Horner v. US .... 126.3.2 & ns. 20, 21

Hornor's Est. v. CIR (3d Cir. 1962) 125.11.2 n.27

Hornor's Est. v. CIR (3d Cir. 1942) 132.5 n.8

Horst v. CIR 123.2.2 n.6

Horton v. US 132.4 n.7

Horton's Est. v. CIR ...... 129.4.2 & n.18

Hoskins' Est. v. CIR 130.3.1 n.10

Hospital Corp. of Am. v. CIR 135.4.5 n.48

Housman v. CIR 121.3.2 n.11, 121.4.5 n.49

Houston's Est. v. CIR 125.6 n.2

Howard's Est. v. CIR (9th Cir.) .. 129.4.5 n.118

Howard's Est. v. CIR (TC) 125.11.4 n.55

Hrobon v. CIR 121.3.2 n.16

Hubbard's Est. v. CIR 126.6.4 n.70, 126.6.6 n.102, 131.3.2 n.12

Hudson United Bank v. US ..... 130.4 & n.10

Huggins v. US 125.5 n.8

Hull v. CIR 121.4.5 n.52

Hull's Est. v. CIR .... 125.8 n.10, 135.7.2 & n.31

Humphreys, Rasquin v. ... 122.4.1 ns. 7, 9

Humphrey's Est. v. CIR ... 126.4.4 ns. 62, 65

TABLE OF CASES

[References are to paragraphs (¶) and notes (n.).]

Hundley's Est. v. CIR 121.4.3 n.35, 123.6.1 n.7, 123.6.2 n.32
Hunt v. US 129.2.3 n.39
Hunter v. US 127.4.6 n.38
Huntington Nat'l Bank v. CIR .. 135.4.10 n.109
Huntsman's Est. v. CIR 127.4.8 n.51, 135.5.1 n.9
Hurd v. CIR ..... 126.5.3 n.63, 126.5.4 & n.73
Hutchings, Helvering v. ..... 121.1 & n.9, 124.2 & ns. 2, 3, 7
Hutchinson v. CIR 124.3.1 n.9
Hutson's Est. v. CIR 127.2 n.1, 127.5 n.5, 131.4.5 n.98

I

Igleheart v. CIR 131.2 n.12
Illinois Nat'l Bank v. US 124.4.2 n.16
Independence Bank Waukesha v. US 128.2.2 n.28
Industrial Trust Co. v. CIR .. 126.5.3 n.52, 126.6.1 n.5, 126.6.3 & ns. 53, 54, 126.6.4 n.71
Infante's Est. v. CIR 127.4.5 n.30, 127.4.8 n.63
Ingalls v. CIR 123.5.1 n.9
Ingram-Richardson, Inc. v. CIR .. 135.2.4 n.46, 135.5.1 ns. 4, 5, 10, 14
Inman's Est. v. CIR 126.5.4 n.73
Iowa-Des Moines Nat'l Bank v. US 129.3.3 n.23
IRS, Detroit Bank & Trust Co. v. 130.3.3 n.22
Irvine v. US 121.7.1 n.8
Ithaca Trust Co. v. US ..... 121.3.3 n.22, 125.7 & ns. 7, 10, 130.4 & ns. 7, 8, 131.4.2 n.19
Iversen's Est. v. CIR 131.4.3 n.76
Ivey v. CIR 135.3.4 n.37

J

Jackson v. CIR 122.2 n.10
Jackson v. US ... 129.3.3 & ns. 18–21, 23, 129.4.3 n.91
Jacobs v. CIR 131.1 n.1
Jacobs, US v. 120.1.2 n.20, 125.11.2 n.12, 125.11.4 n.54
Jaecker v. CIR 121.7.5 n.62

Jaffe v. US 137.4.2 n.25
Jalkut's Est. v. CIR ..... 126.4.2 & ns. 16, 19
Jardell's Est. v. CIR 124.3.2 n.21
Jarre v. CIR 135.4.8 n.90
Jenkins v. US .... 128.2.1 ns. 12, 18, 128.2.2 & ns. 30, 31, 128.3.2 n.7
Jenner's Est. v. CIR 131.3.2 n.47, 131.6.1 n.17
Jennings v. Smith .... 126.5.1 n.16, 126.5.3 & ns. 52, 59, 71, 126.5.6 n.92, 126.6.4 & n.78
Jennings' Est. v. CIR (TC) 129.4.4 n.100
Jennings' Est. v. CIR (TCM) 135.3.7 n.61
Jephson's Est. v. CIR (TC 1986) 135.3.4 n.47, 135.3.8 n.73
Jephson's Est. v. CIR (TC 1983) .... 135.1.2 & n.36
Jeschke v. US 125.11.2 n.22
Jewett v. CIR .... 121.7.1 ns. 4, 7, 8
Johnson, Dulles v. 130.2 n.1, 131.3.2 n.25
Johnson v. CIR 135.1.2 n.32
Johnson's Est. v. CIR (TC 1987) 135.6.6 n.73
Johnson's Est. v. CIR (TC 1981) ... 125.9 n.7
Johnson's Est. v. CIR (TC 1971) 126.4.4 n.56, 126.8.5 n.82
Johnson's Est. v. CIR (TCM) 129.4.3 n.53
Johnson's Est. v. US 130.5.6 n.55
Johnston's Est. v. CIR 126.5.2 n.46
Johnston's Est. v. US 135.7.2 n.25
Jones v. CIR (4th Cir.) 123.5.3 n.22
Jones v. CIR (TC) 124.3.2 n.26
Jones v. CIR (TCM) 131.3.2 n.11
Jones, CIR v. 127.3 n.1
Jones v. US (10th Cir.) 135.5.1 n.7
Jones v. US (ED Ill.) 131.4.1 n.6
Jordahl's Est. v. CIR 126.5.2 n.51, 127.4.2 n.15
Joseloff v. CIR 122.5 n.5
Joslyn's Est. v. CIR (9th Cir. 1977) 131.3.2 n.47
Joslyn's Est. v. CIR (9th Cir. 1974) .... 131.3.2 ns. 43, 47
Joy v. US 126.6.3 n.56

[References are to paragraphs (¶) and notes (n.).]

K

Kammerdiner, Rogan v. 125.11.4 n.47
Kaplan v. US 135.5.1 n.15
Kaplin's Est. v. CIR (6th Cir. 1987)
.... 135.4.1 n.5
Kaplin's Est. v. CIR (6th Cir. 1984)
.... 135.2.1 n.3
Kaplun v. US 130.2 n.17
Karagheusian's Est., CIR v. 127.4.5
n.31
Kasishke v. US 131.6.1 n.11
Kass v. CIR 123.5.2 n.15
Katz v. CIR 124.4.1 n.7
Katz v. US 128.2.1 n.6
Kaufman v. US 122.3.6 n.33, 127.5 n.3
Kavanagh, Heitsch v. 120.1.2 n.10
Kavanagh, Michigan Trust Co. v.
.... 126.5.3 n.64
Keeney, In re 126.6.1 n.7
Keeter v. US .... 128.2.1 ns. 9, 22
Keinath v. CIR 121.7.1 n.8
Keller's Est. v. CIR 126.3.4 n.42,
131.4.3 n.77
Keller's Est., CIR v. 127.2 n.9
Kelley's Est. v. CIR 121.1 n.23, 124.1
n.9
Kellogg-Citizens Nat'l Bank v. US
.... 131.6.2 n.23
Kelly, Blunt v. .. 126.5.1 n.2, 126.5.3 n.53
Kelly's Est. v. CIR 122.2 n.3
Kelm, Struthers v. ... 126.6.3 n.56, 126.6.7
n.113
Kempner, CIR v. 124.3.2 n.16
Kendall's Est. v. CIR 129.3.3 n.23
Kentucky Bar Found. v. CIR ... 130.2 n.1
Kern v. US 127.5 n.7
Kerner v. CIR 135.4.8 n.90
Kess v. US 127.2 n.12
Kieckhefer v. CIR 124.3.3 n.39
Kimmelman v. CIR .... 135.2.3 ns. 29, 39
Kincaid v. US 121.4.5 n.51
King, In re 121.4.5 n.55
King v. Citizens & S. Nat'l Bank
.... 129.7.2 n.18
King v. US 121.4.5
Kinney's Est. v. CIR 126.3.2 n.20,
135.2.2 n.15
Kirschling v. US 121.3.1 n.2
Klauber's Est. v. CIR ... 126.7.3 & ns. 28,
29, 126.7.4 n.48

Kleemeier's Est. v. CIR 126.8.1 n.10,
126.8.5 n.96
Klein v. CIR 124.3.2 n.21
Klein v. US .... 126.7.7 & n.57
Kleine v. US 137.6.2 n.14
Kleinman's Est. v. CIR 129.2.3 n.28
Klein's Est. v. CIR 129.6.4 n.23
Kline v. US 130.4 n.10
Knapp v. CIR 135.3.4 n.51
Kniep v. CIR 124.3.2 n.26
Knipp's Est. v. CIR 125.5 n.8, 127.4.8
n.60
Knoell v. US 135.3.7 n.61
Knowlton v. Moore ... 120.1.1 n.1, 120.1.2
& ns. 7–9, 14, 125.5 n.1, 131.1 & n.1
Koffler v. CIR 135.5.2 n.25
Kolker's Est. v. CIR 124.3.1 n.5
Kolom v. CIR 135.3.7 n.69
Konner v. CIR 124.4.2 n.32
Kopperman's Est. v. CIR 135.3.3 n.16
Korslin v. US .. 126.8.5 n.84, 135.3.5 n.56
Krabbenhoft v. CIR 135.4.6 n.77
Kraemer, Wilson v. 128.4 n.10
Krakoff v. US 121.7.6 n.89
Kramer's Est. v. US ... 122.3.5 n.25, 125.6
n.12, 126.3.2 n.33, 126.5.1 n.8,
126.8.2 n.44
Krampf's Est. v. CIR 129.3.3 n.38
Kraus v. CIR 129.4.3 n.30
Krischer's Est. v. CIR 127.4.2 n.13
Kroger's Est. v. CIR 126.4.4 n.66
Kuhn v. US 126.3.4 n.51
Kurihara's Est. v. CIR 127.8 n.14
Kyle's Est. v. CIR ..... 129.4.5 & ns. 127,
138, 131.4.2 n.24

L

Labombarde's Est. v. CIR ... 131.4.3 n.45
Lacy, New Orleans Baptist
Theological Seminary v. ... 129.7.2 n.18
La Fortune v. CIR 137.4.1 n.11,
137.7.2 ns. 4, 5, 8
Lake Shore Nat'l Bank v. Coyle
.... 129.3.3 ns. 14, 48
Land v. US 135.7.3 n.41
Land, US v. ... 135.1.2 n.34, 135.2.3 n.24,
135.3.5 n.55, 135.3.10 n.104
Landers' Est. v. CIR 131.3.2 n.25,
131.6.1 n.15
Lane v. US 137.5.1 n.6

[References are to paragraphs (¶) and notes (n.).]

Lang's Est. v. CIR (9th Cir. 1980)
..... 121.1 n.22, 121.2 n.3, 132.4 ns. 6, 8
Lang's Est. v. CIR (9th Cir. 1938)
.... 131.4.5 ns. 91, 99
Lanigan's Est. v. CIR 128.2.1 n.20
Lansburgh v. CIR 135.1.2 n.24
Larkin's Est. v. CIR 131.6.1 n.7
La Sala's Est. v. CIR 132.6.2 n.6,
132.6.3 n.34, 132.6.4 n.38
Latta v. CIR .... 122.5 ns. 4, 5
Latty v. CIR 131.4.3 n.40
Laurin's Est. v. CIR 129.4.3 n.81,
129.6.3 n.11
Law v. US 131.4.3 n.77
Law's Est. v. CIR 131.4.1 n.4, 131.4.3
ns. 45, 81
Lazar's Est. v. CIR 131.4.1 n.3
Lazarus v. CIR 126.6.2 n.47
Leavitt's Est. v. CIR 125.2 n.2
Leder's Est. v. CIR ... 126.4.2 n.22, 127.8
ns. 10, 11
Lee v. US 126.3.3 n.41
Lee's Est. v. CIR (TC 1960) 126.6.2
n.21
Lee's Est. v. CIR (TC 1948) 131.4.5
n.92
Leewitz v. US 131.8 n.1
Le Gierse, Helvering v. .... 127.2 & ns. 8,
10, 12
Lehman v. CIR ..... 126.3.1 & ns. 10, 11
Lehman v. US 128.2.1 n.3
Leigh v. CIR 137.7.3 n.23
Leopold v. US 126.5.3 n.70, 131.4.3
n.77
Lepoutre's Est. v. CIR 134.2.4 n.69
Lester's Est. v. CIR 131.4.2 n.30
Levine's Est. v. CIR ...... 124.4.2 & n.35
Levin's Est. v. CIR 126.5.1 n.9
Levitt's Est. v. CIR .... 129.6.4 ns. 21, 22
Levy's Est. v. CIR ... 126.3.1 n.14, 127.4.7
& n.57
Lewald v. US 129.5.2 n.9
Lewellyn v. Frick 120.1.2 n.24
Lewis' Est. v. CIR 131.4.1 n.6
Liberty Nat'l Bank & Trust Co. v. US
.... 129.6.4 n.23
Libeu, Libeu's Est. v. 129.6.4 n.20,
135.6.9 n.148
Libeu's Est. v. Libeu 129.6.4 n.20,
135.6.9 n.148
Lidbury's Est. v. CIR 121.3.3 n.27
Lilly v. Smith 123.4 n.1

Linderme's Est. v. CIR 126.6.2 n.36
Lion's Est. v. CIR 132.6.3 n.23
Lipkowitz v. CIR 129.2.2 n.11
Littick's Est. v. CIR 135.3.10 n.111
Little's Est. v. CIR (TC) 128.2.2 n.28
Little's Est. v. CIR (TCM) 135.2.3
n.34, 135.3.3 n.16, 135.3.7 n.65,
135.3.9 n.82
Lloyd's Est. v. US 132.6.3 n.29
Lober v. US .. 122.4.1 n.15, 126.5.2 & ns.
38, 40, 41
Lockard v. CIR ..... 121.3.5 & ns. 40, 41
Lockie's Est. v. CIR 134.2.3 n.35
Loeb v. McCaughn 131.2 n.7
Logan, Burnet v. .... 125.7 & ns. 4, 5,
135.1.1 & ns. 16, 18, 135.4.7 n.84
Lomb v. Sugden .... 135.3.10 ns. 108, 120
Lombard's Est. v. CIR 128.4 n.17
Long, Binney v. 120.1.2 n.20
Longue Vue Found. v. CIR ... 130.3.1 n.7
Lord Eldon, Crutwell v. Lye 135.4.5
n.55
Loughridge's Est. v. CIR 126.5.5 n.88
Loveland's Est. v. CIR 125.11.4 n.49
Lovering v. US 131.4.3 n.78
Love's Est. v. CIR ... 131.3.2 n.31, 131.6.1
n.14
Lowden, CIR v. 124.3.2 n.19
Lowe v. CIR ... 135.1.1 n.18, 135.2.2 n.15,
135.3.3 n.15, 135.4.8 n.89
Lowe's Est. v. CIR 126.4.4 n.52
Luce v. US 135.2.3 n.25, 135.3.4 n.37
Luehrmann's Est. v. CIR .... 130.6 & n.8
Luff, Bremer v. 125.11.4 n.66
Lumpkin's Est. v. CIR 127.4.2 n.14
Lye, Lord Eldon, Crutwell v. 135.4.5
n.55
Lyeth v. Hoey 126.3.2 n.27, 129.2.3
n.29, 130.3.2 & n.12
Lyman v. CIR 131.8 n.1
Lyon's Est. v. CIR 125.11.4 n.54

M

Maass v. Higgins 135.7.1 n.1, 135.7.2
ns. 16–18
Mackie's Est. v. CIR ... 129.3.3 ns. 24, 28
MacLean v. US 126.6.8 n.129
Madden v. CIR 125.11.4 n.42
Maddox's Est. v. CIR .... 135.6.8 ns. 116,
119
Madsen's Est. v. CIR 127.5 n.7

[References are to paragraphs (¶) and notes (n.).]

Magill v. CIR 131.6.1 n.14

Mallinckrodt v. Nunan 124.3.3 n.43

Malone v. US 131.3.2 n.19

Mandel v. Sturr 125.8 n.10

Mandels' Est. v. CIR 122.3.1 n.9

Mangels' Est. v. US .... 135.6.5 ns. 49, 52

Manly v. Bacon ..... 135.5.1 ns. 9, 11, 12

Manning, Christiernin v. 126.8.3 n.56

Manning v. US 137.5.3 n.46

Manscill's Est. v. CIR 129.4.5 n.123

Manufacturers Nat'l Bank, US v. ... 127.1 n.5

Manufacturers Nat'l Bank of Detroit,
US v. 120.1.2 n.20

Marcus v. DeWitt 131.3.2 n.45

Maresi, CIR v. 131.4.3 n.74

Margrave's Est. v. CIR (8th Cir.)
.... 121.6.2 n.9, 127.4.4 n.28, 127.4.5
n.30, 128.2.1 & ns. 22, 24

Margrave's Est. v. CIR (TC) 125.6
n.10, 127.3 n.3

Marine Midland Trust Co. v.
McGowan 130.2 n.13

Marine Nat'l Bank v. CIR ... 130.3.2 n.13

Marine's Est. v. CIR 130.4 n.4

Markle v. CIR 130.2 n.13

Marks v. Higgins 126.6.4 n.70, 126.6.6
n.102

Marks Est. v. CIR 127.5 n.7, 132.6.3
n.24

Marshall v. US 126.5.4 n.72

Marshall's Est. v. CIR (TC) ... 126.3.1 n.4

Marshall's Est. v. CIR (TCM) 126.6.6
n.100

Marshall's Est., CIR v. 126.7.2 n.17

Martin v. CIR .... 135.6.2 ns. 21, 22

Martin v. US (4th Cir.) 128.2.1 n.13

Martin v. US (7th Cir.) 129.5.2 n.10

Martinez v. CIR 124.3.2 n.18

Maryland Nat'l Bank v. US (4th Cir.)
.... 124.3.2 n.35

Maryland Nat'l Bank v. US (D. Md.)
.... 125.5 n.8

Massey v. US 124.3.1 n.11

Mathey v. US 126.5.1 n.27

Mathias v. CIR 135.5.1 n.16

Matthews v. US (Ct. Cl.) 123.6.1 n.2

Matthews v. US (EDNY) 135.3.10
n.113

Matthews' Est. v. CIR 135.3.10 n.105

Mauldin v. CIR .... 135.4.8 & n.91

Maxant's Est. v. CIR 128.2.3 n.39

Maxwell Trust v. CIR 125.6 n.2

Maxwell v. CIR 121.7.4 n.38

May v. CIR .... 129.4.3 ns. 28, 60, 90

May v. Heiner ... 125.5 & n.5, 126.6.8 &
n.118

May v. Henslee 131.8 n.1

May v. McGowan 135.3.10 n.110

Maytag v. US ... 128.2.1 ns. 7, 20, 128.2.3
ns. 35, 39

McAllister's Est. v. CIR ... 134.2.4 & n.65

McAlpine's Est. v. CIR 135.6.6 n.85

McArdle's Est. v. CIR 128.2.1 n.20

McCabe's Est. v. US 126.3.3 n.40,
129.4.3 n.66

McCann v. CIR 125.2 n.5

McCann, CIR v. .... 135.2.3 & n.23,
135.2.4 & n.42, 135.3.10 n.112,
135.5.2 n.19

McCarthy v. US 125.2 n.4

McCaughn, Bromley v. 120.1.2 n.13

McCaughn, Loeb v. 131.2 n.7

McClennen v. CIR 125.8 n.10

McClure's Est. v. US 131.4.1 n.11,
131.6.2 n.27

McCobb, All v. ... 126.8.2 n.38, 126.8.4 &
n.68

McCoy's Est. v. CIR 127.4.2 n.13

McCue v. CIR 131.4.1 n.9

McCullough v. US 131.4.5 n.96

McCutchan's Est. v. CIR 130.6 n.3,
137.8 n.10

McDonald v. CIR ... 121.7.4 n.38, 135.6.6
n.74

McGauley's Est. v. CIR 132.6.2 n.8

McGehee v. CIR 125.4.1 n.64, 126.4.4
n.64

McGinnes, Bach v. 130.3.2 n.17

McGinnes, Strite v. 128.2.2 n.28

McGinnes, Watson v. 131.7 n.7

McGowan, City Bank Farmers Trust
Co. v. 122.2 n.6

McGowan, Marine Midland Trust
Co. v. 130.2 n.13

McGowan, May v. 135.3.10 n.110

McGrew's Est. v. CIR 125.11.4 n.52

McGuire v. CIR .... 135.1.2 ns. 24, 26

McHugh v. US 122.5 n.9

McKeon's Est. v. CIR 121.4.3 n.26,
126.6.6 n.97

McLean v. US (ND Cal.) 123.5.3 n.24

McLean v. US (ED Mich.) 129.3.3
n.40

TABLE OF CASES

[References are to paragraphs (¶) and notes (n.).]

McLoughlin, Van Beuren v. 126.5.5 n.89

McMillan's Est. v. CIR (8th Cir.) 129.4.3 n.60

McMillan's Est. v. CIR (TC) 129.3.3 n.35

McMurtry v. CIR .... 123.6.1 ns. 2, 15, 124.3.2 n.33, 132.2.2 n.9, 135.4.10 ns. 108, 109

McNichol's Est. v. CIR 126.3.3 n.39

McShain v. CIR 135.1.1 n.18

McTighe's Est. v. CIR 126.5.1 n.27, 126.5.2 n.50, 126.6.2 n.26

Meeske's Est. v. CIR 129.4.3 n.81

Mein v. CIR 122.2 n.13

Mellon, Florida v. 132.4 n.2

Mellon Bank v. US 130.2 n.10

Melman, US v. 137.6.2 n.13, 137.8 n.3

Menkus' Est. v. CIR 129.2.3 n.26

Mercantile-Commerce Bank & Trust Co., Helvering v. 126.6.2 n.17

Mercantile Safe Deposit & Trust Co. v. US (D. Md. 1974) 132.6.3 n.21

Mercantile Safe Deposit & Trust Co. v. US (D. Md. 1970) 124.3.2 n.18

Mercantile Safe Deposit & Trust Co., Stinchcomb v. 129.4.3 n.65

Merchants Nat'l Bank v. CIR 126.6.4 n.71, 130.4 n.9

Merchants Nat'l Bank v. US (ND Iowa) 129.4.3 n.41

Merchants Nat'l Bank v. US (D. Kan.) 132.6.3 n.21

Meres' Est. v. CIR .... 130.5.6 & n.47

Merriam, US v. .... 131.3.2 & n.10

Merrill v. Fahs ..... 121.4.2 & ns. 19, 21, 121.4.3 & n.27, 121.4.4 & n.40, 121.4.5, 123.6.1 & ns. 1, 6, 10, 123.6.2, 125.9 ns. 3, 9

Merrit v. CIR 122.3.1 n.9

Merwin's Est. v. CIR ... 135.6.6 ns. 82, 84

Messing v. CIR 121.4.5 n.52, 124.4.1 n.8, 135.5.2 n.27

Metallics Recycling Co. v. CIR ... 135.4.5 n.59

Metcalf's Est. v. CIR 131.6.2 n.31

Metropolitan Bank v. St. Louis Dispatch Co. 135.4.5 n.56

Metz v. US 137.6.2 n.13

Meyer v. US .... 129.3.3 & ns. 44, 45

Meyer's Est. v. CIR (2d Cir.) 132.6.4 n.44

Meyer's Est. v. CIR (TC) 137.5.1 n.6

Meyer's Est. v. Helvering 121.4.3 n.26

Miami Beach First Nat'l Bank v. US .... 135.4.10 & n.110

Michigan Trust Co. v. Kavanagh 126.5.3 n.64

Miglionico v. US 125.2 n.2

Milbrew, Inc. v. CIR 135.1.2 n.54

Miller v. US (3d. Cir.) 128.2.2 n.28

Miller v. US (MD Fla.) 129.4.3 n.44

Miller v. US (CD Ill.) 135.6.6 n.90

Miller, US v. 135.1.2 n.41

Miller's Est. v. CIR 126.3.2 n.20

Milliken v. US 120.1.2 n.20

Milliken's Est. v. CIR 129.5.2 n.9

Mills, CIR v. 123.2.3 n.10

Mills, Herson v. 129.5.2 n.11

Mills v. US 129.2.3 n.26, 129.3.3 n.26

Milner's Est. v. CIR ... 125.5 n.7, 126.3.2 n.27

Miner v. US 127.5 n.7

Minot's Est. v. CIR 128.4 n.8

Mississippi Valley Trust Co. v. CIR (8th Cir. 1945) 137.4.1 n.11

Mississippi Valley Trust Co. v. CIR (8th Cir. 1934) 130.2 n.16

Mitchell's Est. v. CIR 126.6.2 n.25

Mittleman's Est. v. CIR ... 129.4.3 ns. 26, 29, 41

Moir v. US 137.9 n.6

Mollenberg's Est. v. CIR 126.3.4 n.45

Molter v. US 125.6 n.10

Monroe v. US 121.6.4 n.24

Montagano v. US 137.3 n.12

Montgomery's Est. v. CIR ... 126.8.4 n.65

Moore, Brodrick v. 129.2.3 n.27

Moore, Knowlton v. .... 120.1.1 n.1, 120.1.2 & ns. 7–9, 14, 125.5 n.1, 131.1 & n.1

Moore v. US .... 129.4.3 ns. 29, 66

Morgan v. CIR (US) ..... 128.1 ns. 11, 19

Morgan v. CIR (TC) 124.3.2 n.25, 124.4.1 n.5

Morris v. CIR (6th Cir.) ... 135.1.2 ns. 36, 46

Morris v. CIR (TC) 135.3.7 n.68

Morris v. CIR (TCM) 135.1.2 n.31, 135.2.1 n.6, 135.3.7 n.62

Morris' Est. v. CIR 130.3.2 n.14

Morrow's Est. v. CIR 126.8.4 n.68

Morse's Est. v. CIR .... 131.4.3 ns. 39, 40, 64

[References are to paragraphs (¶) and notes (n.).]

Mortimer's Est. v. CIR ... 122.2 n.1, 125.2 n.5
Morton's Est. v. CIR 126.5.1 n.10, 127.4.2 n.9
Moskowitz v. US 135.3.5 n.56
Moss' Est. v. CIR 125.5 n.13
Mudry v. US .... 134.2.7 ns. 88, 90
Murchie, Delaney v. .... 134.2.3 & ns. 31, 32
Murphy v. Granquist 135.3.4 n.50
Murphy's Est. v. US 129.5.2 n.7
Murphy's Est. v. CIR (TC) ... 128.5.2 n.3
Murphy's Est. v. CIR (TCM 1981)
.... 135.2.1 n.3, 135.2.2 n.18
Murphy's Est. v. CIR (TCM 1966)
.... 125.2 n.5
Murray v. US 129.5.1 n.4

N

Nail's Est. v. CIR 135.2.2 n.16
Nance v. US ... 127.4.5 n.34, 127.4.7 n.47
Narver v. CIR 135.2.1 n.4
Nashville Trust Co. v. CIR 125.11.4 n.51, 131.4.3 n.44
Natchez v. US 131.4.3 n.69
National Bank of Commerce v.
Clauson 126.3.2 n.28
National Bank of Commerce v.
Henslee 126.6.6 n.97
National City Bank v. US ... 126.3.2 n.32, 126.6.8 n.129
National Savings & Trust Co, v. US
.... 130.2 n.17
Naumoff v. CIR 124.3.3 n.41
Neal's Est. v. CIR 126.5.2 n.47
Neel, US v. 125.11.4 n.47
Neely v. US 126.8.2 n.21
Neisen's Est. v. CIR ...... 129.6.4 & n.19
Nelson's Est. v. CIR (2d Cir.) 125.5 n.8
Nelson's Est. v. CIR (TCM 1983)
.... 129.4.3 n.58
Nelson's Est. v. CIR (TCM 1980)
.... 135.2.2 n.15
Nelson's Est., CIR v. 126.3.4 n.54
Nelson Weaver Realty Co. v. CIR
.... 135.4.5 n.55
Nemerov's Est. v. CIR 125.7 n.16
Neugass' Est. v. CIR 129.3.3 n.28
Nevius, CIR v. 134.2.3 n.51
Newberry's Est. v. CIR 126.3.1 n.12

Newhouse's Est. v. CIR .... 135.3.4 & ns. 48, 49, 135.4.3 & ns. 36, 37
Newlin v. CIR 124.3.2 n.30
New Orleans Baptist Theological
Seminary v. Lacy 129.7.2 n.18
Newton Trust So. v. CIR 126.6.4 n.71
New York Trust Co. v. Eisner .... 120.1.2 & ns. 10, 12, 14, 125.5 ns. 1, 3
Nichols v. Coolidge .... 120.1.2 & n.19
Nichols, US v. 131.4.3 n.49
Nicholson's Est. v. CIR 129.4.3 n.40
Nicol's Est. v. CIR 126.6.6 n.96
Nienhuys' Est. v. CIR 134.2.1 n.7
Nilson's Est. v. CIR 131.4.3 n.49
Noel's Est. v. CIR 127.4.7 n.47
Noel's Est., CIR v. ... 127.2 n.2, 127.4.3 & ns. 23, 24
Noriar v. CIR 123.5.1 n.9
Northeastern Pa. Nat'l Bank & Trust
Co. v. US (US) .. 129.4.3 & ns. 68, 72, 76–79
Northeastern Pa. Nat'l Bank & Trust
Co. v. US (MD Pa.) 129.5.2 n.8
Northern Trust Co., Burnet v. (US)
.... 126.6.8 n.119
Northern Trust Co., Burnet v.
(7th Cir.) 125.5 n.5
Northern Trust Co. v. CIR ... 135.3.4 n.40
Northern Trust Co., Reinecke v.
.... 120.1.2 n.20, 126.3.7 ns. 71–73, 126.5.1 n.1
Northern Trust Co. v. US 130.3.2 n.14
Nourse v. Riddell 126.3.4 n.45
Novotny's Est. v. CIR 129.4.5 n.137
Nunan, Mallinckrodt v. 124.3.3 n.43

O

Obermer v. US 135.3.4 n.33, 135.3.8 n.71, 135.5.1 n.11
O'Brian's Est. v. CIR 121.7.4 n.38
Occidental Life Ins. Co. v. CIR .. 137.7.3 n.20
O'Connell's Est. v. CIR (9th Cir.)
...... 135.2.3 n.25, 135.3.5 n.57, 135.3.9 n.82, 135.5.2 n.19
O'Connell's Est. v. CIR (TCM) .. 135.3.2 n.8
O'Connor's Est. v. CIR 126.6.2 n.23, 126.6.3 n.55
Oetting v. US 130.3.2 n.14
O'Hara, Cockrill v. 127.4.7 n.47

[References are to paragraphs (¶) and notes (n.).]

Old Colony Trust Co. v. US (1st Cir.)
.... 122.4.2 & n.26, 126.1 n.7, 126.5.2 &
n.49, 126.6.4 n.77, 130.2 n.17
Old Colony Trust Co. v. US
(D. Mass.) .... 125.7 & n.3
Old Kent Bank & Trust Co. v. US
.... 132.6.3 n.23
Olson v. Reisimer 126.3.1 n.10
Olster v. CIR 135.4.6 n.72
O'Malley, US v. .... 126.3.2 & n.23,
126.6.3 n.54
Opal's Est. v. CIR 129.3.3 n.38
Orcutt's Est. v. CIR 127.3 n.3
Ordway v. US 121.7.1 n.8
O'Reilly v. CIR ...... 135.4.10 & ns. 102,
104–106
Osborn's Est. v. CIR 131.6.2 n.36
Otte's Est. v. CIR 125.11.4 n.68
Otto's Est., In re 130.5.7 n.62
Outwin v. CIR ... 122.3.1 n.10, 122.5 n.14
Oxford Orphanage, Inc. v. US 130.5.6
n.57

P

Pabst v. CIR ... 135.3.4 n.47, 135.3.6 n.58
Pack v. CIR 135.5.1 n.8
Paine, Welch v. 124.3.1 n.5
Paladino v. CIR 135.4.6 n.73
Palmer v. CIR 135.1.2 n.24, 135.5.2
n.19
Palmer's Est. v. CIR 135.2.4 n.43
Paolozzi v. CIR 122.5 n.14
Papson's Est. v. CIR ... 131.3.2 ns. 30, 33
Pardee's Est. v. CIR ... 126.6.2 ns. 21, 22,
131.6.2 n.31
Paris v. US 130.2 n.13
Park Amusement Co. v. CIR 135.1.2
n.27
Parker v. CIR 129.2.3 n.26
Parker v. US 135.6.6 n.89
Park's Est. v. CIR ... 131.3.2 n.41, 131.6.1
& ns. 17, 18, 20, 21
Pascal's Est. v. CIR 125.7 n.1
Pascarelli v. CIR 121.1 n.18, 121.4.5
n.49, 122.3.1 n.9
Paschal, Drummond's Est. v. 125.11.4
n.68
Past, US v. .... 126.3.4 ns. 52, 54
Pastor v. US 129.2.3 n.29
Paul's Est. v. CIR 128.4 n.8
Paxton's Est. v. CIR 126.3.3 n.40

Peacock's Est. v. US 129.4.5 n.137
Pearson v. CIR 126.6.8 n.128
Pelzer, US v. ... 124.3.1 & ns. 3–5, 124.3.2
Penner's Est. v. CIR 128.2.2 n.28
Penney's Est. v. CIR ... 129.5.2 n.8, 137.8
n.10
Pennsylvania Bank & Trust Co. v. US
.... 128.3.5 n.24, 131.3.2 n.25
Peoples First Nat'l Bank v. US ... 126.3.4
n.45
Peoples Trust Co. v. US 126.5.3 n.66,
128.2.2 n.34
Perkins v. CIR 124.3.4 n.54
Perl's Est. v. CIR ... 126.8.5 & ns. 76, 80,
127.4.2 n.7
Perry's Est. v. CIR 126.4.2 n.22, 127.8
ns. 10, 12
Peters' Est. v. CIR 125.11.4 n.45
Peterson v. CIR 137.7.3 n.16
Pettus v. CIR .... 124.4.2 ns. 16, 34
Pfeifer's Est. v. CIR 130.3.1 n.10
Pfeiffer v. US 131.4.3 n.49
Pfohl's Est. v. CIR 137.4.2 n.25
Philadelphia Park Amusement Co. v.
US 135.2.5 n.47
Philip Morris Inc. v. CIR ... 135.4.5 n.67
Phillips v. Dime Trust & Safe Deposit
Co. 125.11.1 n.4
Phillips v. Gnichtel 126.3.4 n.47
Phillips v. US 135.1.2 n.45
Phinney, Bar L Ranch, Inc. v. 135.4.6
n.72
Phipps v. CIR 121.3.1 n.2
Piatt v. Gray 129.4.3 n.59
Pickard's Est. v. CIR 130.3.1 n.5
Piggott's Est. v. CIR 127.4.7 n.47
Pingree's Est. v. Blumenthal .. 137.4.2 ns.
18, 25
Piper's Est. v. CIR 135.3.6 n.58,
135.3.7 n.67, 135.3.8 n.72
Piper's Est. v. US 137.4.2 n.23
Pipe's Est. v. CIR 129.4.3 n.31
Pitner v. US 131.3.2 n.5, 131.3.2 n.25,
131.6.1 ns. 4, 14
Plumb's Est. v. US 132.4 n.23
Poe v. Seaborn .... 123.2.1 & n.1, 126.6.2
n.44
Poinier v. CIR 137.7.2 n.7
Pollard's Est. v. CIR ... 131.4.3 ns. 48, 64
Pollock's Est. v. CIR 132.6.2 n.17,
132.6.3 n.28

[References are to paragraphs (¶) and notes (n.).]

Poor, White v. 126.5.1 n.15, 126.5.6 n.94

Porter v. CIR (US) .... 122.4.1 n.12, 126.5.2 & ns. 35, 44, 131.4.4 n.89

Porter v. CIR (TC) 131.3.2 n.26

Porter v. CIR (BTA) 131.4.3 n.56

Porter, CIR v. ...... 131.4.3 ns. 38, 54, 56

Porter's Est. v. CIR ... 122.3.5 n.25, 125.6 n.12

Posen's Est. v. CIR 131.6.1 n.14

Potemken, US v. 137.6.2 n.9

Powell, US v. 126.5.3 n.61

Prell's Est. v. CIR ... 131.3.2 n.19, 135.7.3 n.42

Premier Packing Co. v. CIR 135.2.2 n.14

Prentice's Est. v. CIR 135.3.4 n.44

Price's Est. v. CIR 126.5.4 n.74

Prichard v. US ... 127.3 n.3, 127.4.2 n.13, 127.4.7 n.47

Procter, CIR v. 121.3.3 n.29, 121.4.5 n.57

Proesel v. US ... 131.4.1 n.2, 131.6.2 n.23

Propstra v. US ..... 125.10 n.3, 131.4.2 & n.22, 135.3.4 ns. 35, 38

Proutt's Est. v. CIR 127.3 n.2

Prouty, CIR v. 122.5 n.2

Provident Nat'l Bank v. US (3d Cir.)
.... 135.3.4 n.43

Provident Nat'l Bank v. US (ED Pa.)
.... 128.4 n.9

Prudowsky's Est. v. CIR .... 126.5.1 ns. 6, 14, 17, 126.6.2 n.29

Prussner v. US 135.6.6 n.84

Publicker v. CIR .... 135.2.1 ns. 8, 9, 135.3.8 n.76

Pullin's Est. v. CIR 135.6.6 n.74

Pyle's Est. v. CIR 126.3.2 n.31

Pyne v. US 129.5.2 n.8

Q

Quinn's Est. v. CIR 135.3.10 n.120

R

Racca's Est. v. CIR 129.2.2 n.14

Radel's Est. v. CIR 129.3.3 n.23

Raimondi's Est. v. CIR 125.11.4 n.39

Rainier Cos. v. CIR 135.2.4 n.46

Randolph v. Craig .... 125.9 ns. 2, 12

Rapelje's Est. v. CIR 126.3.3 n.39, 126.6.2 n.36

Rasquin, Guggenheim v. .... 135.2.1 & ns. 1, 2, 7

Rasquin v. Humphreys ... 122.4.1 ns. 7, 9

Ratterre, Bailey v. 126.3.2 n.28

Rawley v. US 137.3 n.9

Ray v. US 126.6.1 n.4, 126.6.2 n.47

Ray's Est. v. CIR 129.3.3 n.33

Raznatovich v. CIR 135.4.8 n.87

Reardon v. US 135.7.3 n.41

Reed v. CIR 125.2 n.2

Reed v. US (7th Cir.) 120.1.2 n.23

Reed v. US (ED Mo.) 129.5.2 n.9

Reed's Est. v. CIR (8th Cir.) 126.3.2 n.27

Reed's Est. v. CIR (TCM) ... 131.6.2 n.32

Reed's Est. v. US 126.5.1 n.11

Regester's Est. v. CIR 121.6.4 n.24

Reiblich v. US .. 137.5.1 n.6, 137.5.3 n.46

Reichenberger's Est. v. CIR 128.2.1 n.18

Reid's Est. v. CIR (TC) 129.5.2 n.6

Reid's Est. v. CIR (TCM) ... 126.6.3 n.65

Reilly's Est. v. CIR (3d Cir.) 129.3.3 n.45

Reilly's Est. v. CIR (TC) ... 131.3.2 n.26, 131.4.3 n.86

Reinecke v. Northern Trust Co. .. 120.1.2 n.20, 126.3.7 ns. 71–73, 126.5.1 n.1

Reisimer, Olson v. 126.3.1 n.10

Renick's Est. v. US 132.3 n.15

Reno's Est. v. CIR 129.5.2 n.10

Republic Nat'l Bank v. CIR 130.6 n.8

Resch's Est. v. CIR 126.3.1 n.4

Reynolds v. CIR ..... 135.4.8 n.89, 135.5.1 ns. 4, 5, 135.5.2 n.28

Reynolds v. Russell 129.6.4 n.18

Reynolds, Winton v. 137.4.1 n.11

Reynolds' Est. v. CIR ..... 135.1.2 ns. 33, 54, 135.3.9 n.82, 135.3.10 ns. 108, 110

Rhode Island Hosp. Trust Co., US v.
.... 127.4.2 n.7, 127.4.7 & ns. 48, 49

Rhodes v. CIR 125.5 n.7

Rhodes v. US 137.3 n.12

Ribblesdale's Est. v. CIR 131.4.3 n.44

Riccio v. US ..... 132.7.2 n.16, 134.2.3 ns. 50, 55

Richards v. CIR 126.6.2 n.21

Richards v. US 129.7.1 n.10

[References are to paragraphs (¶) and notes (n.).]

Richardson v. CIR (2d Cir. 1945)
.... 135.3.3 ns. 17, 19, 135.3.4 n.45
Richardson v. CIR (2d Cir. 1942)
.... 122.2 ns. 1, 13
Richardson's Est. v. CIR 129.5.3 n.15
Rickenberg v. CIR 129.1 n.3
Riddell, Nourse v. 126.3.4 n.45
Riddle's Est. v. CIR 130.3.2 n.13
Ridgely's Est. v. CIR 135.3.7 n.61
Riegelman's Est. v. CIR ... 125.8 & ns. 4,
5, 10
Riggs v. Del Drago ..... 137.8 & ns. 4, 8
Ritland v. CIR 124.3.2 n.23
Rivera's Est., CIR v. 134.3 n.7
R.M. Smith, Inc. v. CIR (3d Cir.)
.... 135.5.2 n.19
R.M. Smith, Inc. v. CIR (TCM)
.... 135.4.5 n.49
Robbins v. CIR ..... 130.3.2 & ns. 16, 17
Roberts v. CIR 124.3.4 n.53
Robertson v. CIR 123.5.2 n.15
Robertson v. US 129.5.2 n.12
Robinette v. Helvering ..... 121.3.3 & ns.
23, 24, 135.4.10 & n.114
Robinson v. CIR (5th Cir.) ... 122.4.1 n.9
Robinson v. CIR (6th Cir.) 125.11.4
n.42
Robinson v. US (9th Cir.) 129.5.2 n.8
Robinson v. US (SD Ga.) .. 129.4.5 n.127
Robinson v. US (ED Tenn.) 129.4.3
n.37
Robinson's Est. v. CIR (TC 1977)
.... 135.3.8 ns. 78, 79
Robinson's Est. v. CIR (TC 1975)
.... 131.4.3 n.66, 131.5 n.1
Rockefeller Family, John D., Cemetery
Corp. v. CIR 131.2 n.3
Rockwell's Est. v. CIR 127.4.2 n.15
Rodgers v. US 121.7.1 n.5
Rodiek v. CIR .. 125.7 & ns. 8, 9, 134.2.1
n.9
Rodiek v. Helvering 125.4 n.6, 134.2.1
n.9
Roeser v. CIR 123.2.2 n.5
Rogan v. Kammerdiner 125.11.4 n.47
Rogers v. Strong 135.1.2 n.30
Rogers' Est. v. CIR 128.1 n.16
Rohmer v. CIR 134.2.2 n.12, 135.1.2
n.55, 135.3.8 n.78
Rolin's Est. v. CIR .. 121.7.1 n.15, 125.12
n.2, 128.2.1 n.6, 128.3.5 & ns. 26, 27
Rollman v. US 124.4.2 n.29

Rose v. US .... 127.4.6 & ns. 39–41
Rose, US v. 137.7.3 n.25
Rosen v. CIR 124.3.2 n.36
Rosenberg's Est. v. CIR 126.8.5 n.85
Rosenblatt's Est. v. CIR 125.2 n.3
Rosenblum v. Anglim 134.2.3 n.44
Rosenfield v. US 135.7.1 n.7, 135.7.6
n.66
Rosenman v. US .... 131.4.3 & ns. 85, 86
Rosenthal v. CIR .... 121.3.2 & ns. 15–17,
123.6.1 n.19
Rosenwasser's Est. v. CIR ... 126.5.1 n.2,
126.6.4 n.72
Rose's Est. v. CIR 125.2 n.2
Ross v. CIR (9th Cir.) .... 124.4.2 ns. 24,
25
Ross v. CIR (BTA) 122.2 n.1
Ross v. US 124.4.2 n.16
Rosser, CIR v. 125.5 n.8
Roth v. US 132.6.4 n.40
Rothrock v. CIR 121.4.5 n.54
Rott's Est. v. US 126.6.3 n.56
Rountree, Ewing v. 128.1 n.23
Rouse v. US 132.4 n.2
Routzahn, Brown v. .... 121.7.1 & n.3
Rowan's Est. v. CIR .. 131.2 n.14, 131.4.5
n.91
Royce's Est. v. CIR 125.3 n.7
Roy's Est. v. CIR .... 126.7.4 & ns. 41, 42
Rubinow's Est. v. CIR 129.3.3 n.23
Rubin's Est. v. CIR ... 125.9 n.11, 129.4.3
n.78, 131.4.3 n.64
Rundle v. Welch 126.5.1 n.10
Rushton v. CIR .... 135.3.3 ns. 13, 23
Russell, Reynolds v. 129.6.4 n.18
Russell v. US 125.2 n.5, 131.4.2 n.21
Russell's Est. v. CIR 126.4.4 n.57
Ryan's Est. v. CIR 135.7.6 n.68
Ryerson v. US 124.3.1 n.3
Ryerson, US v. .... 135.2.1 & n.7

S

Sachs' Est. v. CIR ... 126.4.3 n.43, 131.4.2
n.25
Safe Deposit & Trust Co., Helvering v.
.... 125.3 & ns. 4, 5, 7, 9, 128.1 n.18
Safe Deposit & Trust Co. v. Tait
.... 126.3.4 n.47
St. Joseph Bank & Tr. Co. v. US
.... 123.6.2 n.21

[References are to paragraphs (¶) and notes (n.).]

St. Louis County Bank v. US 135.3.10
& ns. 117–119
St. Louis Dispatch Co., Metropolitan
Bank v. 135.4.5 n.56
St. Louis Union Trust Co.,
Helvering v. .... 126.7.7 & n.58
Saleh, US v. 137.6.2 n.9
Salisbury v. US .... 126.5.3 ns. 53, 62
Salisbury's Est. v. CIR .... 135.3.4 ns. 31,
33
Salsbury's Est. v. CIR 126.8.5 n.84
Salter's Est. v. CIR 129.4.3 n.62
Saltonstall v. Saltonstall 128.1 n.23
Saltonstall, Saltonstall v. 128.1 n.23
Sam Broadhead Trust v. CIR 130.2
n.13, 131.6.2 n.23
Sampson v. Welch 125.10 n.2
Sanchez v. Bowers 134.2.3 n.54
Sanford's Est. v. CIR 121.3.3 n.25,
122.4.1 & ns. 5, 6, 8, 18, 126.3.2
n.18, 126.3.6 & n.65
Satz' Est. v. CIR ...... 131.4.3 ns. 70, 71
Sauber, Forster v. 126.8.1 n.7
Savage v. US 126.3.2 n.31
Schayek v. CIR 124.3.2 n.30
Scheide's Est. v. CIR 126.6.2 n.24
Schelberg's Est. v. CIR ..... 126.8.2 & ns.
31, 32, 34
Schiffman v. US 131.4.2 n.20
Schildkraut's Est. v. CIR ... 129.4.3 n.78,
131.3.2 n.4
Schindler v. US 135.6.5 n.52
Schlosser's Est. v. CIR 135.7.2 n.24
Schmidlapp v. CIR 121.2 n.5
Schnack v. CIR .... 127.8 & n.13
Schnader, City Bank Farmers Trust
Co. v. 134.2.3 n.34
Schneider, US v. 137.6.2 n.9
Schoonmaker's Est. v. CIR 126.3.2
n.24
Schroeder v. US 129.2.3 n.29
Schuette v. Bowers 125.9 n.2
Schultz, Tax Analysts & Advocates v.
.... 121.9 n.7
Schultz v. US 124.2 n.12
Schuneman v. US 135.6.2 n.23
Schuster v. CIR .... 137.7.3 ns. 14–17,
137.7.4 n.30
Schwager v. CIR 127.4.5 n.31
Schwaner, Cathcart v. 131.4.3 n.61
Schwartz' Est. v. CIR 126.3.1 n.4,
126.6.2 n.48

Schwarzenbach v. CIR 122.2 n.10,
122.5 n.4
Scofield's Est. v. CIR 131.4.2 n.23,
131.4.3 ns. 57, 59
Scott v. CIR (8th Cir.) 131.5 n.3
Scott v. CIR (9th Cir.) 127.5 n.4
Seaboard Automotive, Inc. v. CIR
.... 135.2.1 n.5, 135.4.5 n.67, 135.5.1 n.9
Seaborn, Poe v. ... 123.2.1 & n.1, 126.6.2
n.44
Seagrist's Est. v. CIR 131.6.2 n.31
Seattle First Nat'l Bank v. US 126.4.4
n.50
Second Nat'l Bank v. Dallman ... 128.2.1
n.9, 128.4 n.8
Second Nat'l Bank v. US .... 132.4 & ns.
13, 15
Second Nat'l Bank of New Haven v.
US 129.5.2 n.8
Securities Mortgage Co. v. CIR .. 135.2.3
n.38, 135.2.4 n.45
Security-First Nat'l Bank, US v. .. 137.6.2
ns. 13, 14
Selby's Est. v. US 125.12 n.2
Selecmen's Est. v. CIR 125.11.4 n.58
Self v. US 121.6.3, 121.6.4 n.23
Selig v. US 135.4.5 n.51
Sells' Est. v. CIR .... 130.2 ns. 13, 14
Senft v. US .... 130.3.1 & n.4
Sexton v. US .... 126.3.2 & n.22
Shaeffer's Est. v. CIR 128.5.2 n.6
Shafer's Est. v. CIR 126.3.2 n.19
Sharpe's Est. v. CIR 131.3.2 n.16
Shaughnessy, Singer v. 125.11.4 n.47,
127.4.1 n.3
Shaughnessy, Smith v. .... 121.3.3 & n.21,
122.4.1 & n.19, 126.3.6 & ns. 66, 67,
132.5 & n.2
Shearer's Est. v. CIR 126.6.2 n.36
Sheehan, Wahl v. 122.2 n.12, 126.5.1
n.14
Shenton v. US 134.2.3 n.36
Sherman v. US (5th Cir.) 121.4.3 n.35
Sherman v. US (ED Va.) ... 121.7.3 n.28,
135.3.5 n.56
Sherrod's Est. v. CIR .. 135.6.2 ns. 21, 26
Shively, CIR v. 131.4.2 n.31
Shlensky's Est. v. CIR 131.8 n.1
Short's Est. v. CIR ... 129.5.1 n.4, 129.5.2
n.8
Shriners' Hosp. for Crippled Children
v. US 130.3.3 n.25

[References are to paragraphs (¶) and notes (n.).]

Shukert v. Allen 126.3.7 n.71
Siegel v. CIR .... 135.4.8 ns. 87, 88
Siegel, CIR v. 123.2.2 n.8
Siegel's Est. v. CIR ... 126.5.1 n.8, 126.5.5
         n.86, 126.8.2 n.30
Silberman, Blodgett v. 134.2.3 n.30
Silberman v. CIR 135.5.2 n.25
Silberman v. US 126.8.2 n.43
Silverman v. CIR 135.3.4 n.31, 135.5.2
         & ns. 21, 23
Silverman's Est. v. CIR 126.4.2 n.22,
      126.8.5 ns. 76, 89, 127.8 n.4
Silvester's Est. v. CIR 135.7.6 n.67
Simmie's Est. v. CIR 135.4.6 n.80,
         137.4.2 n.23
Simon, Tax Analysts & Advocates v.
     .... 121.9 n.7
Sinclare's Est. v. CIR 126.3.1 n.4
Singer v. Shaughnessy 125.11.4 n.47,
         127.4.1 n.3
Sirloin Stockade, Inc. v. CIR 135.4.3
     n.30, 135.5.1 n.3, 135.5.2 n.28
Sisto Fin. Corp. v. CIR 135.5.2 n.19
Skifter's Est. v. CIR 126.5.1 n.11,
     127.4.6 & ns. 37, 38
Skinner's Est. v. CIR 126.3.3 n.40,
         126.6.4 n.73
Skouras v. CIR (2d Cir.) 124.3.3 n.39
Skouras v. CIR (TC) 124.3.1 n.10
Slater's Est. v. CIR 135.6.4 n.43
Slocum, Edwards v. .... 130.6 & n.2
Slutsky's Est. v. CIR ... 135.2.3 ns. 26, 33,
         135.4.7 n.82
Smallwood's Est. v. CIR 134.3 n.2
Smead's Est. v. CIR 127.4.3 n.20
Smith, Bull v. 135.3.3 n.18
Smith v. CIR 135.4.5 n.50
Smith, Jennings v. ... 126.5.1 n.16, 126.5.3
     & ns. 52, 59, 71, 126.5.6 n.92,
         126.6.4 & n.78
Smith, Fidelity-Philadelphia Trust
   Co. v. .... 126.6.2 & ns. 39, 40, 46,
     126.7.1 n.2, 127.2 & ns. 11, 12,
         129.3.5 n.51
Smith, Lilly v. 123.4 n.1
Smith v. Shaughnessy .... 121.3.3 & n.21,
     122.4.1 & n.19, 126.3.6 & ns. 66, 67,
         132.5 & n.2
Smith v. US (D. Conn.) 128.2.1 n.22,
         129.4.3 n.87
Smith v. US (D. Mass.) 131.4.3 n.49

Smith's Est. v. CIR (2d Cir. 1975)
     .... 131.3.2 n.41, 131.6.1 ns. 11, 14
Smith's Est. v. CIR (2d Cir. 1972)
     .... 135.1.1 n.18, 135.1.2 ns. 55, 56,
     135.2.2 n.15, 135.3.3 n.15, 135.4.8
         n.89
Smith's Est. v. CIR (7th Cir.) 129.4.3
         n.32, 129.6.3 n.11
Smith's Est. v. CIR (TC 1990) 132.3
         n.4
Smith's Est. v. CIR (TC 1982) ... 129.4.3
         n.58
Smith's Est. v. CIR (TC 1979) ... 127.4.3
         & ns. 17, 18
Smith's Est. v. CIR (TC 1975) ... 135.7.3
         n.36
Smith's Est. v. CIR (TC 1972) 125.7
         n.1
Smith's Est. v. CIR (TCM) 129.7.2
         n.20
Smoot's Est. v. CIR 135.6.3 n.38
Smyth v. Erickson 131.3.2 n.25
Snyder v. CIR (TC 1989) ...... 136.2.4 &
         n.43
Snyder v. CIR (TC 1976) 121.1 n.18,
         121.2 n.3
Snyder v. US .... 137.5.3 & ns. 44, 47
Solitron Devices, Inc. v. CIR ... 135.4.5 &
         ns. 53, 58, 61, 65
Solveson's Will, In re v. 126.5.3 n.68
Southern Rock, Inc. v. B&B Auto
   Supply 137.6.2 n.9
South Seas Shipping Co. v. CIR
     .... 135.2.5 n.47, 135.3.3 n.13
Sowell's Est. v. CIR 128.2.2 n.27
Spaeder v. US 130.6 n.3
Spalding's Est. v. CIR ... 129.2.2 & ns. 11,
         13
Sparling's Est. v. CIR 132.6.3 n.31
Spicer, US v. 129.3.3 n.38
Spiegel's Est. v. CIR ... 126.2 n.5, 126.6.8
     n.127, 126.7.2 n.18, 126.7.3 n.21,
     126.7.4 ns. 33, 34, 126.7.7 n.61
Spohn's Est. v. US 129.4.5 n.127
Spruance v. CIR 123.6.1 n.8
Spruill's Est. v. CIR 126.6.2 n.37
Stalcup v. US 132.3 n.6
Staley v. CIR 121.1 n.15
Stalp, In re 130.5.7 n.62
Stansbury v. US 128.2.1 n.19

[References are to paragraphs (¶) and notes (n.).]

Stapf, US v. .. 129.3.1 n.4, 129.5.3 ns. 15, 16, 131.4.3 & ns. 38, 41, 131.4.5 ns. 91, 94

Stark v. US 124.3.2 n.36

Starrett v. CIR 129.4.3 n.50

State St. Bank & Trust Co. v. US ... 130.2 n.16

State St. Trust Co. v. US ... 126.5.2 n.49, 126.6.4 n.71

Steen v. US 125.11.4 n.47

Steffke's Est. v. CIR .. 129.2.2 & ns. 7, 8, 10

Stephens v. US 129.2.3 n.26

Stern v. US ..... 121.4.5 n.48, 121.9 & n.3

Sternberger's Est., CIR v. .... 135.4.10 ns. 113, 115

Stewart v. US 128.4 n.8

Stewart, US v. 127.5 n.4

Stewart's Est. v. CIR 123.4 n.3

Stifel v. CIR 124.3.3 n.39

Stinchcomb v. Mercantile-Safe Deposit & Trust Co. 129.4.3 n.65

Stix v. CIR 126.5.3 n.55

Stoutz v. US 135.7.3 n.41

Stratton's Est. v. CIR .. 135.3.7 ns. 66, 67

Strauss v. CIR 121.3.6 n.52

Streeter's Est. v. CIR 131.3.2 n.45

Strickland's Est. v. CIR ... 135.6.6 ns. 87, 88

Strite v. McGinnes 128.2.2 n.28

Strong, Rogers v. 135.1.2 n.30

Struthers v. Kelm 126.6.3 n.56, 126.6.7 n.113

Strutz v. CIR ... 135.5.1 n.9, 135.5.2 n.28

Stubblefield's Est. v. CIR ... 126.3.5 n.64, 126.4.4 n.68, 126.6.2 n.36

Sturr, Mandel v. 125.8 n.10

Sugden, Lomb v. ... 135.3.10 ns. 108, 120

Sullivan's Est. v. CIR 125.11.2 n.28, 126.3.5 n.64

Sulovich's Est. v. CIR 122.3.4 n.20, 126.5.2 n.40

Sundquist v. US 135.4.3 n.28

Surloff v. CIR 135.2.1 n.4

Sussman v. US .... 131.3.2 & n.22

Sutton v. CIR .... 131.4.3 ns. 60, 65

Swan's Est. v. CIR .... 134.2.3 & n.45

Swartz v. US ...... 125.11.4 ns. 41, 59, 60

Swayne's Est. v. CIR 131.3.2 n.25, 131.6.1 n.13

Swenson v. CIR 135.4.7 n.83

Swenson's Est. v. CIR 129.2.3 n.28

Swetland v. CIR .... 124.3.2 ns. 18, 38

Symington v. CIR 135.4.1 n.1, 135.5.2 n.27

T

Taft v. CIR ...... 130.3.4 & n.27, 131.4.3 n.38

Tait, Safe Deposit & Trust Co. v. 126.3.4 n.47

Talbott's Est., CIR v. 126.6.8 n.129

Talcott v. US 129.1 n.3

Tarver's Est. v. CIR 126.7.3 n.27, 126.7.4 n.46, 126.7.5 n.49

Tax Analysts & Advocates v. Schultz 121.9 n.7

Tax Analysts & Advocates v. Simon 121.9 n.7

Tebb's Est. v. CIR 129.2.3 n.36

Tennessee Carolina Transp. Inc. v. CIR 135.1.2 n.25, 135.5.2 n.24

Terre Haute First Nat'l Bank v. US 130.3.2 n.17

Terriberry v. US 127.4.3 n.24, 127.4.6 n.39

Teubert v. US 135.6.6 n.81

Thacher's Est. v. CIR 126.7.2 n.13, 126.7.4 n.46

Thalheimer's Est. v. CIR ... 135.3.8 n.72, 135.4.3 n.26

Thayn v. US 129.5.2 n.10

Thebaut, CIR v. 124.4.2 n.29

Theis' Est. v. CIR 131.4.3 n.58, 131.5 n.6

Theopold v. US .... 126.5.2 ns. 41, 47

Third Nat'l Bank & Trust v. White 125.11.2 n.12

Thompson, Townsend v. 126.6.2 n.27, 126.6.6 n.108

Thompson's Est. v. CIR (4th Cir.) 135.6.3 n.38

Thompson's Est. v. CIR (TC) 121.7.5 n.45, 135.6.3 n.32

Thomson's Est. v. CIR 126.6.8 n.128

Tickell, Townson v. 121.7.1 n.12

Tiffany's Est. v. CIR 131.4.3 n.45

Tilton v. CIR 137.4.1 n.11

Tilyou's Est. v. CIR 129.4.2 n.20

Todd's Est. v. CIR ... 129.4.3 n.29, 131.3.2 n.35

Tomec's Est. v. CIR 126.6.1 n.5, 126.6.3 n.60

TABLE OF CASES

[References are to paragraphs (¶) and notes (n.).]

Tomlinson, Barritt v. 128.2.2 n.32
Tomlinson, Union Trust Co. v. 131.6.2 n.31
Tompkins v. CIR 129.3.3 n.28
Tompkins' Est. v. CIR 127.4.8 n.64
Touche v. CIR .. 122.3.1 n.9, 124.4.2 n.11
Towle's Est. v. CIR 128.2.3 n.39
Townsend v. Thompson 126.6.2 n.27, 126.6.6 n.108
Townson v. Tickell 121.7.1 n.12
Trafton's Est. v. CIR 123.4 n.1, 125.11.4 n.47
Treganowan, CIR v. ..... 127.2 & ns. 5, 7
True v. US (Ct. Cl.) ... 123.5.3 n.23, 137.2 n.6
True v. US (D. Wyo.) 135.3.10 n.112
Trunk's Est. v. CIR 130.6 n.3
Trust Co. of Ga., Allen v. 126.3.5 n.58
Trust Serv. of Am., Inc. v. US 137.3 n.18
Tuck v. US 125.11.4 n.64
Tully's Est. v. US .... 121.2 n.7, 122.3.5 & ns. 23, 25, 125.6 & ns. 11, 12, 126.5.4 n.75, 126.6.4 n.67
Turman v. CIR 123.2.2 n.9
Turner v. CIR 135.3.7 n.63
Turner, US v. 128.4 n.6
Twogood's Est. v. CIR 122.3.5 n.21
Twogood's Est., CIR v. 126.8.1 n.8
212 Corp. v. CIR 135.1.2 n.33
Tyler v. US (US) .... 120.1.2 ns. 6, 18, 125.5 ns. 1, 2, 125.11.1 & ns. 2, 10–12
Tyler v. US (10th Cir.) 129.4.3 n.62

U

Uhl's Est., In re 126.6.1 n.5, 126.6.4 n.73
Ujvari v. US 135.2.4 n.44
Underwood v. US ... 130.3.2 n.17, 131.3.2 n.8
Union Commerce Bank v. CIR ... 126.3.2 n.30, 131.3.3 n.59
Union Pac. RR v. US 135.1.2 n.31
Union Planters Nat'l Bank & Trust Co., Henslee v. 130.4 n.9
Union Trust Co. v. Tomlinson 131.6.2 n.31
United States Nat'l Bank v. US .. 126.7.3 n.25

United States Trust Co. v. Helvering 127.2 n.1
United States Trust Co., Helvering v. 121.4.3 n.26
Untermyer v. Anderson 120.1.2 n.20
Upjohn v. US 124.4.2 n.17
Usry, Fatter v. 126.4.4 n.57

V

Vaccaro v. US ... 122.3.1 n.9, 126.5.1 n.14, 126.5.6 n.93
Valentine's Est. v. CIR 126.7.3 n.23
Van Beuren v. McLoughlin 126.5.5 n.89
Vandenhoeck's Est. v. CIR ... 134.2.4 n.69
Van Den Wymelenberg v. US 124.4.2 n.11
Vander Hook v. CIR .... 135.4.8 n.87, 135.5.1 ns. 7, 13
Vanderlip v. CIR 126.6.1 n.6
Vander Weele, CIR v. 122.5 n.11
Van Horne's Est. v. CIR .... 131.4.2 & ns. 34–36, 135.7.3 n.47
Van Wye's Est. v. US 126.8.2 n.31
Vardell's Est. v. CIR 126.3.4 n.51
Varian's Est. v. CIR 126.5.2 n.40
Varick's Est. v. CIR 130.3.1 n.7
Vatter's Est. v. CIR 131.3.2 n.42
Vaughan, Clauson v. 128.1 n.19
Vaughn v. US 125.5 n.7, 125.11.1 n.1, 128.2.1 n.3
Vease's Est., CIR v. ... 126.3.1 n.7, 126.3.2 n.28
Vermilya's Est. v. CIR 129.3.3 n.38
Vernon v. CIR 135.4.10 n.101
VGS Corp. v. CIR ...... 135.4.5 & ns. 59, 60, 63
Vinal, Hansen v. 129.4.2 n.17
Virginia Nat'l Bank v. US ... 129.4.3 n.44
Visintainer v. CIR 122.2 n.12
Vissering's Est. v. CIR 128.2.2 n.34
Vitt's Est. v. US 137.9 n.1
Voelbel's Est. v. CIR 131.6.1 n.7
Vogel's Est. v. CIR 125.10 n.10
Vohland, US v. ... 137.6.1 n.6, 137.6.2 n.9
Voorhis v. US 135.6.6 n.82
Vriniotis' Est. v. CIR 134.2.1 n.1

[References are to paragraphs (¶) and notes (n.).]

W

Wadewitz' Est. v. CIR ...... 126.8.2 & ns. 45, 46, 53

Wagner v. US 126.8.5 n.102

Wahl v. Sheehan 122.2 n.12, 126.5.1 n.14

Wahlfeld's Est. v. US 128.2.2 n.27

Waldrop v. US 130.6 n.7

Waldrup v. US 129.2.3 n.32

Walker's Est. v. CIR 135.4.6 n.73

Wallace v. US ... 135.3.2 n.9, 135.4.3 n.32

Walston, CIR v. 121.6.4 n.23

Walter v. US 126.5.1 n.19

Wang v. CIR 123.5.2 n.15

Want v. CIR 137.7.3 n.19

Ward v. CIR ... 135.3.4 n.35, 135.3.8 n.72

Ward's Est. v. CIR 135.6.5 n.52

Ware's Est. v. CIR ... 126.3.2 n.24, 126.5.1 ns. 17, 25

Warner, Bergh v. 121.4.3 n.31

Warner, CIR v. 121.1 n.17, 122.3.1 n.8

Warner, US v. 137.6.2 n.9

Warren Jones Co. v. CIR 135.4.6 n.74

Warren's Est. v. CIR 130.6 n.8

Watson v. CIR 127.4.7 n.50

Watson v. McGinnes 131.7 n.7

Watson's Est. v. Blumenthal 137.4.2 n.25

Watson's Est. v. CIR 129.3.3 n.23

Watts' Est. v. CIR 135.4.4 n.40

Webber v. CIR 135.1.2 n.45

Webster v. CIR 131.2 n.2

Webster's Est. v. CIR .... 126.3.1 n.7, 126.5.4 n.74, 131.3.2 ns. 35, 39

Wegman's Est. v. CIR 129.2.3 n.32

Weil v. CIR (5th Cir.) 122.2 n.10

Weil v. CIR (TCM) 135.5.1 n.7

Weil's Est. v. CIR 135.4.4 n.43

Weinstein's Est. v. US ..... 132.6.3 ns. 28, 29

Weisberger's Est. v. CIR 132.4 n.19

Welch, Cadden v. 131.3.2 n.17

Welch, Central Trust Co. v. 131.3.3 n.60

Welch, Hassett v. 120.1.2 n.24, 126.6.8 n.125

Welch v. Paine 124.3.1 n.5

Welch, Rundle v. 126.5.1 n.10

Welch, Sampson v. 125.10 n.2

Weller v. CIR .... 121.4.5 ns. 42, 43, 124.4.2 n.31, 135.4.10 n.100

Welliver's Est. v. CIR 126.8.1 n.7, 126.8.3 n.56, 135.7.4 n.52

Wells v. Gay 132.4 n.3

Wells, US v. ..... 122.2 n.17, 126.4.1 n.3, 126.4.4 & ns. 44, 47

Well's Est. v. CIR 129.4.3 n.40

Wells' Est. v. CIR 126.6.4 n.73

Wells Fargo Bank v. US 130.5.7 n.62

Wells Fargo Bank, US v. 137.9 n.6

Wemyss, CIR v. ... 121.4.1 & n.1, 121.4.2 & ns. 10, 11, 14, 121.4.5, 123.6.1 n.1, 131.4.3 & ns. 40, 60

Werbe's Est. v. US 129.4.4 n.100

Wheaton v. US 129.3.3 n.29

Whelan v. US 128.2.2 n.28

Wheless v. CIR 131.3.2 n.40

Whipple's Est. v. US 129.5.2 n.12

White v. Poor 126.5.1 n.15, 126.5.6 n.94

White, Third Nat'l Bank & Trust v. 125.11.2 n.12

White v. US 128.4 n.8

White, US v. 131.6.1 n.14

Whiteley v. US 126.3.2 n.32

Whittemore v. Fitzpatrick 135.1.2 n.39

Whittle's Est. v. CIR 132.6.3 n.30

Whitworth's Est. v. CIR 122.3.5 n.27

Wiener, Fernandez v. ...... 120.1.2 & ns. 16–18, 120.2.3 & n.16, 123.2.1 n.1, 125.5 n.2, 125.10 & ns. 5, 6, 126.6.2 n.44, 129.1 & ns. 5, 6

Wien's Est. v. CIR 127.7 n.4

Wier's Est. v. CIR 126.6.4 n.71

Wilcoxen v. US 129.3.3 n.40

Wildenthal's Est. v. CIR 131.5 n.11

Wildman v. CIR 135.4.8 n.87

Willcuts, Brooks v. 135.1.2 n.24

Williams v. US 124.4.2 n.16

Williams' Est. v. CIR 125.5 n.8

Williamson v. CIR ... 135.6.2 n.21, 135.6.9 n.132

Willow Terrace Dev. Co. v. CIR 135.5.1 n.2

Wilmot Fleming Eng'g Co. v. CIR .... 135.4.5 ns. 57, 59

Wilson v. Bowers 135.3.10 n.107

Wilson v. CIR 125.11.2 n.20

Wilson v. Kraemer 128.4 n.10

Wilson v. US 131.6.3 n.47

Wilson's Est. v. CIR ... 126.5.3 ns. 60, 67

Wiltshire v. CIR 135.1.2 n.25, 135.4.8 n.87

TABLE OF CASES

[References are to paragraphs (¶) and notes (n.).]

Winchell, US v. 126.5.2 n.48
Winer v. US 132.7.1 n.13
Winkle v. US (SD Ohio) ..... 129.3.3 ns. 33, 38
Winkle v. US (WD Pa.) 125.8 n.10
Winn-Dixie Montgomery, Inc. v. US 135.4.5 n.53
Winton v. Reynolds 137.4.1 n.11
Wisely's Est. v. US 129.4.3 n.40
Wishard v. US 126.6.2 n.19
Witkowski's Est. v. US 128.2.3 n.35
Wittemore v. Fitzpatrick 135.3.4 n.33
Wodehouse v. CIR 134.2.2 n.12
Wolder v. CIR 131.4.3 n.44
Wolf's Est. v. CIR 128.2.1 n.8, 128.5.2 n.7
Wolfe's Est. v. CIR 135.3.7 n.61
Wolfsen Land & Cattle Co. v. CIR .... 136.2.2 & ns. 13, 17
Wolfson, US v. 135.1.2 n.24, 135.5.1 n.13
Woodward's Est. v. CIR 125.2 n.8
Woodworth's Est. v. CIR .... 130.4 & ns. 3–5
Woody's Est. v. CIR .... 131.4.3 & ns. 61, 80

Worcester County Trust Co. v. CIR 135.3.10 n.106
Worthington's Est. v. CIR .... 134.2.3 ns. 44, 48
Wragg, CIR v. .. 125.7 n.3, 131.4.3 ns. 54, 55
Wright v. CIR (BTA 1941) ... 135.1.2 n.44
Wright v. CIR (BTA 1933) ... 137.7.3 n.24
W.T. Grant Co. v. Duggan ... 135.1.2 n.35
Wycoff's Est. v. US .... 129.5.1 & n.4
Wyly's Est. v. CIR ... 126.3.3 n.41, 126.6.2 ns. 44, 45

Y

Yalem v. US 122.2 n.4
Yawkey's Est. v. CIR .... 126.5.3 n.66, 126.5.4 n.74, 126.6.3 ns. 61, 62, 126.6.4 n.71, 126.6.6 n.97
YMCA v. Davis 125.6, 137.8 n.7
Young v. US 131.4.3 n.46

Z

Zaiger's Est. v. CIR 126.4.4 n.55
Zietz's Est. v. CIR 125.5 n.7

Table of IRC Sections

[References are to paragraphs (¶) and notes (n.).]

SECTION

16(b) .... 135.3.7 & n.69
61(a) 125.3
61(a)(1) 135.1.1 n.6
72(a) 126.8.2 n.14
83(a) 135.4.7 n.81
101(a) .... 127.2 ns. 1, 13
101(a)(1) 127.2
102(a) 120.3, 121.5, 130.3.2
151(e) 121.5
152(a) 121.5
162 .... 120.3, 135.6.2 & n.26, 137.5.2
162(a) 131.3.2 n.28
164(a)(5) 133.2.7 n.50
165 .... 131.8 n.3
165(c)(3) .... 120.3, 131.4.5, 131.8 & n.1
165(h)(2) 131.6.4 n.48
168 .... 135.2.3
170 .... 130.2 n.5
170(b)(1)(A) 130.5.2
170(b)(1)(A)(ii) .... 121.5 & n.10
170(b)(2) 121.1 n.3
170(c) .... 121.8.1, 130.2 & ns. 8, 11,
                                130.5.2 & n.2
170(c)(4) 130.2 n.11
170(c)(5) 130.2 n.9, 131.2 n.3
170(f)(2) 121.8.2 n.9, 130.5.1 n.2,
                                130.5.4 n.40
170(f)(2)(A) 130.5.2 n.16
170(f)(3)(A) 130.5.4 n.40
170(f)(3)(B) 121.8.2, 130.5.3 n.23,
                                130.5.4 n.40
170(f)(3)(B)(i) 130.5.5 n.42
170(f)(3)(B)(ii) 130.5.4 n.36
170(h) ...... 121.8.2, 125.3 n.7, 135.3.10 &
                                       n.89
212 .... 120.3, 131.5 n.12, 131.6.4
213 .... 121.5
213(b) 121.5 n.11
213(c) 131.4.5 n.93
213(d) .... 121.5 & n.11, 129.7.1 n.6

SECTION

267(b) .... 136.3.3 & n.39
267(c)(4) 137.5.2 n.26
274(b) 121.4.5 n.41
274(b)(1) .... 121.1 & n.4
280A 136.4.6 n.97
280A(d) 136.4.6 n.97
303 ...... 125.11.3 & n.34, 133.6.4 & n.16,
                            137.5.4 & n.52
303(a) .... 126.4.2 & n.26
303(b) 126.4.2
303(b)(2)(A) 126.4.2 n.24
303(d) 133.6.4 n.16
318 .... 126.6.5
318(a)(1)(A)(ii) 126.6.5 n.87
318(a)(2)(B)(i) 126.6.5 n.87
351(a) .... 134.2.2 n.13, 135.7.3 & n.36
354–355 .... 135.7.3
354–356 .... 135.7.3 n.36
354 .... 135.7.3 n.36
401(a) .... 126.8.2, 126.8.5 & n.78
402(a)(2) 126.8.5 n.85
402(e) 126.8.5 n.85
402(e)(1) 126.8.5
402(e)(4) 126.8.5
402(e)(4)(J) 126.8.5 n.86
403(a) 126.8.5
403(b) .... 126.8.5 & n.91
403(e)(3) .... 129.6.3 ns. 18, 19
404 .... 126.8.5
441(c)(2) 124.1 n.6
453B(f) 121.1 n.24
469(h)(1) 135.6.5 n.48
483 .... 135.4.6 n.77
483(a) 135.4.6 n.77
501(c)(3) .... 121.8.1 & ns. 1, 7, 130.1,
           130.5.1, 130.5.2 & ns. 1, 5, 134.2.3
                                       n.33
501(c)(13) 130.2 n.10
501(j) 121.8.1 n.1
507(c) 130.2 n.21

TAXATION OF INCOME, ESTATES AND GIFTS

[References are to paragraphs (¶) and notes (n.).]

SECTION

508(2) 130.2 n.21
508(a) 130.2 n.21
508(d) 121.8.1 n.7
508(d)(1) 130.2 n.21
508(e) 130.2 n.21
527(e) 121.9
533(b) 126.4.3 n.61
642(g) 120.3, 129.7.1 n.5, 130.4,
 131.3.2 n.39, 131.8 n.2, 133.3.2 ns.
 10, 14
644 .... 123.6.2 n.21
644(c)(5)(A) 130.5.2 n.20
644(d) 130.2 n.11
644(d)(1)(A) 130.6 n.1
644(d)(1)(C) 130.5.2 n.20
644(d)(2)(C) 130.5.2 n.20
671–677 .... 126.5.5 n.80
674(a) 136.2.10
676–677 .... 122.5
676 .... 125.3
691 .... 120.3 n.7, 125.8 & n.6
691(a) 120.3
691(c) 120.3, 125.7 n.14, 125.8
702(i) 126.6.5
707 .... 136.2.4 n.47
707(c) ..... 136.2.2 & n.16, 136.2.4 & n.47
811(c) 126.6.8 n.127
861(a)(1)(A) 134.2.3 n.47
861(c) 334.2.3 n.47
871(h)(1) 134.2.3
897 .... 134.2.2 n.13
958(a) 134.4 n.9
958(b) 134.4 n.9
1001(a) 126.3.4 n.44
1001(b) 135.1.2 n.20
1014 .... 120.3, 128.5.2, 128.5.4, 133.4 &
 n.1
1014(a) 129.4.5 n.152, 135.7.5
1014(a)(1) 135.1.1 n.17
1014(a)(3) 120.3 n.6
1014(b) 135.6.3
1014(b)(9) 125.11.3 n.35, 125.11.4
 n.42, 126.4.2, 126.4.3 n.57
1014(b)(10) 129.4.5 n.153
1014(c) 120.3 n.7
1014(e) 120.3 n.8
1015 .... 120.3, 126.4.2 & n.32, 128.5.2,
 128.5.4, 133.4 & n.1
1015(a) 129.4.5 n.152
1015(d) .... 133.4 & n.4

SECTION

1016(c) .... 135.6.9 & n.145
1031 ...... 135.6.5 & n.64, 135.6.9 & n.129
1033 ...... 135.6.5 & n.64, 135.6.9 & n.122
1223(11) 120.3
1274(d) 130.5.3 n.35, 135.4.10 n.96
1286 .... 126.6.2 n.42
1402(a)(1) 135.6.5
1852(e)(3) 126.8.5 n.71
2001 ..... 125.5, 125.6, 125.9, 129.2.5 n.63,
 132.4, 132.5, 132.7.1, 136.2.12
2001(a) 120.2.2
2001(b) ... 125.11.1 n.7, 125.11.2, 132.3 &
 n.8, 135.6.4 n.43, 136.4.4, 137.3 n.2
2001(c) 132.2.1, 132.3, 133.3.4 n.44,
 134.2.2, 134.2.5, 134.4
2001(c)(3) 132.1 n.12
2001(d) 123.5.1 n.8, 132.3 n.12
2001(e) .... 123.5.1 & n.10, 132.3 n.14
2002 .... 137.7.1 n.1, 137.7.3 n.12, 137.8
2010 .... 129.6.2 n.6, 132.5, 132.6.4,
 134.2.7 n.90
2010(b) 120.1 n.22, 132.2.1 n.8, 132.3
 n.15
2011 ...... 129.2.5, 129.5.2 n.5, 129.6.2 n.8,
 131.6.2 n.40, 131.7 & n.3, 132.4 &
 ns. 1, 2, 132.5, 132.6.4, 132.7.1 ns. 6,
 11, 134.2.5
2011(a) .... 132.4 & n.1
2011(b) .... 132.4 & n.4, 134.2.5
2011(c) .... 132.4 & n.23
2011(d) 132.4, 132.8 n.1
2011(e) 132.4 n.33
2011(f) .... 132.4 & n.28
2012 .... 125.11.1 n.7, 125.11.4, 126.4.1
 n.7, 132.3, 132.4 n.2, 132.5, 132.6 &
 n.36, 134.2.5
2012(a) 132.5
2012(c)(1) 132.5 n.10
2012(d)(1) 132.5
2012(e) 132.5 n.3
2013 ...... 129.2.5 & n.78, 132.6.1, 132.6.2,
 132.6.4 & n.38, 134.2.5
2013(a) 132.6.2, 132.6.4
2013(b) 132.6.3 n.19, 132.6.4
2013(c)(1) 132.6.3 n.19, 132.6.4
2013(d) 132.6.3
2013(d)(1) 132.6.3 n.30
2013(d)(2) 132.6.3 n.31
2013(d)(3) 132.6.3 n.32
2013(e) 132.6.2

TABLE OF IRC SECTIONS

[References are to paragraphs (¶) and notes (n.).]

SECTION

2013(g) 132.6.1 n.5
2014 .... 129.2.5, 129.5.2 n.5, 131.6.2 n.40,
  131.7 & n.3, 132.4 n.1, 132.7.1 &
  n.6, 132.7.2, 132.7.3, 132.7.4, 134.2.5
  & n.78
2014(a) 132.7.1, 132.7.2 n.15
2014(b) 132.7.1 n.10
2014(b)(1) .... 132.7.3 ns. 30, 33
2014(b)(2) 132.7.3 n.37
2014(c)(1) 132.7.3 n.34
2014(c)(2) 132.7.3 n.38
2014(e) 132.7.1 n.11
2014(f) 132.7.1 n.10, 132.7.4 n.40
2014(g) 132.7.1 n.6
2014(h) 132.7.1 n.7
2015 .... 132.4 n.24, 132.7.1 n.12, 133.5,
  137.4.4 n.36,
2016 .... 132.4 n.20, 132.7.2 n.15
2031–2044 .... 134.2.3
2031–2046 .... 120.2.2
2031 .... 135.1.1 & n.4, 135.7.1
2031(b) 135.2.2
2032 ...... 126.4.3 n.62, 129.2.5, 129.5.1 &
  n.1, 129.7.1 n.4, 133.3.4 n.60,
  135.7.1, 135.7.2, 135.7.5, 137.3 & n.5
2032A ..... 120.3 & n.6, 125.11.3 & ns. 31,
  34, 126.4.2 & n.27, 129.2.5, 131.3.2
  & n.38, 131.6.2 n.42, 137.6.1 & n.4,
  133.3.2, 133.3.3, 133.3.4 & n.60,
  133.4 n.6, 135.6.5, 135.6.6, 135.6.7 &
  n.97, 135.6.8, 135.6.9, 135.6.10, 137.3
  & n.6, 137.5.1 & n.4, 137.5.2 n.16
2032A(a)(1) 135.6.7 n.95
2032A(b)(1) 135.6.3 n.28
2032A(b)(1)(A) 135.6.4 n.39, 135.6.7
  n.97
2032A(b)(1)(B) .... 135.6.5 ns. 45, 68,
  135.6.6 n.90, 135.6.7 n.97
2032A(b)(1)(C) .... 135.6.5 ns. 44, 65
2032A(b)(1)(D) 135.6.6 n.71
2032A(b)(3) 135.6.4 n.41
2032A(b)(4)(A) 135.6.5 n.61
2032A(b)(4)(B) 135.6.5 n.62
2032A(b)(5)(A) 135.6.5 n.55
2032A(b)(5)(B) 135.6.5 n.55
2032A(b)(5)(C) 135.6.5 n.63
2032A(c) 133.3.2 n.6, 133.3.3 n.33,
  135.6.6 n.70
2032A(c)(1) 135.6.9 n.120
2032A(d)(1) 135.6.6 n.72

SECTION

2032A(d)(2) 135.6.6 n.74
2032A(d)(3) .... 135.6.6 & n.84, 135.6.8
  n.116
2032A(e)(1) 135.6.3 n.29
2032A(e)(2) 135.6.3 n.29
2032A(e)(6) 135.6.5 n.46
2032A(e)(7) 135.6.7 n.98
2032A(e)(7)(A) 135.6.7 n.103
2032A(e)(7)(B) 135.6.7 n.107
2032A(e)(7)(C) 135.6.7 n.10
2032A(e)(8) .... 135.6.7 ns. 98, 113
2032A(e)(9)(A) 135.6.3 n.31
2032A(e)(12) 135.6.5 n.56
2032A(e)(14) 135.6.5 n.64
2032A(g) .... 135.6.1 & n.3, 135.6.3 &
  n.35, 135.6.8
2032(a) .... 135.7.1 n.6, 135.7.2 & n.14,
  135.7.5
2032(a)(1) 135.7.1 n.9, 135.7.2, 135.7.3
2032(a)(2) 135.7.1 n.10
2032(a)(3) 135.7.2 n.11, 135.7.4
2032(b) .... 135.7.5 & ns. 58, 60, 62
2032(c) 135.7.1
2032(d) 135.7.5 n.61
2032(d)(1) .... 135.7.6 ns. 66, 71
2032(d)(2) 135.7.6 n.67
2033–2042 .... 132.7.1, 135.1.1 n.4, 135.7.1
2033 ..... 122.2 n.12, 125.1, 125.2, 125.3 &
  n.7, 125.4, 125.5 & n.7, 125.6 & ns.
  3, 7, 12, 125.7 & ns. 6, 13, 125.8,
  125.9, 125.11.2 & n.17, 125.11.4,
  125.12, 126.5.1 & n.2, 126.5.2,
  126.7.1, 126.7.2, 126.7.4, 126.8.1,
  126.8.2 ns. 23, 52, 126.8.5 n.76,
  127.1, 127.2 n.13, 127.3, 127.4.1 &
  n.1, 3, 127.4.8, 127.5 & n.6, 127.6,
  127.7, 128.1, 128.2.1 ns. 3, 6, 128.2.2
  n.24, 128.5.1, 131.5, 132.4 n.7, 132.5,
  134.2.3
2033(a)(4) .... 125.4 & n.4
2034–2042 .... 137.6.2, 137.7.3
2034 .... 125.1, 125.9 ns. 1, 10, 125.10
2035–2038 .... 126.2, 126.3.1, 126.3.2,
  126.3.4 & n.42, 127.1, 127.6, 128.1,
  128.3.3 & n.16, 128.4, 128.5.1,
  131.4.3 n.38, 134.2.3 & n.22, 134.4,
  135.7.3 & n.33
2035–2042 ...... 129.6.2, 136.2.12, 137.3 &
  n.2

[References are to paragraphs (¶) and notes (n.).]

SECTION

2035 .... 120.3 n.8, 121.7.1 & n.3, 122.2 n.19, 125.2, 125.6 n.12, 126.1, 126.4.1, 126.4.2 ns. 11, 12, 16, 126.4.3, 126.5.7, 127.8 & ns. 1, 3, 128.3.3, 128.4 n.4, 128.5.1, 132.3 & n.14, 133.2.5, 133.3.2, 133.3.3 n.24, 135.3.10 n.111

2035(a) ..... 126.3.5 & n.56, 126.4.1 & n.1, 126.4.2 & ns. 11, 34, 126.4.3, 126.7.6, 127.8

2035(b) 126.4.2, 126.4.3 n.38

2035(b)(1) 126.3.5 n.60, 126.4.2 n.33

2035(c) .... 126.3.7, 126.4.1 & n.1, 126.4.2, 126.4.3 & n.36, 127.8, 128.3.4 n.18

2035(d)(1) 126.4.2, 127.8

2035(d)(2) .... 126.3.5, 126.4.2 & ns. 14, 17, 21, 22, 126.5.7, 126.6.6 n.105, 126.6.8, 126.7.6, 127.1 n.2, 127.8 & n.7, 128.3.3 n.16, 133.3.3

2035(d)(3)(A) .... 121.4.2 & n.26

2035(d)(3)(B) 135.6.4 n.42

2035(d)(3)(C) 126.4.2, 126.4.3 n.39

2035(d)(4) 126.4.2, 137.5.2 n.29

2035(e) 126.4.2

2036–2038 .... 125.9, 125.11.2, 126.3.3, 126.3.5, 126.4.1, 126.4.2, 126.5.7, 126.8.1, 128.3.3, 131.3.3, 131.8, 134.2.3

2036–2039 .... 126.3.3, 126.8.3, 127.8

2036–2042 .... 127.4.6

2036 .... 123.5.1 & n.6, 125.2, 125.5, 125.11 n.4, 125.11.2 ns. 27, 29, 126.1, 126.2, 126.3.1, 126.3.2 & n.19, 126.3.3, 126.3.4 & n.51, 126.3.5, 126.3.6, 126.4.2, 126.4.3 n.67, 126.5.2 n.49, 126.5.5 n.90, 126.6.1, 126.6.2 & ns. 16, 29, 37, 47, 126.6.5, 126.6.6 & ns. 100, 104, 126.6.7, 126.6.8, 126.8.1, 126.8.2 & n.50, 127.2 & n.11, 127.4.6, 128.1, 128.3.3 & n.12, 128.4, 128.5.1, 129.3.3, 129.4.5 & n.149, 130.3.1 & n.3, 132.1 n.5, 132.6 & n.4, 133.3.3 & n.25, 134.2.3 n.22, 135.3.10 & n.111, 136.4.4 & n.84, 137.8

2036(a) .... 126.3.2 n.32, 126.3.3 n.39, 126.3.4, 126.3.5, 126.5.1 n.15, 126.6.1, 126.6.2, 126.6.4, 126.6.6 & ns. 95, 105, 126.6.7 & n.111, 126.6.8,

SECTION

126.8.2 & n.54, 129.4.5, 130.3.1, 133.2.6

2036(a)(1) .... 125.5, 126.3.3, 126.3.4, 126.3.5 & n.61, 126.4.2, 126.5.1 & n.6, 126.5.3 & n.53, 126.6.1, 126.6.2 & ns. 16, 21, 25, 29, 34, 126.6.4, 126.6.5, 126.6.6, 126.6.7

2036(a)(2) .... 126.3.3, 126.3.5, 126.5.1, 126.5.3 n.52, 126.6.1, 126.6.3 & ns. 52, 54, 56, 126.6.4, 126.6.5, 126.6.5 n.92, 126.6.6, 126.6.7, 126.6.8, 126.7.3 & n.28

2036(b) 126.3.2, 126.5.2 n.51, 126.6.1, 126.6.5

2036(b)(1) 126.6.5

2036(b)(2) .... 126.6.5 & n.93

2036(b)(3) 126.4.2, 126.6.5

2036(b)(7) 129.4.5

2036(c) .... 120.1 n.25, 125.5, 126.3.2 n.31, 126.6.8 ns. 116, 122, 129, 126.7.3, 136.1 ns. 3, 4

2037–2039 .... 126.3.3

2037 .... 125.3 n.10, 125.11.1 n.4, 125.11.2 n.29, 126.1, 126.2 & n.5, 126.4.2, 126.6.8 n.126, 126.7.3 n.20, 126.7.4 & n.46, 126.7.5, 126.7.6, 126.7.7, 128.5.1, 133.3.3, 137.7.3 n.14

2037(a) ..... 120.1 n.25, 126.7.1, 126.7.2 & n.13, 126.7.3, 126.7.4

2037(a)(1) 126.7.7, 126.8.2

2037(a)(2) 126.5.1 n.15, 126.7.7

2037(b) .... 126.7.2, 126.7.3 & n.28, 126.7.4 & n.45

2038 .... 122.4.1 & n.15, 124.4.2 n.38, 125.2, 125.3 n.10, 125.7 n.13, 125.11.1 n.29, 126.1, 126.2, 126.3.1 & n.3, 4, 126.3.2, 126.3.3 & n.33, 126.3.5, 125.4.2, 126.5.1 & ns. 2, 6, 19, 126.5.2 & n.35, 47, 126.5.3 ns. 52, 53, 126.5.4. 126.5.5, 126.5.6, 126.6.1, 126.6.2 n.29, 126.6.3, 126.6.4 & n.38, 126.6.6 & n.100, 126.6.7, 126.8.1 n.6, 126.8.5, 127.4.1 & n.4, 127.4.2 n.14, 127.4.6, 127.6, 128.1 & n.21, 128.2.2, 128.2.3 n.35, 128.3.2, 130.5.1, 131.3.3, 133.5, 135.3.10 n.111, 135.6.1 n.2

2038A(a)(1)(A) 135.6.1 n.10

TABLE OF IRC SECTIONS

[References are to paragraphs (¶) and notes (n.).]

SECTION

2038(a) ..... 120.1 n.25, 126.3.4, 126.5.2 & n.45, 126.5.3, 126.5.6, 126.5.7, 126.6.3
2038(a)(1) .... 125.6 n.12, 126.3.5, 126.4.2, 126.5.1 & n.15, 126.5.2, 126.5.3 n.55, 126.5.4, 126.5.5, 126.5.6, 127.4.1, 127.4.5 & n.30
2038(a)(2) 126.5.1 n.15, 126.5.6, 126.6.5
2038(b) 126.5.4, 126.6.6 n.100, 128.3.2 n.5
2039 .... 125.1, 125.6 n.5, 125.8, 126.2, 126.3.1, 126.3.2, 126.8.1, 126.8.2 ns. 11, 20, 43, 49, 126.8.3, 126.8.4, 126.8.5, 129.2.3 n.18, 131.3.3
2039A(e)(9)(B) 135.6.3 n.32
2039A(e)(9)(C) 135.6.3 n.32
2039(a) ..... 126.1, 126.3.4, 126.8.1, 126.8.2 & ns. 11, 20, 126.8.3, 126.8.4, 126.8.5 & n.71, 127.1 n.1, 127.2 & n.1, 128.5.2 & n.10
2039(b) 126.3.4, 126.8.1, 126.8.3, 126.8.5 n.72
2039(c) .... 126.8.1, 126.8.2 ns. 11, 16, 126.8.5 & ns. 72, 76, 89, 96
2039(c)(4) .... 126.8.5 & n.83
2039(d) 126.8.5 n.76
2039(e) .... 126.8.5 ns. 72, 99
2039(f) .... 126.8.5 & n.85
2039(f)(2) 126.8.5 n.85
2039(g) 126.8.5
2040 .... 125.1, 125.11.1, 125.11.2 & ns. 17, 27, 125.11.4 ns. 42, 50, 131.3.3 & n.26
2040(a) .... 125.11.1, 125.11.2 & ns. 15, 22, 125.11.3 & n.30, 125.11.4 & ns. 38, 41, 129.2.5 n.52, 131.8
2040(b) .... 125.11.1, 125.11.2, 125.11.3 & ns. 30, 32, 125.11.4, 126.4.3 n.42, 129.2.3 n.21, 129.2.5
2040(c) 125.11.3 n.31
2040(d) 123.4
2041 ..... 125.1, 125.6 n.5, 126.4.2, 126.5.3 n.62, 126.8.5 n.96, 126.4.2, 126.5.3 n.62, 126.8.5 n.96, 127.1, 127.4.6, 127.6, 128.1, 128.2.1 & ns. 3, 6, 128.2.2, 128.2.3, 128.3.2, 128.3.3 n.16, 128.4, 128.5.1, 129.4.3 n.53, 130.3.1 n.9, 131.3.3, 132.6.2, 133.2.2 n.6

SECTION

2041(1) 127.3, 127.4.8 n.51
2041(a)(1) .... 125.3, 128.4 & ns. 8, 17, 128.5.1, 129.4.3
2041(a)(1)(B) 126.4.2 n.14, 128.4
2041(a)(2) 128.1, 128.2.1, 128.3.2, 128.3.3, 128.3.4, 128.3.5, 128.5.1, 128.5.4, 129.4.3,
2041(a)(3) .... 128.1 n.3, 128.5.1 & n.2
2041(b) .... 129.4.3 & n.48
2041(b)(1) 121.6.1 n.6, 128.1, 128.2.1 n.11, 128.2.3, 128.3.2, 129.2.3
2041(b)(1)(A) 128.2.2
2041(b)(1)(B) 128.2.3 n.36, 128.4
2041(b)(1)(C) 121.6.1 n.7
2041(b)(1)(C)(i) 128.2.3 n.37
2041(b)(1)(C)(ii) .... 128.2.3 ns. 38, 44
2041(b)(2) 128.1 n.15, 128.3.3 n.17, 128.3.4, 128.5.2
2041(b)(3) 128.4, 128.5.1 n.3
2042 ...... 125.6 ns. 5, 13, 126.1, 126.4.2 & n.14, 126.8.4, 127.1 & n.2, 127.2 & n.14, 127.4.1 & n.3, 127.4.6, 127.5 n.6, 127.6, 127.7, 127.8, 128.1, 128.3.3 n.16, 128.5.1, 131.3.3, 133.3.3, 133.5, 134.2.3
2042(1) .... 127.3 & n.1, 127.5, 128.2.1 n.21
2042(2) .... 122.3.6 n.30, 125.l6 n.10, 126.4.2 n.15, 127.3, 127.4.1, 127.4.2 & ns. 7, 13, 127.4.3, 127.4.4, 127.4.5 & ns. 31, 32, 127.4.6 & ns. 36, 39, 127.4.8, 127.4.9, 127.5, 127.8
2043(a) .... 126.3.4 & n.52, 131.4.3 n.38
2043(b) .... 121.4.2 & n.20, 121.4.3 & n.26, 123.6.1, 123.6.2, 125.9 & n.9, 126.3.4 & n.53
2043(b)(1) 131.4.3
2043(b)(2) 131.4.3
2044 .... 123.3.3, 129.4.5 n.111, 137.8 & n.6
2044(b)(2) 129.4.5
2044(c) 129.4.5 n.136
2046 .... 121.7.1 n.2
2053 ...... 120.2.2, 126.4.2, 129.4.5, 129.7.1 & n.3, 130.3.4, 131.1 & n.3, 131.3.1, 131.3.2 & n.31, 131.4.3, 131.4.5, 131.6.4, 131.7, 132.4, 132.5, 132.6.4, 133.3.2, 134.2.4 & n.59, 135.1.2, 137.5.2 & n.10, 137.5.3

[References are to paragraphs (¶) and notes (n.).]

SECTION

2053(a) 131.1, 131.2, 131.3.1, 131.3.3, 131.4.1, 131.4.2, 131.5, 131.6.1, 131.6.2, 137.5.3

2053(a)(1) 125.1, 131.2, 131.3.3 n.50, 131.4.1

2053(a)(2) .... 120.3, 131.3.1 & n.1, 131.3.2 & ns. 5, 12, 31, 39, 45, 47, 131.3.3 n.62, 131.4.1, 131.6.1, 131.6.2, 131.8 n.6, 135.1.2 n.48

2053(a)(3) .... 121.4.3, 121.4.4, 123.6.1, 125.11.4 n.49, 126.4.3, 130.3.4, 131.1 n.5, 131.3.2, 131.4.1 & n.2, 10, 131.4.2 & n.21, 131.4.3, 131.4.4 & n.86, 131.5 & n.4, 12, 131.6.1, 131.6.2, 132.4, 137.6.2 & ns. 12, 19, 137.7.2 n.10

2053(a)(4) .... 131.3.3 n.49, 131.4.1 & n.10, 131.4.2 n.20, 131.5 & n.4, 135.6.4 & n.41, 135.6.7

2053(b) .... 131.1 n.5, 131.3.1, 131.3.2, 131.3.3, 131.4.3 n.62, 131.6.1 & n.1

2053(c)(1) 131.3.3

2053(c)(1)(A) .... 121.4.2 n.20, 121.4.3, 121.4.4, 123.6.1, 125.9, 131 n.5, 131.4.1, 131.4.3 & ns. 40, 60, 64, 131.4.4 & ns. 87, 89, 131.5

2053(c)(1)(B) ... 131.4.1, 131.6.2, 132.4 & n.31

2053(c)(1)(C) 129.4.5 n.150

2053(c)(2) .... 131.1 n.5, 131.2, 131.4.1, 131.6.2 & n.43, 135.7.5 & n.63, 137.9

2053(c)(3) ...... 131.6.2, 131.7 & n.2, 3, 7, 132.4, 132.7.1 n.10, 132.7.3

2053(d) .... 131.6.2, 131.7 & ns. 2,3,7, 132.4, 132.7.1 n.10, 132.7.3

2053(d)(2) 131.7 n.7

2054 ..... 120.2.2, 120.3, 126.4.2, 129.7.1 & n.3, 131.1, 131.4.5, 131.8, 134.2.4 & n.59, 135.7.5 n.59, 137.4.4, 137.5.2 & n.10, 137.5.3

2055 ...... 120.2.2, 126.4.3, 129.2.5, 129.4.5 & n.142, 130.1, 130.2 & n.8, 130.3.1 n.4, 130.3.2, 130.3.3, 130.5.1, 130.5.3, 130.5.6, 131.4.4 & n.87, 131.7, 134.2.4 & n.64, 135.7.5 & n.60

2055(a) .... 121.7.5 n.62, 126.3.2 n.24, 130.2, 130.3.1, 130.3.3 n.22, 130.5.1, 130.5.2 & n.21, 130.5.4

2055(a)(1) .... 130.2 & ns. 1, 10

SECTION

2055(a)(2) ...... 130.2 & ns. 1, 10, 130.3.2, 131.2 n.3

2055(a)(3) 130.2

2055(a)(4) .... 130.2 & n.12

2055(b) 130.3.1 n.9

2055(c) ...... 129.5.2 n.5, 130.3.1 n.6, 130.6 & n.2

2055(d) 129.2.4 n.42, 130.3.1, 130.5.1, 134.2.4 n.68

2055(e)(1) 130.2 n.21, 130.3.1 n.6

2055(e)(2) .... 121.8.2 & n.9, 130.5.7, 130.3.2 & ns. 18, 20, 130.4, 130.5.1 & ns. 3, 10, 12, 13, 130.5.3, 130.5.4 & n.36, 40, 130.5.5 & n.42, 130.5.6 & n.55

2055(e)(2)(A) 130.2 n.11

2055(e)(2)(B) 130.5.3 n.23

2055(e)(3) .... 130.4, 130.5.6 & ns. 47, 57, 130.5.7 & n.62

2055(e)(3)(A) 130.5.6 n.47

2055(e)(3)(B) .... 130.5.6 ns. 47, 54, 56

2055(e)(3)(C)(i) 130.5.6 n.49

2055(e)(3)(C)(ii) 130.5.6 n.50

2055(e)(3)(C)(iii) 130.5.6 n.52

2055(e)(3)(E) 130.5.7 n.58

2055(e)(3)(F) 130.5.6 n.54

2055(e)(3)(G) 130.5.7 n.59

2055(e)(4) 121.8.2 n.14, 130.5.1 n.12

2055(g) 121.8.1 n.4, 130.2 n.3

2056 .... 123.5.1 & n.3, 125.9 & n.13, 125.10, 127.5 n.8, 128.2.3 n.35, 129.2.2 & n.10, 129.2.4 n.42, 129.2.5, 129.3.2, 129.3.3, 129.4.5, 129.5.1, 129.5.2, 129.7.2, 130.5 n.1, 131.4.5, 132.6.4, 134.2.4

2056(a) .... 127.5, 129.2.1, 129.2.3 n.16, 129.2.4, 129.4.3 n.23, 129.4.5 & n.114, 129.5.1

2056(b)(1) .... 129.2.3 n.17, 129.3.1, 129.3.2 n.8, 129.3.3 & n.45, 129.4.1 & n.1, 129.4.3 & n.23, 129.4.7, 129.5.3

2056(b)(1)(A) 123.3.2, 129.3.3 n.42

2056(b)(1)(B) 123.3.2

2056(b)(1)(C) 129.3.5

2056(b)(2) 129.2.4 n.43, 129.3.4

2056(b)(3) ...... 129.4.2 & n.8, 17, 129.4.3 & n.92, 129.4.4 & n.92

2056(b)(4) 129.5.1, 129.5.2 n.5, 129.5.3

2056(b)(4)(B) 129.5.3

TABLE OF IRC SECTIONS

[References are to paragraphs (¶) and notes (n.).]

SECTION

2056(b)(5) .... 123.3.3, 128.2.3, 129.5.2, 129.6.1, 129.3.1, 129.3.3 & n.17, 129.4.3 & ns. 23, 26, 30, 48, 129.4.4 & n.92, 129.4.5 & n.116, 129.4.7 & n.160, 129.5.1 n.3
2056(b)(6) 123.3.3 n.22, 129.4.4
2056(b)(7) .... 123.3.3 & n.27, 129.2.5 n.64, 129.3.1, 129.3.3 & n.47, 129.4.5, 129.5.1 n.1
2056(b)(7)(B)(i)(I) 129.4.5 n.113
2056(b)(7)(B)(i)(II) 129.4.5 n.115
2056(b)(7)(B)(ii)(I) ...... 129.4.5 & n.140
2056(b)(7)(B)(ii)(II) 129.4.5 n.122
2056(b)(7)(B)(iv) 129.4.5 n.129
2056(b)(7)(C) .... 129.4.5 ns. 119, 121
2056(b)(8) 123.3.3 n.30, 129.2.5 n.75, 129.4.6
2056(b)(9) 129.4.5 n.143
2056(c) .... 129.2.2 n.10, 129.2.3 & n.18, 129.4.3 n.23
2056(c)(1) 129.2.3 n.19
2056(c)(1)(A)(ii) 129.7.1 n.2
2056(c)(2) 129.2.3 n.19
2056(c)(2)(A) 129.7.1 n.3
2056(c)(2)(B)(i)–(iii) 129.7.1 n.10
2056(c)(3) 129.2.3 n.19
2056(c)(4) 129.2.3 n.23, 129.2.4
2056(c)(5) 129.2.3 n.20
2056(c)(6) 129.2.3 n.24
2056(c)(7) 129.2.3 n.22
2056(d) 129.2.5 n.46
2056(d)(1)(A) 129.2.5 n.49
2056(d)(1)(B) 129.2.5 n.50
2056(d)(2)(A) 129.2.5 n.54
2056(d)(2)(B) 129.2.5 n.58
2056(d)(3) 129.2.5 n.77
2056(d)(4) 129.2.5 n.53
2056(d)(5) 129.2.5
2056A(a) 129.2.5 n.55
2056A(b)(1) 129.2.5 n.60
2056A(b)(2)(A) 129.2.5 n.62
2056A(b)(2)(B) 129.2.5 n.63
2056A(b)(2)(C) 129.2.5 n.63
2056A(b)(3) 129.2.5 n.60
2056A(b)(4) 129.2.5 n.60
2056A(b)(5)(A) 129.2.5
2056A(b)(6) 129.2.5 n.74
2056A(b)(7) 129.2.5 n.77
2056A(b)(9) 129.2.5 n.61
2056A(b)(10)(A) 129.2.5 n.65

SECTION

2056A(b)(10)(B) 129.2.5 n.72
2056A(b)(11) 129.2.5 n.64
2056A(b)(12) 129.2.5 n.76
2056A(b)(14) 129.2.5 n.64
2056A(d) 129.2.5 n.56
2101–2108 .... 132.7.2
2101 .... 132.7.1
2101(a) 134.2.1
2101(b) .... 134.2.5 ns. 72, 81
2101(c)(1) 134.2.5 n.73
2101(d) 134.2.5 n.72
2102(a) 134.2.5 n.77
2102(b) 134.2.5 n.79
2102(c) 134.2.7 n.90
2102(c)(1) 134.2.5 n.74
2102(c)(2) 134.3 n.10
2102(c)(3)(A) 134.2.7
2102(c)(3)(B) 134.2.5 n.77
2103 .... 132.7.1, 134.2.3 n.21
2104 .... 134.2.3
2104(a) 134.2.3 n.25
2104(c) ...... 132.7.2 ns. 19, 24, 134.2.3 ns. 25, 30, 39, 41, 47, 48, 57
2105 .... 132.7.2 n.20, 133.2.4 n.42, 134.2.3
2105(a) .... 132.7.2 n.25, 134.2.3 ns. 49, 50
2105(b)(1) .... 132.7.2 n.22, 134.2.3 ns. 44, 52
2105(b)(2) 134.2.3 n.46
2105(c) 132.7.2 n.29, 134.2.3 n.33
2106 .... 134.2.4
2106(a)(2) 134.2.4
2106(a)(3) 134.2.4 n.67
2106(b) 134.2.3 n.23
2107 .... 134.2.3 & n.23, 134.4 n.1
2107(a) .... 134.4 ns. 8, 11
2107(b) 134.4 n.9
2107(c) 134.4 n.12
2107(d) 134.4 n.3
2107(e) 134.4 n.2
2201 .... 132.4 n.30, 132.8
2203 .... 131.3.2 n.6, 137.7.1 n.1
2204 .... 132.3 n.2, 137.6.2 & n.19
2204(a) 135.7.6 n.68, 137.7.4
2204(b) 137.7.4
2204(d) 137.7.4
2205 .... 137.8
2206 .... 137.8 & ns. 5, 8
2207 .... 137.8 & n.8
2207A .... 129.4.5 & n.151, 137.8
2207A(b) 123.3.3 n.25

[References are to paragraphs (¶) and notes (n.).]

SECTION

2207B 137.8
2208 .... 134.3
2209 .... 134.3 & n.7
2210 .... 137.7.3
2501(a) 120.2.1, 121.3.1, 121.3.2,
 121.3.3, 121.4.2, 122.2
2501(a)(1) 121.1, 121.2, 121.3.1,
 121.4.1, 121.4.3, 121.6.1, 121.6.2,
 122.1, 123.6.1, 124.1, 134.2.2
2501(a)(2) .... 134.2.1, 134.2.2 & n.10,
 134.2.3 n.22
2501(a)(3) ..... 134.2.2 n.10, 134.4 ns. 1, 4
2501(a)(3)(A) 134.4 n.3
2501(a)(4) 134.4 n.2
2501(a)(5) 121.9, 124.2 n.9
2501(b) 134.3
2501(c) 134.3
2502(a) .... 124.1, 132.2.1 & n.1, 132.2.2
 & n.9, 134.2.2 n.19
2502(b) 132.2.1 n.5
2502(c) 137.4.1 n.6, 137.7.1 n.1
2503 .... 135.6.3 n.34
2503(a) 136.4.4
2503(a)(3) 125.9
2503(a)(5) 121.9
2503(b) 121.9 n.7, 123.3.4, 123.3.5,
 123.5.1, 123.5.3, 124.1 & n.6, 124.2,
 124.3.1 & n.1, 124.3.2, 124.4.2 n.11,
 129.4.5 & n.146, 132.2.1 & n.3,
 132.2.2, 132.5, 133.3.4 & n.48,
 134.2.2, 136.4.4, 137.2 & n.1
2503(c) .... 121.3.2, 124.4.2 & ns. 10, 11
2503(c)(1) 124.4.2
2503(c)(2) 124.4.2
2503(e) .... 121.1, 121.4.3 n.37, 121.5 &
 n.3, 123.6.1, 123.6.2, 129.1, 132.2.2,
 132.5, 133.2.13 & n.69, 133.3.4 n.48,
 137.2 & n.1
2503(e)(2) 121.5
2503(e)(2)(A) 121.5
2503(e)(2)(B) .... 121.5 & n.11
2504(a) 132.2.1 n.6
2504(a)(3) 132.2.1 n.7
2504(b) 132.2.1 n.6
2504(c) 132.2.2, 132.3 n.7
2505(b) 132.3 n.15
2511(a) 121.1, 121.3.1, 121.3.3, 134.2.2,
 134.4 n.5
2511(b) 134.2.2 n.10, 134.4 n.6
2511(b)(2) 134.4 n.7

SECTION

2512 .... 135.1.1 n.5
2512(b) 120.2.1, 121.4.3, 121.4.5,
 123.6.1 & n.10, 123.6.2
2513 ..... 120.2.1 n.5, 121.1 & n.24, 123.1,
 123.2.1, 123.5.1, 123.5.2, 123.5.3 &
 n.21, 124.1 & n.7, 125.10, 126.3.1
 n.4, 126.4.2, 126.5.1 n.6, 129.1,
 131.6.2, 132.2.1 & n.2, 132.3, 132.5
 & n.11, 133.2.2 & n.5, 134.2.2 &
 n.16, 136.2.12 n.145, 136.4.4 n.80,
 137.4.1 & n.7
2513(a)(1) ...... 123.5.2 ns. 11, 16, 123.5.3
 n.19
2513(b) 123.5.3 n.24
2513(c) 123.5.3 n.25
2513(d) ...... 123.5.3 & n.26, 126.4.3 n.40
2514 .... 121.2 n.5, 121.6.1, 121.6.2,
 121.6.3, 123.3.2 & n.13, 129.4.3 ns.
 25, 85
2514(a) 121.6.4
2514(b) 121.6.1, 121.6.2, 121.6.3,
 121.7.1 n.13
2514(c) .... 121.6.1 ns. 2, 6, 124.4.2 &
 n.23, 129.4.3 & n.48
2514(c)(3) 121.6.1 n.7, 121.6.4
2514(d) 121.6.3 n.21, 121.6.4, 128.5.1
 n.2
2514(e) 121.6.2, 121.6.4
2515 .... 123.4, 133.1
2515(c)(1) 123.4
2515(c)(2) 123.4
2515(c)(3) 123.4
2515A 123.4
2516 .... 123.6.1 & n.9, 123.6.2 & n.21,
 131.4.3 & n.78, 136.4.2
2516(1) .... 123.6.2 & n.30
2516(2) 123.6.2
2517 .... 126.8.5
2517(b) 126.8.5 n.104
2518 .... 121.3.3, 121.6.2 & ns. 17, 18,
 121.7.1 & ns. 2, 6, 14, 121.7.3,
 121.7.4 ns. 29, 38, 121.7.5 n.62,
 121.7.6 & n.89, 121.7.7 & n.95,
 125.12 & n.1, 126.3.2 & n.24,
 128.3.5, 129.2.3 & ns. 38, 39, 129.4.5
 n.128, 129.6.3, 129.7.2 n.15, 130.3.3
 & n.22, 133.2.10 n.61, 136.2.3,
 136.4.2
2518(a) 121.7.1
2518(b) .... 121.7.2 & n.21, 121.7.6, 137.2

[References are to paragraphs (¶) and notes (n.).]

SECTION

2518(b)(1) 121.7.3 n.25
2518(b)(2) 121.7.3 n.27, 121.7.4 n.29,
121.7.7
2518(b)(3) 121.7.5 n.43
2518(b)(4) 121.7.5 n.74, 121.7.6
2518(c)(1) 121.7.5 n.58
2518(c)(2) 121.7.1
2518(c)(3) 121.7.2, 121.7.6
2519 .... 123.3.3, 129.4.5 n.110
2519(a) 129.4.5 n.145
2522 .... 121.8.1 ns. 4, 8, 124.2, 132.5,
136.4.7
2522(a) .... 121.8.1, 121.9, 130.2 & n.8,
134.2.2 n.17
2522(a)(2) 121.9 n.7
2522(a)(4) 130.2 n.12
2522(b) 134.2.2
2522(c)(1) 121.8.1 n.7
2522(c)(2) ..... 121.8.2 & n.11, 130.5.1 n.2
2522(c)(2)(A) 130.5.2 n.16
2522(c)(2)(B) 130.5.3 n.23
2522(c)(3) 121.8.2 n.14
2522(c)(4) 121.8.2 n.11
2522(d) 121.8.2 n.17
2523 .... 120.2.1, 121.4.2 n.24, 121.4.3,
123.1, 123.2.1, 123.2.3 & n.11,
123.3.1, 123.5.1, 123.5.2, 123.6.3 &
n.34, 125.10, 132.5, 137.2
2523(a)(1) 123.3.2
2523(a)(2) 123.3.5 n.35
2523(b) 121.4.3, 123.3.1, 123.3.2, 123.4
2523(b)(1) 123.3.2
2523(b)(2) 123.3.2
2523(c) 123.3.2
2523(d) 123.3.2, 123.4
2523(e) .... 123.3.3 & n.22
2523(f) 123.3, 123.3.3, 123.3.5 n.33,
123.5.2 n.15, 129.4.5
2523(i) 134.2.2 n.15
2602 .... 133.3.1 n.1, 133.3.4 n.42
2603(a) 133.6.1
2603(a)(1) 133.2.6 n.47
2603(b) 133.6.1 n.1
2604 .... 133.3.5 n.74
2611(a) 133.2.5 n.26
2611(b)(1) 133.2.13 n.69
2611(b)(2) 133.2.9 n.59
2612(a)(1) 133.2.6 n.37
2612(a)(2) 133.2.6 n.40
2612(b) 133.2.6 n.44

SECTION

2612(c)(1) 133.2.5 n.27
2612(c)(2) .... 132.2.5 ns. 30, 31
2612(c)(3) 132.2.5 n.29
2613(a)(1) 133.2.4 n.20
2613(a)(2)(A) 133.2.4 n.22
2613(a)(2)(B) 133.2.4 n.24
2613(b) 133.2.4 n.21
2621(a) 133.3.2 n.13
2621(b) 133.2.6 n.48, 133.3.2 n.15
2622 .... 133.3.2 n.8
2623 .... 133.3.2 n.4
2624(a) 133.3.2 n.3
2624(b) 133.3.2 n.5
2624(c) 133.3.2 n.11
2624(d) 133.3.2 n.16
2631(a) 133.3.3 n.18
2631(b) .... 133.3.3 ns. 34, 41
2632(a) 133.3.3 n.32
2632(a)(1) 133.3.3 n.39
2632(b) 133.3.3 n.21
2632(c)(1)(A) 133.3.3 n.35
2632(c)(2) 133.3.3 n.36
2641(a) 133.3.4 n.43
2641(b) 133.3.4 n.44
2642(a)(1) 133.3.4 n.45
2642(a)(2)(A) 133.3.4 n.46
2642(a)(2)(B) 133.3.4 n.47
2642(a)(2)(B)(ii)(I) 133.3.4 n.55
2642(a)(2)(B)(ii)(II) 133.3.4 n.73
2642(b)(1) 133.3.4 n.57
2642(b)(2)(A) 133.3.4 n.59
2642(b)(3) 133.3.3 n.40, 133.3.4 n.58
2642(b)(4) 133.3.4 n.62
2642(c)(1) 133.2.13 n.69, 133.3.4 n.48
2642(c)(2) 133.3.4 n.50
2642(c)(3) 133.3.4 n.48
2642(d) 133.3.4 n.67
2642(e) 133.3.4 n.71
2642(f) 133.3.2 n.7, 133.3.4 n.61
2642(f)(1) 133.2.5 n.35, 133.3.3 n.23
2642(f)(2) 133.3.3 n.30
2642(f)(3) .... 133.3.3 ns. 27, 29
2642(f)(4) 133.3.3 n.31
2651(a) 133.2.3 n.9
2651(b)(1) 133.2.3 n.10
2651(b)(2) 133.2.3 n.12
2651(b)(3) .... 133.2.3 ns. 11, 13
2651(c)(1) 133.2.3 n.14
2651(c)(2) 133.2.3 n.15
2651(d) 133.2.3 n.17

[References are to paragraphs (¶) and notes (n.).]

SECTION

2651(e)(1) 133.2.3 n.16

2651(e)(2) 133.2.3 n.19, 133.2.4 n.25,
133.2.5 n.29, 133.2.12 n.65

2651(e)(3) 133.2.3 n.18

2652(a)(1) 133.2.2 n.4, 133.2.5 n.33,
133.3.3 n.37

2652(a)(2) 133.2.2 n.5, 133.3.3 n.20

2652(a)(3) 133.2.2 n.8, 133.2.5, 133.3.3
n.38, 133.3.4 n.63

2652(b) 133.2.12 n.64

2652(b)(2) 133.2.12 n.67

2652(c)(1) 133.2.8 n.51

2652(c)(2) .... 133.2.8 ns. 52, 58

2652(c)(3) 133.2.8 n.55

2653(a) 133.2.9 n.58

2654(a)(1) .... 133.4 ns. 2, 5, 6

2654(a)(2) 133.4 n.7

2654(b)(1) 133.2.10 n.62, 133.3.4 n.56

2654(b)(2) 133.2.11 n.63, 133.3.4 n.68

2654(c) 121.7.1 n.2, 133.2.10 n.61

2654(d) 133.2.13 n.71, 133.3.4 n.53,
133.6.1 n.6

2662(a)(1) 133.6.12 n.8

2662(a)(2)(A) 133.6.2 n.12

2662(a)(2)(B) 133.6.2 n.13

2701–2704 .... 131.1 & ns. 1, 2

2701 .... 135.3.10 n.92, 135.4.4 n.38,
136.2.1 & ns. 1, 8, 136.2.2 & n.15,
136.2.3, 136.2.5, 136.2.7, 136.2.10,
136.2.12

2701(a) 135.3.4 n.41, 136.2.1, 136.2.2,
136.2.3 & n.23, 136.2.4 & n.61,
136.2.5, 136.2.6, 136.2.7, 136.2.8,
136.2.9, 136.2.11, 136.2.12, 136.3.2 &
n.22

2701(a)(1) 136.2.3 n.29

2701(a)(2) 136.2.3 n.37

2701(a)(2)(A) 136.2.3 n.30

2701(a)(2)(B) 136.2.3 n.31

2701(a)(2)(C) .... 136.2.3 ns. 32, 34

2701(a)(3)(A) 136.2.4 n.41

2701(a)(3)(B) 136.2.5 n.64

2701(a)(4) 136.2.8 n.94

2701(a)(4)(B)(i) 136.2.2 n.17

2701(b)(1) 136.2.2 n.12

2701(b)(2)(A) 136.2.2 n.13, 136.2.4
n.53, 136.3.4 n.44

2701(b)(2)(B) 136.2.2 n.14, 136.2.4
n.55, 136.3.4 n.45

2701(c)(1) 136.2.2 n.16

SECTION

2701(c)(2)(A) 135.2.2. n.18

2701(c)(2)(B) 136.2.4 n.48

2701(c)(2)(C) 136.2.4 n.50

2701(c)(3)(A) 136.2.4 n.41

2701(c)(3)(B) 136.2.4 n.57

2701(c)(3)(C)(i) 136.2.6 n.68

2701(c)(3)(C)(ii) 136.2.7 n.72

2701(c)(3)(C)(iii) 136.2.6 n.71, 136.2.7
n.74

2701(d) 136.2.1, 136.2.7 n.77, 136.2.9
n.98

2701(d)(1) 136.2.9 n.103

2701(d)(2)(A) .... 136.2.9 ns. 111, 112

2701(d)(2)(B) 136.2.9 n.117

2701(d)(2)(C) 136.2.9 n.114

2701(d)(3)(A)(i) 136.2.9 n.104

2701(d)(3)(A)(ii) 136.2.9 n.106

2701(d)(3)(A)(iii) .... 136.2.9 ns. 101, 120

2701(d)(3)(B)(i) 136.2.9 n.105

2701(d)(3)(B)(ii) 136.2.9 n.107

2701(d)(4)(A) 136.2.9 n.102

2701(d)(4)(B) 136.2.9 n.108

2701(d)(5) 136.2.9 n.109

2701(e)(1) 135.3.10 n.93, 136.2.2 n.10

2701(e)(2) 136.2.2 n.11

2701(e)(3)(A) 136.2.2 n.15, 136.2.10
ns. 123, 137, 136.3.4 n.46

2701(e)(3)(B) 136.2.2 n.15

2701(e)(5) .... 136.2.3 ns. 20, 24

2701(e)(6) 136.2.12 n.143

2701(e)(7) 136.2.3 n.39

2702 .... 135.4.10 n.103, 136.2.8 n.85,
136.4.1 n.7, 136.4.7

2702(a) .... 136.4.1 & n.2, 136.4.2, 136.4.3,
136.4.4, 136.4.5, 136.4.6, 136.4.7,
136.4.8

2702(a)(2) 136.4.3 n.28

2702(a)(3)(A)(i) 136.4.5 n.87

2702(a)(3)(A)(ii) 136.4.6 n.92

2702(a)(3)(B) 136.4.5 n.88

2702(b) 136.4.3 n.29

2702(c)(4) 136.4.3 n.62

2702(c)(4)(B) 136.4.3 n.66

2702(e) 135.3.10 n.93

2702(3)(1) 135.3.10 n.93

2703 .... 135.3.10, 136.3.3 n.42

2703(a) 135.3.10

2703(b) 135.3.10 n.90

2704 .... 121.3.3, 136.3.1

TABLE OF IRC SECTIONS

[References are to paragraphs (¶) and notes (n.).]

SECTION

2704(a) .... 136.3.1, 136.3.2 & ns. 3, 19, 136.3.4
2704(a)(1) 136.3.2 n.3
2704(a)(2) .... 136.3.2 ns. 25, 27
2704(b) .... 136.3.1, 136.3.2, 136.3.3 & n.29, 136.3.4
2704(b)(3)(A) 136.3.3 n.38
2704(b)(3)(B) 136.3.3 n.41
2704(b)(4) 136.3.3 n.43
2704(c)(1) .... 136.3.4 ns. 44, 45
2704(c)(2) 136.3.4 n.47
2704(c)(3) 136.3.4 n.46
3466–3477 .... 137.7.3
3466 .... 137.7.2 n.11
3467 .... 137.7.2 n.11
3713 .... 137.7.3 & n.25, 137.7.4
4941 .... 130.5.3
4943 .... 130.5.3
4944 .... 130.5.3
4945 .... 130.5.3
4947(a)(2) .... 130.5.3 ns. 33,34
4947(b)(3)(A) 130.5.3 n.34
4948(c) 130.2 n.21
4948(c)(4) 121.8.1 n.7, 130.2 n.21
4980A(d) .... 131.6.2, 132.6.1 & n.5
6013 .... 123.5.1
6018(a)(1) .... 125.4 n.5, 131.5 & n.9, 137.3 ns. 1, 5
6018(a)(2) 137.3 n.3
6018(a)(3) .... 137.3 & ns. 1, 3
6019 .... 137.2
6019(a)(10) 133.6.2 n.11
6020 .... 137.2 n.9
6020(b) 137.6.3
6075(a) .... 129.4.2 & n.14, 135.7.6 n.67, 137.3 n.7
6075(b)(1) 137.2 n.10
6075(b)(2) 137.2 n.12
6075(b)(3) 137.2 n.13
6081(a) .... 137.3 & n.11
6091(b)(3) 137.3 n.7
6151(a) 137.4.1 n.1, 137.4.2 n.13
6161 .... 132.4 & n.21, 132.7.1 & n.11, 137.7.4
6161(a)(1) 137.2 n.14, 137.3 n.15, 137.4.1, 137.4.4, 137.4.3
6161(a)(2) ..... 137.4.2, 137.4.3, 137.5.3 & n.49
6161(b)(2) 137.4.3 n.26
6161(b)(3) 137.4.3 n.26

SECTION

6163 ...... 132.7.1, 137.4.2, 137.4.4, 137.7.4
6163(a) .... 132.4 & n.24, 137.4.4
6163(b) .... 136.4.4 & n.37
6165 .... 137.4.1 n.5, 137.4.3, 137.4.4, 137.5.3 & n.48
6166 .... 125.11.3 & n.34, 129.2.5, 132.4 & n.21, 132.6.3 & n. 30, 132.6.4 & n.37, 133.6.3 & n. 15, 134.1 n.3, 135.4.6, 137.4.2 & n.19, 137.4.3 & n.27, 137.5.1 & n.6, 137.5.2 & n.16, 137.5.3 & ns. 46, 48, 137.5.4 & n.52, 137.6.1 n.5, 137.7.3
6166(a)(1) 137.5.2 n.9, 137.5.3 n.38
6166(a)(2) 137.5.3 n.32
6166(a)(3) .... 137.5.3 ns. 35, 38
6166(b)(1) .... 135.6.8 & n.115, 137.5.2 ns. 12, 14
6166(b)(1)(A) 137.5.2
6166(b)(1)(B) .... 137.5.2 n. 24
6166(b)(2)(B) .... 137.5.2 n. 25
6166(b)(2)(C) 137.5.2 n.27
6166(b)(2)(D) 137.5.2 n.26
6166(b)(3) 137.5.2 n.23
6166(b)(4) 137.5.2 n.4
6166(b)(5) 137.5.3 n.33
6166(b)(6) 137.5.2 n.10, 137.5.3 n.34
6166(b)(7) 137.5.2 n.28, 137.5.3 n.37
6166(b)(8) 137.5.2 n.18, 137.5.3 n.37
6166(b)(9) .... 137.5.3 n.216166(e)
6166(c) 137.5.2 n.11
6166(e) 137.5.3 n.42
6166(f)(1) 137.5.3 n.36
6166(f)(3) 137.5.3 n.43
6166(g)(1)(B) 137.5.4 n.52
6166(g)(1)(C) 137.5.4 n.53
6166(g)(1)(D) 137.5.4 n.54
6166(g)(2) 137.5.4 n.55
6166(g)(3)(A) 137.5.4 n.57
6166(g)(3)(B) 137.5.4
6166(h) 137.5.2
6166(i) 133.6.3 n.15
6166(k)(1) 137.5.4 n.48
6212(a) 123.5.3
6212(b)(3) 137.3 n.16
6321–6327 .... 126.4.2
6321 .... 137.6.1 n.2
6323(b) .... 137.6.2 & n.20
6323(h)(1) 137.6.2 n.17
6323(h)(6) 137.6.2 n.17
6323(i)(2) 137.6.3 n.30

[References are to paragraphs (¶) and notes (n.).]

SECTION

6324 .... 126.4.2, 132.5 & n.8, 133.6.5
n.18, 137.6.1 ns. 1, 2, 137.6.2
6324(a) 137.6.1, 137.6.2, 137.8 n.3
6324(a)(1) 137.6.2 n.11, 137.7.4
6324(a)(2) ...... 137.6.2 ns. 16, 17, 137.7.3
& ns. 14, 17, 137.7.4
6324(b) .... 122.4.1 n.11, 137.4.1 ns. 9, 11,
12, 137.6.1, 137.6.3, 137.7.2 & n.8
6324(c) 137.6.1 n.7, 137.6.3 n.28
6324(c)(1) 137.6.2 n.20
6324(c)(2) 137.6.2 n.21
6324A 137.5.3, 137.6.1
6324B 137.6.1
6325 .... 137.6.3 n.29
6325(a) 137.6.2 n.23
6325(b) 137.6.2 n.24
6325(c) 137.6.2 n.24
6402 .... 137.5.3
6403 .... 137.5.3 n.44
6501 .... 125.4 n.6, 132.4 n.20
6501(c)(9) .... 136.2.11 ns. 139, 141,
136.4.8
6503(d) 137.5.3
6601(a) .... 137.5.3 ns. 41, 43
6601(b)(1) .... 137.4.4 n. 42
6601(e)(1) 137.7.2 n.6
6601(j) ... 137.5.2, 137.5.3 n.40, 137.5.4 &
n.58
6621 .... 121.3.4

SECTION

6651 .... 135.7.6 & n.68
6901 .... 137.7.2 & n.8
6901(a) 137.4.1 n.11, 137.7.2
6901(a)(1) .... 137.7.3 & n.17
6901(a)(1)(A) 137.4.1, 137.7.2
6901(a)(1)(A)(ii) 137.7.3
6901(a)(1)(A)(iii) 137.7.2
6901(h) 137.7.3 n.17
6903 .... 137.3 n.16, 137.7.2 n.8
7520 .... 121.3.3, 124.3.2 & ns. 31, 32,
125.7 n.6, 126.7.1 & ns. 4, 5, 126.7.4
n.40, 126.8.3 n.55, 127.4.4 & n.26,
135.7.4 & n.56, 136.4.3 & n.41,
136.4.4, 136.4.7
7520(a) .... 130.5.3 n.35, 135.4.10 & ns.
95, 99
7520(b) 135.4.10 n.95
7520(c)(3) .... 135.4.10 ns. 98, 109
7701(a)(1) 124.2 n.1
7701(a)(3) 134.2.3 n.51
7701(a)(4) 132.7.2 n.17, 134.2.2 n.17,
134.2.3 n.35
7701(a)(9) 134.2.3 n.21
7701(a)(30) 134.2.3 n.39
7701(b) 134.2.1 n.4
7871(a) 130.2 n.2
7871(a)(1) 121.8.1 n.4
7872 .... 135.4.6

Table of Treasury Regulations

[References are to paragraphs (¶) and notes (n.).]

TREAS. REGS.

20.0-1(b)(1) ... 134.2.1 n.2, 134.2.3 ns. 21, 26
20.0-1(b)(2) 134.2.1 n.2
5h.5(a) 133.3.3 n.22
23.1 .... 125.11.3 n.31
37, Article 12 (1919) 125.5 n.4
70, Article 27 (1929) 127.4.2 n.9
79 .... 121.1 n.3
1.83-7(b)(1) 135.4.7 n.81
1.170A-1(c)(2) .... 135.1.2 ns. 20, 28, 50
1.170A-4(b)(3) 130.5.1 n.12
1.170A-7(b)(1)(i) 130.5.4 n.38
1.170A-7(b)(3) 130.5.5 n.43
1.170A-7(b)(4) 130.5.5 n.43
1.421-7(e)(2) 135.4.2 n.11
1.664-1(a)(5)(i) 130.5.2 n.22
1.664-3(a)(1)(iii) 136.4.3 n.43
1.664-3(a)(1)(v) 136.4.3 n.43
1.901-2(e)(5) 132.4 n.25
1.1001-1(a) .... 135.1.1 ns. 3, 15
1.1402(a)-4(b) 135.6.5 n.47
20.2002-1 .... 137.7.3 ns. 12, 19
20.2011-1(c)(2) .... 132.4 ns. 16, 18
20.2011-1(d) 128.4 n.10
20.2012-1(a) .... 132.5 ns. 5, 7
20.2012-1(b) 132.5 n.13
20.2012-1(c) 132.5 n.11
20.2012-1(d)(2) 132.5 n.12
20.2012-1(e) .... 132.5 ns. 10, 11
20.2013-3(c) 132.6.4 n.44
20.2013-4(a) Ex. 2 .... 132.6.3 n.20
20.2013-4(b)(1) 132.6.3 n.30
20.2013-4(b)(2) 132.6.3 n.32
20.2013-4(b)(3) 132.6.3 n.31
20.2013-5(a) 132.6.2 n.14
20.2013-5(b) .... 132.6.2 ns. 7, 12
20.2013-6 Ex. 1 .... 132.6.4 n.43
20.2013-6 Ex. 2 .... 132.6.4 n.45
20.2014-1(a) .... 132.7.1 ns. 5, 6
20.2014-1(a)(3) ...... 132.7.2 ns. 18, 23, 26

TREAS. REGS.

20.2014-2(a) .... 132.7.3 ns. 30, 31
20.2014-2(b) 132.7.3 n.35
20.2014-2(b) Ex. 132.7.3 n.36
20.2014-3(b) 132.7.3 n.38
20.2014-3(c) 132.7.3 n.38
20.2014-4(a)(1) 132.7.4 n.51
20.2014-7 .... 132.7.3 n.40
20.2015-1(c) Exs. 1–3 .... 132.4 n.24
20.2016-1 .... 132.4 n.20, 132.7.1 n.14
20.2031-1–20.2031-10 .... 135.1.1 n.2
20.2031-1(a) 134.2.3 n.27
20.2031-1(a)(1) 125.1 n.1
20.2031-1(b) .... 135.1.2 ns. 20, 24, 28, 47, 135.4.1 n.5, 135.4.10 n.100, 135.7.3 n.46
20.2031-2(b) 135.4.2 n.6
20.2031-2(b)(1) 135.4.2 n.8
20.2031-2(b)(2) .... 135.4.2 ns. 12, 13
20.2031-2(b)(3) Exs. 1–3 .... 135.4.2 n.9
20.2031-2(b)(3) Exs. 4–6 ...... 135.4.2 n.13
20.2031-2(c) 135.4.2 n.14
20.2031-2(e) .... 135.2.2 n.15, 135.3.3 n.13, 135.3.4 ns. 24, 34, 135.4.2 n.15
20.2031-2(f) ..... 127.4.8 n.51, 135.4.2 n.6, 135.4.3 ns. 22, 24, 135.4.6 n.69
20.2031-2(f)(2) 135.5.1 n.1
20.2031-2(h) .... 135.3.10 ns. 104, 114
20.2031-3 .... 135.4.4 ns. 40, 42
20.2031-4 .... 135.4.6 n.70
20.2031-6(b) 135.5.1 n.1
20.2031-7 .... 135.4.10 n.95
20.2031-8(a)(1) 125.7 n.6, 127.7 n.3, 135.4.9 n.93
20.2031-8(a)(3) Ex. 2 .... 127.7 n.3
20.2031-8(a)(3) Ex. 3 .... 127.7 n.3
20.2031-8(b) 135.4.2 n.18
20.2031-8(b)(1) 135.1.2 n.52
20.2032-1(b)(1) 135.7.1 n.3
20.2032-1(b)(2) .... 135.7.1 n.7, 135.7.2 n.14, 135.7.6 ns. 67, 71

[References are to paragraphs (¶) and notes (n.).]

TREAS. REGS.

20.2032-1(c)(1)	135.7.3 ns. 32, 35
20.2032-1(c)(3)	135.7.3 ns. 34, 44
20.2032-1(d)	135.7.2 n.15
20.2032-1(d)(1)	135.7.2 ns. 18, 21
20.2032-1(d)(2)	135.7.2 ns. 18, 20
20.2032-1(d)(3)	135.7.2 n.18, 135.7.4 n.51
20.2032-1(d)(4)	135.7.2 n.22
20.2032-1(e)	135.7.2 ns. 15, 19
20.2032-1(f)	135.7.4 n.50
20.2032-1(f)(1)	135.7.4 n.55
20.2032-1(f)(2)	135.7.4 n.54
20.2032-1(g)	135.7.5 n.58
20.2032A-3	135.6.5 n.48
20.2032A-3(a)	135.6.5 n.51, 135.6.7 n.100
20.2032A-3(b)(1)	135.6.2 ns. 16, 25
20.2032A-3(c)	135.6.5 ns. 58, 59
20.2032A-3(d)	135.6.5 n.66
20.2032A-3(e)(1)	135.6.5 ns. 44, 50, 53, 60
20.2032A-3(e)(2)	135.6.5 n.49
20.2032A-3(f)(1)	135.6.5 n.53
20.2032A-3(f)(2)	135.6.5 n.54
20.2032A-3(g) Ex. 3	135.6.5 n.67
20.2032A-3(g) Ex. 8	135.6.5 n.58
20.2032A-4(b)(2)	135.6.7 n.109
20.2032A-4(b)(2)(iv)	135.6.7 n.106
20.2032A-4(d)	135.6.7 n.108
20.2032A-4(e)	135.6.7 n.104
20.2032A-8(a)(2)	135.6.3 n.36, 135.6.6 n.90
20.2032A-8(a)(3)	135.6.6 ns. 73, 79
20.2032A-8(b)	135.6.6 n.93
20.2032A-8(c)(1)	135.6.6 n.77
20.2032A-8(c)(2)	135.6.6 n.74
20.2032A-8(c)(3)	135.6.6 n.75
20.2032A-8(c)(4)	135.6.9 n.147
20.2032A-8(d)	135.6.6 ns. 72, 73
20.2033-1(a)	125.1 n.1, 125.2 n.1
20.2033-1(a)(1)	125.1 n.1
20.2033-1(b)	125.1 n.1, 125.5 n.11
20.2034-1	125.9 n.6
20.2035-1(c)	126.4.4 n.46
20.2035-1(e)	126.4.4 ns. 62, 64, 127.8 n.4
20.2036-1(a)	126.3.3 n.39, 126.6.1 n.3, 126.6.3 n.60, 126.6.8 n.122
20.2036-1(b)(1)(i)	126.6.6 n.99

TREAS. REGS.

20.2036-1(b)(1)(ii)	126.6.4 n.70, 126.6.6 n.102, 126.6.7 n.115
20.2036-1(b)(2)	126.6.2 ns. 17, 20
20.2036-1(b)(3)	126.6.3 ns. 61, 63, 126.6.7 n.111
20.2036-1(b)(3)(i)	126.6.3 n.62
20.2036-1(b)(3)(iii)	126.6.4 n.66, 126.6.7 n.110
20.2037-1(b)	126.7.2 n.16, 126.8.2 n.18
20.2037-1(c)(2)	126.7.3 ns. 22, 24
20.2037-1(c)(3)	126.7.4 n.45
20.2037-1(c)(4)	126.7.4 n.47
20.2037-1(e) Ex. 1	126.7.2 n.14, 126.7.4 n.32
20.2037-1(e) Ex. 2	126.3.7 n.75, 126.7.4 n.38
20.2037-1(e) Ex. 3	126.7.1 n.3, 126.7.4 n.39, 126.7.5 ns. 49, 50
20.2037-1(e) Ex. 4	126.7.5 ns. 49, 51
20.2037-1(e) Ex. 5	126.7.2 ns. 15, 17, 126.7.3 n.21, 126.8.2 n.18
20.2037-1(e) Ex. 6	126.7.2 n.19
20.2037-1(g)	126.7.7 ns. 54, 60
20.2038-1(a)	126.5.1 n.4, 126.5.2 ns. 42, 43, 126.5.5 n.79
20.2038-1(a)(3)	126.5.5 n.88
20.2038-1(b)	126.5.4 ns. 74, 78, 126.6.7 n.110
20.2038-1(c)	126.5.1 n.15
20.2038-1(d)	126.5.5 n.80
20.2038-1(f)	126.5.4 n.73
20.2039-1(b)	126.8.2 ns. 13, 15, 16
20.2039-1(b) Ex. 2	126.8.2 n.42
20.2039-1(b) Ex. 5	126.8.2 n.51
20.2039-1(b)(1)	126.8.2 ns. 21, 24, 126.8.2 ns. 36, 42
20.2039-1(b)(2) Ex. 2	126.8.2 n.19, 126.8.3 n.57
20.2039-1(b)(2) Ex. 4	126.8.2 n.22
20.2039-1(b)(2) Ex. 6	126.8.2 ns. 37, 40
20.2039-1(d)	126.8.4 ns. 66, 67, 127.2 n.3
20.2039-1(d) Ex.	126.8.4 n.67
20.2039-2(b)	126.8.5 n.84
20.2039-2(b) Ex. 3	126.8.5 n.73
20.2039-2(b)(5) Ex. 4	126.8.5 n.88
20.2039-2(c)(2)	126.8.5 n.92
20.2039-2(c)(2) Ex.	126.8.5 n.93
20.2039-4(c)(3)	126.8.5 n.87

TABLE OF TREASURY REGULATIONS

[References are to paragraphs (¶) and notes (n.).]

TREAS. REGS.

20.2039-5(c)(2) 126.8.5 n.101
20.2040-1(a) 125.11.2 n.26
20.2040-1(a)(2) ... 125.11.4 ns. 41, 42, 46, 52
20.2040-1(b) ..... 125.11.1 n.5, 125.11.2 ns. 17, 24
20.2040-1(c)(2) 125.11.4 n.43
20.2040-1(c)(4) .... 125.11.4 ns. 52, 61
20.2040-1(c)(5) 125.11.4 n.55
20.2040-1(c)(8) 125.11.4 n.39
20.2041-1(b) 129.1 n.3
20.2041-1(b)(1) .... 121.6.1 n.5, 128.2.1 ns. 2–4
20.2041-1(b)(2) ...... 128.1 n.7, 128.5.2 ns. 5, 8
20.2041-1(c)(1) .... 128.2.1 ns. 14, 15
20.2041-1(c)(2) .... 128.2.2 ns. 26, 28
20.2041-1(e) ..... 121.6.1 n.4, 128.4 ns. 4–6
20.2041-1(d) .... 128.4 ns. 7, 12
20.2041-2(c) Ex. 2 .... 128.3.3 n.12
20.2041-2(c) Ex. 3 .... 128.3.4 n.11
20.2041-2(d) .... 128.4 ns. 13, 14
20.2041-2(e) .... 128.4 ns. 16, 17
20.2041-2(f) 128.4 n.9
20.2041-3(b) 128.3.2 n.6
20.2041-3(c)(2) .... 128.2.3 ns. 39, 40
20.2041-3(c)(2) Ex. 1 .... 128.2.3 n.41
20.2041-3(c)(3) 128.2.3 n.45
20.2041-3(d) 128.3.3 n.12
20.2041-3(d)(4) 128.3.4 n.20
20.2041-3(d)(5) 128.3.4 n.23
20.2041-3(d)(6) 121.7.1 n.5
20.2041-3(d)(6)(i) 128.3.5 n.24
20.2041-3(f) Ex. 2 .... 128.3.4 n.22
20.2041-3(f) Ex. 4 .... 128.5.2 n.8
20.2041-3(f) Ex. 5 .... 128.5.2 n.9
20.2042-1 .... 126.8.5 n.84
20.2042-1(a)(1) 127.2 n.4
20.2042-1(a)(3) 127.7 n.2
20.2042-1(b)(1) 127.3 n.3
20.2042-1(b)(2) 127.5 n.2
20.2042-1(c)(2) 127.4.2 n.8, 127.4.2 n.11, 127.4.8 n.53
20.2042-1(c)(3) .... 127.4.4 ns. 25, 28
20.2042-1(c)(4) .... 127.4.2 ns. 12, 14, 127.4.5 n.30, 127.4.6 n.35
20.2042-1(c)(5) 127.4.7 n.47, 127.5 n.3
20.2042-1(c)(6) ...... 127.4.8 ns. 52, 54, 56, 127.7 n.2, 127.8 n.6
20.2053-1(a) 131.1 n.5

TREAS. REGS.

20.2053-1(a)(1) 131.2 n.11, 131.6.1 n.2
20.2053-1(b)(2) .... 131.6.1 ns. 6, 9, 10
20.2053-1(b)(3) .... 131.2 ns. 4, 5
20.2053-1(c) Ex. 2 .... 131.6.3 n.44
20.2053-1(c)(2) .... 131.6.3 ns. 42, 45
20.2053-2 .... 131.2 ns. 1, 2, 4, 6
20.2053-3(a) .... 131.3.2 ns. 3, 20, 28
20.2053-3(b)(1) 131.3.2 n.4
20.2053-3(b)(2) .... 131.3.2 ns. 7, 9
20.2053-3(b)(3) 131.3.2 n.13
20.2053-3(c)(1) 131.3.2 n.18
20.2053-3(c)(2) 131.3.2 n.19, 137.9 n.7
20.2053-3(c)(3) .... 131.3.2 ns. 21, 23
20.2053-3(d)(1) ..... 131.3.2 ns. 27, 29, 30, 32
20.2053-3(d)(2) .... 131.3.2 ns. 41, 44, 131.6.1 n.19, 135.1.2 n.48
20.2053-4 ... 131.3.2 n.39, 131.4.1 ns. 1, 5, 131.4.2 n.17, 131.4.3 n.49
20.2053-5(b) 131.4.4 n.88
20.2053-6(a) 131.6.2 n.22
20.2053-6(b) 131.6.2 n.29
20.2053-6(c) 132.4 n.27
20.2053-6(d) 131.6.2 n.23
20.2053-6(e) 131.6.2 n.32
20.2053-6(f) ..... 131.6.2 ns. 23, 27, 28, 34
20.2053-7 .... 131.5 n.7, 131.6.2 n.30
20.2053-8(a) 131.3.3 n.52
20.2053-8(b) 131.3.3 n.53
20.2053-8(d) Ex. 1 .... 131.3.3 n.54
20.2053-8(d) Ex. 2 .... 131.3.3 n.62
20.2053-8(d) Ex. 3 .... 131.3.3 ns. 58, 61
20.2053-8(d) Ex. 4 .... 131.3.3 n.57
20.2053-9(b)(1) 131.7 n.7
20.2053-9(b)(2) 131.7 n.6
20.2053-9(d) 131.7 n.4
20.2053-9(e) Ex. 2 .... 131.7 n.7
20.2054-1 .... 131.8 ns. 2, 5, 7
20.2055-1(a) 130.3.1 n.1
20.2055-1(d) 130.2 n.3
20.2055-2(b)(1) 130.4 n.1
20.2055-2(c) .... 121.7.1 n.5, 130.3.3 ns. 22, 24
20.2055-2(e)(1)(i) 130.5.1 n.1
20.2055-2(e)(1)(i) Ex. 3 .... 130.5.1 n.9
20.2055-2(e)(1)(i) Ex. 5 .... 130.6 n.12
20.2055-2(e)(1)(i) Ex. 6 .... 130.3.1 n.8
20.2055-2(e)(1)(ii)(e) Ex. 1 .... 130.5.1 n.14

[References are to paragraphs (¶) and notes (n.).]

TREAS. REGS.

20.2055-2(e)(1)(ii)(e) Ex. 2 .... 130.5.1 n.15
20.2055-2(e)(2)(i) .... 130.5.1 n.12, 130.5.4 ns. 37–40
20.2055-2(e)(2)(ii) .... 130.5.5 ns. 43, 45
20.2055-2(e)(2)(iii) ...... 130.5.5 ns. 44, 45
20.2055-2(e)(2)(v) 130.2 n.11
20.2055-2(e)(2)(vi)(a) 130.5.3 n.26
20.2055-2(e)(2)(vi)(b) 130.5.3 n.28
20.2055-2(e)(2)(vi)(d) .... 130.5.3 ns. 27, 30
20.2055-2(e)(2)(vi)(e) .... 130.5.3 ns. 25, 34
20.2055-2(e)(2)(vi)(f) 130.5.3 n.31
20.2055-2(e)(2)(vi)(g) .... 130.5.3 ns. 31, 34
20.2055-2(e)(2)(vii)(a) 130.5.3 n.29
20.2055-2(e)(2)(vii)(c) 130.5.3 n.25
20.2055-2(e)(2)(vii)(d) 130.5.3 n.30
20.2055-2(e)(2)(vii)(e) 130.5.3 n.31
20.2055-2(e)(3)(i) 130.5.7 n.60
20.2055-2(e)(3)(ii) 130.5.7 n.61
20.2055-3(a) 130.6 n.1
20.2056-1(b) 129.4.5 n.131
20.2056(a)-1 .... 129.2.5 n.45
20.2056(a)-2(b)(2) 129.2.4 n.44
20.2056(a)-2(b)(3) 129.2.4 n.44
20.2056(b)-1(b) 129.3.2 n.9
20.2056(b)-1(e)(2) 129.3.3 n.42
20.2056(b)-1(f) 129.3.5 n.50
20.2056(b)-1(g) Ex. 2 .... 129.3.2 n.10
20.2056(b)-1(g) Ex. 4 .... 129.3.2 n.10
20.2056(b)-1(g) Ex. 6 .... 129.3.3 n.16
20.2056(b)-1(g) Ex. 8 .... 129.3.3 n.22
20.2056(b)-2(d) Ex. 129.3.4 n.49
20.2056(b)-3(c) 129.4.2 n.16
20.2056(b)-3(d) Ex. 2 .... 129.4.2 n.9
20.2056(b)-3(d) Ex. 3 .... 129.4.2 n.9
20.2056(b)-3(d) Ex. 4 .... 129.4.2 n.17
20.2056(b)-4(a) ...... 129.4.3 n.45, 129.5.1 ns. 2, 3
20.2056(b)-5(b) 129.4.3 n.70
20.2056(b)-5(c) .... 129.4.3 ns. 73, 74, 129.4.4 n.105
20.2056(b)-5(c) Ex. 1 .... 129.4.3 n.75
20.2056(b)-5(d) .... 129.4.3 ns. 70, 71
20.2056(b)-5(e) ...... 129.4.3 ns. 30, 31, 42
20.2056(b)-5(f)(1) 129.4.3 n.33
20.2056(b)-5(f)(2) 129.4.3 n.35
20.2056(b)-5(f)(3) 129.4.3 n.36

TREAS. REGS.

20.2056(b)-5(f)(4) 129.4.3 n.37
20.2056(b)-5(f)(5) 129.4.3 n.34
20.2056(b)-5(f)(6) 129.4.3 n.32
20.2056(b)-5(f)(7) .... 129.4.3 ns. 39, 44
20.2056(b)-5(f)(8) .... 129.4.3 ns. 43, 46
20.2056(b)-5(f)(9) ... 129.4.3 n.45, 129.5.1 n.3
20.2056(b)-5(g)(1) 129.4.3 n.49
20.2056(b)-5(g)(1)(i) 129.4.3 n.56
20.2056(b)-5(g)(2) 129.3.3 n.17, 129.4.3 n.57
20.2056(b)-5(g)(3) 129.4.3 n.53
20.2056(b)-5(g)(4) 129.4.3 n.54
20.2056(b)-5(g)(5) 129.4.3 n.51
20.2056(b)-5(h) 129.4.3 n.92
20.2056(b)-5(j) 129.4.3 n.67
20.2056(b)-5(j) Ex. 1 .... 129.4.3 n.69
20.2056(b)-6(b) 129.4.4 n.98
20.2056(b)-6(c) 129.4.4 n.105
20.2056(b)-6(c)(1) 129.4.4 n.98
20.2056(b)-6(c)(2) 129.4.4 n.96
20.2056(b)-6(c)(3) 129.4.4 n.97
20.2056(b)-6(d) 129.4.4 n.98
20.2056(b)-6(e) 129.4.4 n.98
20.2056(c)-2 ..... 129.5.2 n.13, 129.7.1 n.10
20.2056(c)-2(d) 129.2.3 n.19
20.2056(d)-1 .... 129.2.3 n.38
20.2056(d)-1(a) 121.7.1 n.5
20.2056(e)-1(b) 129.2.3 n.19
20.2056(e)-2(b)(iii) 129.4.7 n.159
20.2056(e)-2(b)(3)(iv) 129.4.4 n.94
20.2056(e)-2(b)(3)(v) 129.4.4 n.95
20.2056(e)-2(c) 129.2.3 n.26
20.2056(e)-2(d) 129.2.3 n.29
20.2056(e)-2(d)(2) .... 129.2.3 ns. 30, 31
20.2056(e)-2(e) .... 129.2.2 ns. 14, 15
20.2102-1(b)(2) 134.2.5 n.79
20.2103-1 .... 134.2.3 ns. 20, 23, 27
20.2104-1(a)(1) 132.7.2 n.27, 134.2.3 n.26
20.2104-1(a)(2) 132.7.2 n.28, 134.2.3 n.29
20.2104-1(a)(3) 134.2.3 n.39
20.2104-1(a)(4) .... 134.2.3 ns. 50, 55
20.2104-1(a)(5) 134.2.3 n.35
20.2104-1(a)(7) ...... 134.2.3 ns. 30, 39, 58
20.2104-1(a)(8) 134.2.3 n.41
20.2104-1(b) 134.2.3 n.22
20.2105-1(a)(1) 134.2.3 n.26
20.2105-1(a)(2) 134.2.3 n.29

TABLE OF TREASURY REGULATIONS

[References are to paragraphs (¶) and notes (n.).]

TREAS. REGS.

20.2105-1(b) 132.7.2 n.29
20.2105-1(d) 134.2.3 n.48
20.2105-1(e) .... 134.2.3 ns. 40, 50, 56
20.2105-1(f) .... 134.2.3 ns. 36, 38
20.2105-1(g) 132.7.2 n.25, 134.2.3 n.49
20.2105-1(i) 134.2.3 n.44
20.2105-1(j) 134.2.3 n.46
20.2105-1(m) 134.2.3 n.48
20.2106-1(b) 134.2.3 n.23
20.2106-2(a)(1) 134.2.4 n.63
20.2106-2(a)(2) 134.2.4 n.61
20.2203-1 .... 137.3 n.17, 137.7.1 n.1
20.2204-1(a) 137.7.4 n.27
20.2204-2(b) 137.7.4 n.31
20.2205-1 .... 137.8 ns. 2, 3
20.2209-1 .... 134.3 n.7
20.2209-1 Exs. 1–5 .... 134.3 n.7
25.2501-1(b) 134.2.1 n.3
25.2501-1(d) 134.3 n.7
25.2501-1(d) Exs. 1–5 .... 134.3 n.7
25.2502-2 .... 137.4.1 ns. 7, 8
25.2503-3(a) .... 124.3.1 n.6, 124.3.4 ns.
 51–54
25.2503-3(b) .... 124.3.2 ns. 14, 22, 28,
 124.3.4 n.51
25.2503-3(c) Ex. 1 .... 124.3.2 n.23
25.2503-3(c) Ex. 2 .... 124.3.4 n.54
25.2503-3(c) Ex. 3 .... 124.3.2 n.23
25.2503-3(c) Ex. 4 .... 124.3.2 n.29
25.2503-3(c) Ex. 5 .... 124.3.1 n.11
25.2503-3(c) Ex. 6 .... 124.3.4 n.53
25.2503-4(b) .... 124.4.2 ns. 26, 28
25.2503-4(b)(1) 124.4.2 n.15
25.2503-4(b)(2) 124.4.2 n.19
25.2503-4(c) 124.4.2 n.11
25.2503-6(a) 121.5 n.2
25.2503-6(b)(2) 121.5 n.9
25.2503-6(b)(3) .... 121.5 ns. 12, 13
25.2503-6(c) Ex. 1 .... 121.5 n.10
25.2503-6(c) Ex. 2 .... 121.5 n.6
25.2503-6(c) Ex. 3 .... 121.5 n.2
25.2503-6(c) Ex. 4 .... 121.5 n.5
25.2504-1(b) 132.2.1 n.7
25.2504-1(d) 132.2.2 n.9
25.2511-1(a) 121.1 n.22, 121.2 n.3
25.2511-1(b) 134.2.2 n.11
25.2511-1(b)(2) 134.2.2 n.12
25.2511-1(c) .... 121.2 ns. 2, 4
25.2511-1(c)(1) 121.7.7 n.95

TREAS. REGS.

25.2511-1(c)(2) 121.7.1 n.5, 121.7.4
 n.31, 121.7.7 n.95
25.2511-1(d) 121.1 n.23, 123.5.2 n.27
25.2511-1(e) 121.3.3 n.26
25.2511-1(g)(1) 121.1 n.10, 121.4.2
 n.12, 121.4.5 n.46
25.2511-1(g)(2) .... 121.1 n.10, 122.4.2 ns.
 21–24
25.2511-1(h) Ex. 7 .... 121.3.3 n.22
25.2511-1(h)(1) .... 121.1 ns. 3, 6, 13,
 124.2 ns. 4, 10
25.2511-1(h)(2) 121.1 n.15
25.2511-1(h)(3) 121.1 n.16
25.2511-1(h)(4) 122.3.2 n.12, 125.11.1
 n.8
25.2511-1(h)(5) 122.3.3 n.17
25.2511-1(h)(8) 122.3.6 n.28, 124.3.4
 n.53
25.2511-1(h)(9) 123.2.2 n.7, 127.5 n.3
25.2511-1(h)(10) 122.3.5 n.22, 126.8.5
 n.102
25.2511-2(b) 122.4.1 n.17, 122.5 n.8
25.2511-2(c) 122.3.1 n.4, 122.4.2 n.21,
 125.11.1 n.8
25.2511-2(d) 122.4.1 n.14
25.2511-2(e) .... 122.5 ns. 2, 5
25.2511-2(f) ..... 122.2 n.18, 122.3.1 ns. 5,
 8, 122.4.1 ns. 10, 16, 122.5 n.17
25.2511-2(g) 122.4.2 n.21
25.2511-3(b) 134.4 n.6
25.2511-3(b)(4) 134.4 n.7
25.2512-1–25.2512-9 .... 135.1.1 n.2
25.2512-1 .... 135.1.2 ns. 20, 28, 47,
 135.4.1 n.5
25.2512-1(b) 135.4.2 n.10
25.2512-1(b)(2) 135.4.2 n.13
25.2512-1(b)(3) 135.4.2 n.13
25.2512-1(c) 135.4.2 n.14
25.2512-2(b) 135.4.2 n.6
25.2512-2(e) ...... 135.2.2 n.15, 135.3.3 ns.
 13, 22, 135.3.4 ns. 24, 34, 135.4.2
 n.15
25.2512-2(f) ... 135.4.2 n.6, 135.4.3 ns. 22,
 24, 135.4.6 n.69, 135.5.1 n.1
25.2512-3 .... 135.4.4 n.40
25.2512-4 .... 135.4.6 n.70
25.2512-5 .... 135.4.10 n.95
25.2512-6 .... 127.7 n.3
25.2512-6(a) 135.4.9 n.93
25.2512-6(b) 135.4.2 n.18

[References are to paragraphs (¶) and notes (n.).]

TREAS. REGS.

25.2512-7 .... 135.3.8 n.76
25.2512-8 ...... 121.4.1 n.2, 121.4.2 ns. 11,
　　　　17, 121.4.5 ns. 41, 46, 121.9 n.3,
　　　　　　123.6.1 n.3, 123.6.2 n.27
25.2513-1(b)(1) 123.5.2 n.20
25.2513-1(b)(2) 123.5.2 n.18
25.2513-1(b)(4) 123.5.2 n.13
25.2513-1(c) 123.5.2 n.23
25.2513-2(a) 123.5.2 n.22
25.2513-2(a)(1) 123.5.2 n.24
25.2513-2(a)(2) 123.5.2 n.24
25.2513-2(b)(2) 123.5.2 n.24
25.2513-2(c) 123.5.2 n.22
25.2513-3 .... 123.5.2 n.25
25.2513-4 .... 137.4.1 n.7
25.2514-1(b)(1) 121.6.1 n.5
25.2514-1(b)(2) 121.6.3 n.22
25.2514-1(c)(2) 121.6.3 n.22
25.2514-1(e) 121.6.1 n.4
25.2514-2(b) 121.6.4 n.25
25.2514-2(c) 121.6.4 n.25
25.2514-2(d) 121.6.4 n.25
25.2514-3(c)(1) 121.6.2 n.13
25.2514-3(c)(2) 121.6.2 n.15
25.2514-3(c)(3) 121.6.2 n.15
25.2514-3(c)(4) 121.6.2 n.20
25.2514-3(c)(5) 121.6.2 n.18
25.2514-3(c)(6) 121.6.2 n.18
25.2515-1–25.2515-4 .... 123.4 n.1
25.2515-1(d)(2) 123.4 n.3
25.2515-2(d) Ex. 123.4 n.2
25.2515-4(b) 123.4 n.4
25.2516-1(a) 123.6.2 n.21
25.2516-1(b) 123.6.2 n.21
25.2516-2 .... 123.6.2 n.24
25.2517-1(a) 126.8.5 n.102
25.2517-1(c) 126.8.5 n.104
25.2518-1(a)(1) 121.7.1 n.14
25.2518-1(b) 121.7.7 n.95
25.2518-1(c)(1)(i) .... 121.7.6 ns. 77, 90
25.2518-1(c)(2) 121.7.2 n.22, 121.7.6
　　　　　　　　　　　　　　　　　n.89
25.2518-1(c)(3) Ex. 1 .... 121.7.6 n.91
25.2518-1(c)(3) Ex. 2 .... 121.7.6 n.94
25.2518-1(c)(3) Ex. 3 .... 121.7.6 n.91
25.2518-2(b)(1) 121.7.3 n.26
25.2518-2(b)(2) 121.7.3 n.27
25.2518-2(c)(2) 121.7.4 n.30
25.2518-2(c)(3) .... 121.7.4 ns. 32, 34, 41
25.2518-2(c)(4)(i) 121.7.4 n.38

TREAS. REGS.

25.2518-2(c)(4)(ii) 121.7.4 n.38
25.2518-2(c)(5) Ex. 1 .... 121.7.4 n.36
25.2518-2(c)(5) Ex. 2 .... 121.7.4 n.37
25.2518-2(c)(5) Ex. 5 .... 121.7.4 n.29
25.2518-2(c)(5) Ex. 6 .... 121.7.4 n.35
25.2518-2(c)(5) Ex. 7 .... 121.7.4 n.38
25.2518-2(c)(5) Ex. 8 .... 121.7.4 n.38
25.2518-2(c)(5) Ex. 9 .... 121.7.4 n.40
25.2518-2(c)(5) Ex. 10 .... 121.7.4 n.38
25.2518-2(d)(1) .... 121.7.5 ns. 44, 46
25.2518-2(d)(2) 121.7.5 n.47
25.2518-2(d)(3) 121.7.5 n.48
25.2518-2(d)(4) Ex. 1 .... 121.7.5 n.62
25.2518-2(d)(4) Ex. 2 .... 121.7.5 n.45
25.2518-2(d)(4) Ex. 3 .... 121.7.5 n.44
25.2518-2(d)(4) Ex. 4 .... 121.7.5 n.44
25.2518-2(d)(4) Ex. 5 .... 121.7.5 n.44
25.2518-2(d)(4) Ex. 7 .... 121.7.5 n.44
25.2518-2(d)(4) Ex. 8 .... 121.7.5 n.44
25.2518-2(d)(4) Ex. 9 .... 121.7.5 n.49
25.2518-2(d)(4) Ex. 10 .... 121.7.5 n.50
25.2518-2(e)(1) 121.7.6 n.78
25.2518-2(e)(2) 121.7.6 n.85
25.2518-2(e)(3) 121.7.6 n.83
25.2518-2(e)(4) 121.7.6 n.76
25.2518-2(e)(5) Ex. 1 .... 121.7.6 n.84
25.2518-2(e)(5) Ex. 4 .... 121.7.6 n.86
25.2518-2(e)(5) Ex. 5 .... 121.7.6 n.88
25.2518-2(e)(5) Ex. 6 .... 121.7.6 n.87
25.2518-2(e)(5) Ex. 7 .... 121.7.6 n.87
25.2518-2(e)(5) Ex. 8 .... 121.7.6 n.76
25.2518-2(e)(5) Ex. 9 .... 121.7.6 n.81
25.2518-2(e)(5) Ex. 10 .... 121.7.6 n.82
25.2518-2(e)(5) Ex. 11 .... 121.7.6 n.79
25.2518-2(e)(5) Ex. 12 .... 121.7.6 n.80
25.2518-3(a)(1)(i) .... 121.7.5 ns. 58, 64
25.2518-3(a)(1)(ii) 121.7.5 n.51
25.2518-3(a)(1)(iii) 121.7.5 n.72
25.2518-3(a)(1)(iv) 121.7.5 n.66
25.2518-3(a)(2) 121.7.5 n.69
25.2518-3(b) 121.7.5 n.59
25.2518-3(c) 121.7.5 n.53
25.2518-3(d) Ex. 1 .... 121.7.5 n.52
25.2518-3(d) Ex. 2 .... 121.7.5 n.60
25.2518-3(d) Ex. 3 .... 121.7.5 n.58
25.2518-3(d) Ex. 4 .... 121.7.5 n.61
25.2518-3(d) Exs. 5–7 .... 121.7.5 n.71
25.2518-3(d) Ex. 9 .... 121.7.5 n.73
25.2518-3(d) Ex. 10 .... 121.7.5 n.75
25.2518-3(d) Ex. 11 .... 121.7.5 n.63

TREAS. REGS.

25.2518-3(d) Ex. 12	121.7.5 n.65
25.2518-3(d) Ex. 13	121.7.5 n.67
25.2518-3(d) Ex. 14	121.7.5 n.68
25.2518-3(d) Ex. 15	121.7.5 n.70
25.2518-3(d) Ex. 16	121.7.5 n.54
25.2518-3(d) Ex. 18	121.7.5 n.55
25.2518-3(d) Ex. 20	121.7.5 n.57
25.2522-1(a)	121.8.1 n.6
25.2522(c)-3(b)(1)	121.8.3 n.18
25.2522(c)-3(c)(1) Ex. 2	121.8.2 n.13
25.2522(c)-3(c)(1) Ex. 4	121.8.3 n.21
25.2522(c)-3(c)(2)(i)	121.8.2 n.15
25.2522(c)-3(c)(2)(ii)	121.8.2 n.16
25.2522(c)-3(c)(2)(iii)	121.8.2 n.16
25.2522(d)-1	121.8.1 n.4
25.2523(a)-1(a)	123.3.1 n.3, 123.3.4 n.31
25.2523(b)-1(b)(3)	123.3.2 n.9
25.2523(b)-1(b)(3)(i)	123.3.2 n.17
25.2523(b)-1(b)(3)(ii)	123.3.2 n.18
25.2523(b)-1(b)(6)(iii)	123.3.2 n.10
25.2523(b)-1(b)(6)(v)	123.3.2 n.9
25.2523(b)-1(b)(6)(vi)	123.3.2 n.15
25.2523(b)-1(c)(2) Ex.	123.3.3 n.29
25.2523(b)-1(d)(2)	123.3.2 n.14
25.2523(b)-1(d)(3) Ex.	123.3.2 n.12
25.2523(c)-1(c) Ex.	123.3.2 n.21
25.2523(e)-1(b)	123.3.3 n.23
25.2523(e)-1(c)	123.3.3 n.23
25.2523(f)-1	123.3.5 n.33
26.2601-1(a)(2)	133.5 n.21
26.2601-1(b)(1)(ii)(B)	133.5 ns. 3, 6
26.2601-1(b)(1)(ii)(C)	133.5 n.8
26.2601-1(b)(1)(ii)(D) Ex. 1	133.5 n.5
26.2601-1(b)(1)(ii)(D) Ex. 3	133.5 n.7
26.2601-1(b)(1)(ii)(D) Ex. 4	133.5 n.9
26.2601-1(b)(1)(iv)	133.5 n.12
26.2601-1(b)(1)(v)	133.5 n.14
26.2601-1(b)(1)(vi)	133.5 n.13
26.2601-1(b)(2)(i)	133.5 n.24
26.2601-1(b)(2)(ii)	133.5 n.23
26.2601-1(b)(3)(i)	133.5 n.15
26.2601-1(b)(3)(ii)	133.5 n.17
26.2601-1(b)(3)(iii)	133.5 n.18
26.2601-1(b)(3)(iv)	133.5 n.18
26.2601-1(b)(3)(v)	133.5 n.16
26.2601-1(d)	133.5 n.19
26.2662-1(b)(1)	133.6.2 n.9
26.2662-1(b)(2)	133.6.2 n.10

TREAS. REGS.

26.2662-1(b)(3)	133.3.4 n.54, 133.6.2 n.11
26.2662-1(c)(2)(ii)	133.6.1 n.3
26.2662-1(c)(2)(iv) Ex. 1	133.6.1 n.4
26.2662-1(c)(2)(iv) Ex. 2	133.6.1 n.5
26.2662-1(c)(3)	133.2.13 n.72, 133.6.1 n.7
26.2662-1(c)(4)(i)	133.6.2 n.14
26.2662-1(d)(2)(i)	133.6.2 n.12
25.2701-1(a)(2)	136.2.1 n.2
25.2701-1(a)(3) Ex.	136.2.1 n.7
25.2701-1(b)(2)(i)	136.2.2 n.21
25.2701-1(b)(2)(i)(B)	136.2.2 n.22
25.2701-1(b)(3)(i)	136.2.3 n.26
25.2701-1(b)(3)(ii)	136.2.3 n.27
25.2701-1(b)(3)(iii)	136.2.3 n.28
25.2701-1(c)(1)	136.2.3 n.29
25.2701-1(c)(2)	136.2.3 n.30
25.2701-1(c)(3)	136.2.3 ns. 34, 35, 37
25.2701-1(c)(4)	136.2.3 n.38
25.2701-1(d)(1)	136.2.2 n.10
25.2701-1(d)(2)	136.2.2 n.11
25.2701-2(a)(1)	136.2.4 n.45
25.2701-2(a)(2)	136.2.4 n.45
25.2701-2(a)(3)	136.2.5 n.64
25.2701-2(b)(1)	136.2.4 ns. 44, 52
25.2701-2(b)(2)	136.2.4 n.46
25.2701-2(b)(3)	136.2.4 n.46
25.2701-2(b)(4)(i)	136.2.4 n.48
25.2701-2(b)(4)(ii)	136.2.4 n.49
25.2701-2(b)(4)(iv)(A)	136.2.4 n.50
25.2701-2(b)(4)(iv)(B)	136.2.4 n.51
25.2701-2(b)(5)(i)	136.2.4 n.52, 136.2.8 n.78
25.2701-2(b)(5)(ii)(A)	136.2.4 n.53
25.2701-2(b)(5)(ii)(B)	136.2.4 n.54
25.2701-2(b)(5)(iii)	136.2.4 n.55
25.2701-2(b)(6)(i)(B)	136.2.4 n.56
25.2701-2(b)(6)(ii)	136.2.4 n.57
25.2701-2(c)(1)	136.2.6 n.70
25.2701-2(c)(2)	136.2.7 n.75
25.2701-2(c)(2)(ii)	136.2.7 n.72
25.2701-2(c)(3)	136.2.4 n.61, 136.2.6 n.71, 136.2.7 n.74
25.2701-2(c)(4)	136.2.4 ns. 59, 61, 136.2.9 n.102
25.2701-2(c)(5)	136.2.4 n.61
25.2701-2(d) Ex. 3	136.2.5 n.65
25.2701-2(d) Ex. 5	136.2.7 n.76
25.2701-3(a)(1)	136.2.8 n.78

[References are to paragraphs (¶) and notes (n.).]

TREAS. REGS.

25.2701-3(a)(2)(i) 136.2.8 n.78
25.2701-3(a)(2)(ii) 136.3.2 n.15
25.2701-3(a)(2)(iii) 136.3.2 n.15
25.2701-3(b)(1)(i) 136.2.8 n.79
25.2701-3(b)(1)(ii) 136.2.8 n.82
25.2701-3(b)(2)(i) 136.2.8 n.80
25.2701-3(b)(2)(i)(B) 136.2.8 n.81
25.2701-3(b)(2)(ii) 136.2.8 n.83
25.2701-3(b)(3) 136.2.8 n.84
25.2701-3(b)(4)(i) 136.2.8 n.85
25.2701-3(b)(4)(ii) 135.3.4 n.41,
                                 136.2.8 n.87
25.2701-3(b)(4)(iii) 136.2.8 n.93
25.2701-3(b)(4)(iv) 136.2.8 n.85
25.2701-3(b)(5) 136.2.8 n.91
25.2701-3(c)(1) 136.2.8 n.96
25.2701-3(c)(3)(i)(A) 136.2.8 n.97
25.2701-3(d) Ex. 1 .... 136.2.8 n.86
25.2701-3(d) Ex. 2 .... 136.2.8 n.92
25.2701-3(d) Ex. 3 .... 135.3.4 n.42,
                                 136.2.8 n.89
25.2701-3(d) Ex. 4 .... 136.2.3 n.23
25.2701-3(d) Ex. 5 .... 136.2.3 n.23
25.2701-4(a) 136.2.9 n.100, 136.2.10
                                          n.138
25.2701-4(b)(1) 136.2.9 n.109
25.2701-4(b)(2)(i) 136.2.9 n.108
25.2701-4(b)(2)(ii) .... 136.2.9 ns. 105, 107
25.2701-4(c)(1)(ii)(C) 136.2.9 n.116
25.2701-4(c)(2) 136.2.9 n.112
25.2701-4(c)(5) 136.2.9 n.113
25.2701-4(c)(6) 136.2.9 n.117
25.2701-4(d) 136.2.9 n.120
25.2701-4(d)(4) Ex. 136.2.9 n.122
25.2701-6(a)(1) 136.2.10 n.134
25.2701-6(a)(2) 136.2.10 n.124
25.2701-6(a)(3) 136.2.10 n.126
25.2701-6(a)(4)(i) .... 136.2.10 ns. 127,
                                     128, 130
25.2701-6(a)(4)(ii)(A) 136.2.10 n.127
25.2701-6(a)(4)(ii)(B) 136.2.10 n.127
25.2701-6(a)(4)(ii)(C) 136.2.10 n.133
25.2701-6(a)(5)(i) 136.2.10 n.135
25.2701-6(a)(5)(ii) 136.2.10 n.136
25.2701-6(b) Ex. 1 .... 136.2.10 n.125
25.2701-6(b) Ex. 2 .... 136.2.10 n.125
25.2701-6(b) Ex. 3 .... 136.2.10 n.129
25.2701-6(b) Ex. 4 .... 136.2.10 n.131
25.2702-1(b) 136.4.1 n.1
25.2702-1(c)(1) .... 136.4.5 ns. 87, 90

TREAS. REGS.

25.2702-1(c)(3) 136.4.7 n.121
25.2702-1(c)(4) 136.4.7 n.121
25.2702-1(c)(5) 136.4.7 n.123
25.2702-1(c)(6) 136.4.1 n.11
25.2702-1(c)(7) 136.4.1 n.12
25.2702-2(a)(1) 136.4.2 n.13
25.2702-2(a)(2) 136.4.2 n.14
25.2702-2(a)(3) 136.4.2 n.18
25.2702-2(a)(4) 136.4.2 n.16
25.2702-2(b)(1) 136.4.3 n.28
25.2702-2(b)(2) 136.4.3 n.28
25.2702-2(c)(1) .... 136.4.3 ns. 66, 69
25.2702-2(c)(2) 136.4.3 n.64
25.2702-2(c)(2)(i)(B) 136.4.3 n.62
25.2702-2(c)(3) 136.4.3 n.68
25.2702-2(c)(4) 136.4.3 n.70
25.2702-2(c)(5)(i) 136.4.3 n.71
25.2702-2(c)(5)(ii) 136.4.3 n.72
25.2702-2(d) Ex. 1 .... 136.4.3 n.31
25.2702-2(d) Ex. 2 .... 136.4.3 n.42
25.2702-2(d) Ex. 3 .... 136.4.2 n.17
25.2702-2(d) Ex. 4 .... 136.4.5 n.89
25.2702-2(d) Ex. 5 .... 136.4.5 n.90
25.2702-2(d) Ex. 6 .... 136.4.5 n.91
25.2702-2(d)(2) Ex. 8 .... 136.4.3 n.65
25.2702-2(d)(2) Ex. 9 .... 136.4.3 n.68
25.2702-2(d)(2) Ex. 10 .... 136.4.3 n.70
25.2702-3(a) 136.4.3 n.29
25.2702-3(b)(1)(i) .... 136.4.3 ns. 33, 40
25.2702-3(b)(1)(ii) 136.4.3 n.34
25.2702-3(b)(1)(iii) 136.4.3 n.38
25.2702-3(b)(2) 136.4.3 n.34
25.2702-3(b)(3) 136.4.3 n.33
25.2702-3(b)(4) 136.4.3 n.33
25.2702-3(c)(1)(i) .... 136.4.3 ns. 43, 46
25.2702-3(c)(1)(ii) 136.4.3 n.43
25.2702-3(c)(1)(iii) 136.4.3 n.47
25.2702-3(c)(2) 136.4.3 n.43
25.2702-3(c)(3) 136.4.3 n.43
25.2702-3(d)(1) 136.4.3 n.48
25.2702-3(d)(2) 136.4.3 n.49
25.2702-3(d)(3) 136.4.3 n.51
25.2702-3(d)(4) 136.4.3 n.52
25.2702-3(e) Ex. 1 .... 136.4.3 ns. 32, 39
25.2702-3(e) Ex. 2 .... 136.4.3 n.36
25.2702-3(e) Ex. 3 .... 136.4.3 n.37
25.2702-3(e) Ex. 5 .... 136.4.3 n.44
25.2702-3(e) Ex. 6 .... 136.4.3 n.44
25.2702-3(e) Ex. 7 .... 136.4.3 n.50
25.2702-3(f)(1)(ii) 136.4.3 n.61

TABLE OF TREASURY REGULATIONS

[References are to paragraphs (¶) and notes (n.).]

TREAS. REGS.

25.2702-3(f)(1)(iii) 136.4.3 n.55
25.2702-3(f)(1)(iv) .... 136.4.3 ns. 53, 57
25.2702-3(f)(2) 136.4.3 n.59
25.2702-3(f)(3) Ex. 1 .... 136.4.3 n.54
25.2702-3(f)(3) Ex. 2 .... 136.4.3 n.58
25.2702-3(f)(3) Ex. 3 .... 136.4.3 n.60
25.2702-3(f)(3) Ex. 4 .... 136.4.3 n.56
25.2702-4(a) .... 136.4.2 ns. 20, 23
25.2702-4(b) 136.4.2 n.25
25.2702-4(c) 136.4.2 n.26
25.2702-4(d) Ex. 1 .... 136.4.2 n.27
25.2702-4(d) Ex. 2 .... 136.4.2 n.22
25.2702-4(d) Ex. 3 .... 136.4.2 n.24
25.2702-5(a) .... 136.4.6 ns. 92, 98
25.2702-5(b)(1) .... 136.4.6 ns. 93, 95, 102
25.2702-5(b)(2)(i) 136.4.6 n.97
25.2702-5(b)(2)(ii) ...... 136.4.6 ns. 99, 101
25.2702-5(b)(2)(iii) .... 136.4.6 ns. 103, 112
25.2702-5(b)(2)(iv) 136.4.6 n.96
25.2702-5(b)(3) 136.4.6 n.94
25.2702-5(c)(2) 136.4.6 n.105
25.2702-5(c)(3) 136.4.6 n.106
25.2702-5(c)(4) 136.4.6 n.106
25.2702-5(c)(5)(ii)(A) 136.4.6 n.107
25.2702-5(c)(5)(ii)(B) 136.4.6 n.108
25.2702-5(c)(5)(ii)(C) 136.4.6 n.115
25.2702-5(c)(5)(ii)(D) 136.4.6 n.113
25.2702-5(c)(6) 136.4.6 n.120
25.2702-5(c)(7)(i) 136.4.6 n.109
25.2702-5(c)(7)(ii) 136.4.6 n.116
25.2702-5(c)(7)(iii) 136.4.6 n.114
25.2702-5(c)(8) 136.4.6 n.118
25.2702-5(d) Ex. 1 .... 136.4.6 n.104
25.2702-5(d) Ex. 2 .... 136.4.6 n.111
25.2702-5(d) Ex. 3 .... 136.4.6 n.100
25.2702-5(d) Ex. 5 .... 136.4.6 n.110
25.2702-5(d) Ex. 6 .... 136.4.6 ns. 117, 119
25.2702-6(a)(1) 136.4.4 n.74
25.2702-6(a)(2) 136.4.4 n.86
25.2702-6(a)(3) 136.4.4 n.80
25.2702-6(b) 136.4.4 n.86
25.2702-6(b)(1) 136.4.4 n.75
25.2702-6(b)(2) 136.4.4 n.78
25.2702-6(c) Ex. 1 .... 136.4.4 n.73
25.2702-6(c) Ex. 2 .... 136.4.4 n.77
25.2702-6(c) Ex. 3 .... 136.4.4 n.79
25.2702-6(c) Ex. 6 .... 136.4.4 n.81
25.2702-6(c) Ex. 7 .... 136.4.4 n.82
25.2703-1(a)(1) 135.3.10 n.84

TREAS. REGS.

25.2703-1(a)(2) 135.3.10 n.87
25.2703-1(a)(3) 135.3.10 n.88
25.2703-1(a)(4) 135.3.10 n.89
25.2703-1(b)(1) 135.3.10 n.90
25.2703-1(b)(2) 135.3.10 n.91
25.2703-1(b)(3) .... 135.3.10 ns. 92, 93
25.2703-1(b)(4) .... 135.3.10 ns. 94, 95, 97
25.2703-1(c)(1) .... 135.3.10 ns. 99–101
25.2703-1(c)(2) 135.3.10 n.102
25.2703-1(d) 135.3.10 n.98
25.2704-1(a) .... 136.3.2 ns. 3, 4
25.2704-1(a)(2)(iv) .... 136.3.2 ns. 6, 8
25.2704-1(a)(2)(v) 136.3.2 n.7
25.2704-1(a)(2)(vi) 136.3.2 n.15
25.2704-1(a)(3) 136.3.2 n.17
25.2704-1(a)(4) .... 136.3.2 ns. 9, 11
25.2704-1(b) 136.3.2 n.10
25.2704-1(c)(1) .... 136.3.2 ns. 10, 15
25.2704-1(c)(2)(i)(A) 136.3.2 n.19
25.2704-1(c)(2)(i)(B) 136.3.2 n.20
25.2704-1(c)(2)(ii) 136.3.2 n.22
25.2704-1(c)(2)(iii) 136.3.2 n.24
25.2704-1(d) .... 136.3.2 ns. 25, 27
25.2704-1(f) Ex. 1 .... 136.3.2 n.26
25.2704-1(f) Ex. 2 .... 136.3.2 n.5
25.2704-1(f) Ex. 3 .... 136.3.2 n.12
25.2704-1(f) Ex. 4 .... 136.3.2 n.13
25.2704-1(f) Ex. 5 .... 136.3.1 n.2
25.2704-1(f) Ex. 6 .... 136.3.2 n.21
25.2704-1(f) Ex. 7 .... 136.3.2 n.16
25.2704-1(f) Ex. 8 .... 136.3.2 n.23
25.2704-1(f) Ex. 9 .... 136.3.2 n.18
25.2704-2(a) 136.3.3 n.29
25.2704-2(b) .... 136.3.3 ns. 29, 35, 37, 38, 41, 42
25.2704-2(c) 136.3.3 n.30
25.2704-2(d) Ex. 1 .... 136.3.3 n.33
25.2704-2(d) Ex. 2 .... 136.3.3 n.34
25.2704-2(d) Ex. 3 .... 136.3.3 n.36
25.2704-2(d) Ex. 4 .... 136.3.3 n.40
25.6018-1(a) 137.3 n.5
25.6018-2 .... 137.3 n.16
25.6019-1(b)(2) 137.2 n.5
25.6019-1(c) 137.2 n.7
25.6019-1(d) 137.2 n.8
25.6019-3(b) 123.6.2 n.21
20.6075-1 ..... 129.4.2 n.13, 137.3 ns. 8, 10
20.6075-2 .... 137.2 n.10
20.6081-1 .... 137.2 n.11
20.6081-1(a) 137.3 n.12

T-49

TAXATION OF INCOME, ESTATES AND GIFTS

[References are to paragraphs (¶) and notes (n.).]

TREAS. REGS.

20.6081-1(b)	137.3 n.13
20.6081-1(c)	137.3 n.14
20.6091-1(b)	137.3 n.7
20.6161-1(a)(1) Exs. 1–4	137.4.3 n.29
20.6161-1(a)(2)	137.4.3 n.28
25.6161-1(b)	137.4.1 n.2, 137.4.3 n.35
25.6161-1(c)	137.4.1 n.3
25.6161-1(d)	137.4.1 n.4
20.6161-2(c)	137.4.3 n.31
20.6163-1(a)(1)	137.4.4 n.40
20.6163-1(b)	137.4.3 n.36
20.6163-1(c)	137.4.4 n.39
25.6165-1(a)	137.4.1 n.5
20.6165-1(b)	137.4.4 n.43
20.6166-1(b)	137.5.1 n.1, 137.5.3 n.31
20.6166-1(d)	137.5.2 n.30
20.6166A-2(c)(1)	137.5.2 n.21

TREAS. REGS.

20.6166A-2(c)(2)	137.5.2 n.21
20.6166A-3(b)	137.5.4 n.56
301.6323(i)-1(b)(2)	137.6.2 n.22
301.6324-1(a)(1)	137.6.2 n.9
301.6324-1(a)(iv)	137.6.2 n.23
301.6324-1(b)	137.6.3 n.27
301.6324-1(d)	137.6.1 n.2
301.6325-1	137.6.2 n.24
301.6325-1(c)	137.6.2 n.23
301.6501(c)-1(e)	136.4.8 n.124
301.6501(c)-1(e)(1)	136.2.11 n.139
301.6501(c)-1(e)(2)	136.2.11 n.142
301.6601-1	137.5.3 n.41
301.7502-1(c)(1)	121.7.4 n.31
301.7502-1(c)(2)	121.7.4 n.31
301.7502-1(d)	121.7.4 n.31
301.7701-2(a)(3)	134.2.3 n.51

PROPOSED REGULATIONS

PROP. REGS.

20.2036-2	126.6.5 n.79
20.2039-2(a)	126.8.5 n.72
26.2611-4(b) Ex. 7	133.2.12 n.66
26.2613-1(e)	133.2.7 n.49
25.2701-5	136.2.12 n.143
25.2701-5(a)(1)	136.2.12 n.145
25.2701-5(a)(2)	136.2.12 n.151
25.2701-5(b)(1)(i)	136.2.12 n.145
25.2701-5(b)(1)(ii)	136.2.12 n.147

PROP. REGS.

25.2701-5(b)(2)	136.2.12 n.147
25.2701-5(b)(2)(iii)	136.2.12 n.149
25.2701-5(c)	136.2.12 n.152
25.2701-5(d) Ex. 1	136.2.12 n.146
25.2701-5(d) Ex. 2	136.2.12 n.148
25.2701-5(d) Ex. 3	136.2.12 n.150
25.2701-5(d) Ex. 4	136.2.12 n.151
301.7701-4(a)	133.2.4 n.22

Table of Revenue Rulings, Revenue Procedures, and Other IRS Releases

[References are to paragraphs (¶) and notes (n.).]

REVENUE RULINGS

REV. RUL.

156	137.4.2 n.24
158	126.8.1 n.8, 128.2.1 n.8, 128.5.2 n.7
187	134.2.3 n.31
189	135.3.10 n.112
243	128.2.1 n.18
260	126.8.1 n.8
279	129.3.3 n.25
53-146	123.5.1 n.5
54-6	123.5.2 n.22
54-19	125.6 n.1
54-91	124.3.3 n.39, 124.4.1 n.6
54-121	129.4.2 n.22, 129.4.4 n.99
54-153	128.2.1 n.19
54-246	123.5.1 n.7
54-344	124.3.2 n.17
54-382	131.4.1 n.11
54-400	124.3.3 n.44, 124.4.1 n.3, 124.4.2 n.11
54-410	123.3.2 n.10
54-444	135.7.3 n.38
54-445	135.7.6 n.69
54-537	122.5 n.19
54-538	122.5 n.11
55-71	121.4.3 n.34
55-143	134.2.3 ns. 30, 44
55-163	134.2.3 n.51
55-227	128.2.1 n.9
55-241	123.5.2 n.17
55-278	135.1.2 n.52, 135.4.6 n.78
55-334	131.6.2 n.25, 135.7.2 n.27
55-335	130.2 n.15
55-378	126.6.2 n.47

REV. RUL.

55-408	124.3.4 n.53
55-438	125.5 n.8
55-524	131.4.5 n.95
55-581	125.6 n.4
55-601	131.6.2 n.33
55-622	127.2 n.1
55-643	129.7.1 n.5
55-678	124.3.2 n.20
55-679	124.3.2 n.20
55-683	126.3.1 n.6
55-701	134.2.3 n.53
55-759	130.3.1 n.5
55-760	130.3.1 n.4
56-144	137.6.2 n.18
56-230	132.4 n.25
56-324	126.6.6 n.105
56-529	137.6.2 n.15
56-604	131.3.2 n.34
56-637	125.6 n.4
57-54	127.2 n.13
57-78	131.4.1 n.11, 131.6.2 n.28
57-315	121.3.5 n.44
57-366	124.4.3 n.38, 126.5.1 n.6, 126.6.2 n.29
57-368	129.2.2 n.5
57-446	127.5 n.5
57-495	135.7.3 n.39
57-530	131.2 n.3
58-167	132.6.2 n.9
58-307	122.3.5 n.22
58-395	122.5 n.4
58-436	135.7.2 n.26
58-576	135.7.2 n.18

[References are to paragraphs (¶) and notes (n.).]

REV. RUL.

59-9 .... 132.6.2 n.16
59-60 ...... 135.2.2 n.20, 135.2.3 ns. 27, 41,
135.3.4 ns. 25, 29, 135.3.5 n.55,
135.3.10 n.115, 135.4.3 ns. 25, 26,
135.4.4 n.40
59-78 .... 124.4.1 n.6
59-123 .... 132.6.3 n.34
59-195 .... 135.4.9 n.94
59-213 .... 135.7.3 n.34
59-357 .... 124.4.3 n.37, 126.5.1 n.6,
126.6.2 n.29
60-70 .... 126.8.2 n.25
60-88 .... 132.4 n.26
60-160 .... 123.6.1 n.19, 131.4.3 n.71
60-218 .... 124.4.2 n.22
60-247 .... 131.4.2 n.28, 132.6.2 n.11
61-55 .... 137.5.2 n.16
61-88 .... 125.7 ns. 4, 6, 135.1.1 n.13,
135.4.10 n.117
63-52 .... 135.7.2 n.28, 135.7.4 n.53
63-223 .... 135.7.4 n.49, 135.7.5 n.65
64-225 .... 121.3.6 n.51
65-57 .... 127.2 ns. 6, 12
65-144 .... 129.4.3 n.29
65-193 .... 135.2.2 n.20, 135.3.5 n.55,
135.3.10 n.115, 135.4.3 ns. 25, 26
65-217 .... 125.6 n.7
65-222 .... 127.2 n.7
65-245 .... 134.2.3 n.44
65-274 .... 131.6.2 n.31
66-20 .... 125.8 n.10
66-21 .... 131.4.5 n.95
66-40 .... 123.4 n.10
66-49 .... 135.5.1 n.1
66-60 .... 125.11.1 n.1
66-86 .... 126.3.2 n.27
66-139 .... 129.2.3 ns. 32, 37
66-167 .... 121.3.6 n.51
66-211 .... 131.6.2 n.30
66-234 .... 131.2 n.8
66-236 .... 134.2.3 ns. 39, 57
66-271 .... 132.6.2 n.16
66-272 .... 135.7.3 n.39
66-300 .... 131.4.1 n.6
66-348 .... 135.7.2 n.25
67-53 .... 132.6.3 n.26
67-55 .... 123.5.2 n.22
67-97 .... 125.6 n.10
67-107 .... 130.2 n.10
67-229 .... 130.4 n.4

REV. RUL.

67-270 .... 124.4.2 n.16
67-276 ..... 135.4.2 n.15, 135.4.6 ns. 72, 74
67-277 .... 125.6 n.4
67-278 .... 126.8.5 n.97
67-370 .... 125.7 n.13
67-371 .... 126.8.5 ns. 74, 90
67-384 .... 124.4.2 n.10
67-396 .... 121.3.2 n.13
67-442 .... 129.2.2 n.11
68-88 .... 125.6 ns. 4, 5, 127.2 n.14
68-89 .... 126.8.5 n.90
68-269 .... 122.3.2 n.13, 125.11.2 n.19
68-335 .... 131.6.2 n.31
68-379 .... 121.4.3 n.25, 123.6.1 ns. 5, 7,
123.6.2 ns. 22, 25, 131.4.3 n.73
68-538 .... 126.5.4 n.74
68-554 .... 129.4.7 n.161
68-556 .... 126.8.5 n.95
68-558 .... 121.4.5 ns. 47, 48
68-609 .... 135.4.4 n.40, 135.4.5 n.67
68-670 .... 124.4.2 ns. 30, 31
69-8 .... 125.6 n.4
69-56 .... 129.4.3 n.38
69-148 .... 122.3.2 n.13, 125.11.2 n.23
69-193 .... 131.4.5 ns. 92, 95
69-285 .... 130.2 n.8
69-341 .... 135.7.4 n.53
69-344 .... 124.3.2 n.36
69-345 .... 124.4.2 n.16
69-346 .... 121.3.3 n.20
69-347 .... 121.3.3 n.19
69-402 .... 131.3.2 n.39
69-411 .... 131.8 n.1, 137.8 n.5
69-551 .... 131.3.2 n.17
69-577 .... 125.11.2 n.27
70-84 .... 126.3.2 n.32
70-155 .... 126.6.2 n.35
70-211 .... 126.8.5 ns. 74, 90
70-237 .... 121.3.6 n.51
70-272 .... 132.4 n.26
70-348 .... 126.5.1 n.15
70-400 .... 129.4.2 n.12
70-452 .... 121.8.3 n.22, 130.4 n.6
70-512 .... 135.2.1 n.3, 135.2.2 n.12,
135.7.3 n.47
70-513 .... 126.5.1 n.19, 126.5.5 n.83
70-514 .... 126.8.5 n.104
70-600 .... 131.6.2 n.24
71-51 .... 129.3.3 n.41

TABLE OF IRS RELEASES

[References are to paragraphs (¶) and notes (n.).]

REV. RUL.

71-67 ...... 121.4.3 n.25, 131.4.3 ns. 75, 76, 135.4.10 n.113
71-168 .... 131.2 ns. 14, 15, 131.4.5 n.92
71-200 .... 130.2 n.8
71-317 .... 135.7.2 n.25
71-355 .... 132.4 n.7
71-396 .... 135.7.3 n.39
71-422 .... 131.3.2 n.39
71-441 .... 130.2 n.15
71-442 .... 135.4.10 n.116
71-443 .... 124.2 n.4, 124.3.1 n.8
71-480 .... 132.6.2 n.13
71-481 .... 126.8.5 n.79
71-483 .... 121.7.5 n.62
71-497 .... 127.8 n.8
71-507 ..... 125.8 n.10, 126.8.1 n.2, 126.8.2 n.43, 126.8.3 ns. 58, 62

72-7 .... 129.3.3 ns. 25, 26
72-8 .... 129.3.2 n.12, 129.3.3 n.26
72-62 .... 123.3.2 n.10, 123.3.3 n.29
72-153 .... 129.3.3 ns. 13, 23, 26
72-282 .... 126.4.4 n.63
72-307 .... 122.3.5 n.27, 127.4.3 n.22
72-355 .... 121.9 n.7
72-383 .... 129.4.3 n.47
72-442 .... 130.4 n.5
72-443 .... 134.2.4 n.69
73-21 .... 126.6.3 n.65, 126.6.4 n.68
73-47 .... 132.6.4 n.45
73-97 .... 135.7.3 n.39
73-142 ..... 126.5.1 ns. 18, 24, 126.5.5 n.88
73-143 .... 126.5.3 n.58
73-207 .... 123.5.2 n.21
73-287 .... 124.4.2 n.18, 124.4.3 n.39
73-311 .... 137.4.4 n.41
73-316 .... 125.6 n.6, 126.8.2 n.25
73-399 .... 135.7.3 n.41
73-405 ...... 124.3.3 ns. 39, 45, 124.4.1 n.6, 124.4.2 n.11
73-612 .... 122.2 n.6
74-25 .... 134.3 n.7
74-42 .... 129.2.4 n.42
74-43 .... 124.4.2 n.22
74-120 .... 129.4.3 n.63
74-179 .... 130.2 n.2
74-199 .... 124.2 n.9
74-260 .... 135.7.1 n.10
74-345 .... 124.2 n.6, 124.3.1 n.6
74-363 .... 132.5 n.8
74-365 .... 122.2 n.18, 126.4.1 n.10

REV. RUL.

74-410 .... 135.4.10 n.116
74-424 .... 137.3 n.9
74-491 .... 132.5 n.12
74-492 ...... 121.7.3 n.28, 125.5 n.9, 125.12 n.2, 128.2.1 n.6, 128.3.5 n.24
74-523 .... 130.2 n.18
74-533 .... 132.5 n.8
74-556 ..... 123.5.1 n.7, 126.3.1 n.4, 126.5.1 n.6
74-557 .... 126.8.5 n.79
74-623 .... 134.2.3 n.39
75-1 .... 121.4.2 n.18
75-8 .... 123.4 n.2
75-24 .... 131.4.2 n.27
75-63 .... 132.4 n.7
75-71 .... 121.3.3 n.28
75-73 .... 123.6.2 n.29
75-100 .... 127.5 n.4
75-126 .... 125.6 n.3, 128.2.1 n.24
75-127 .... 125.6 ns. 3, 5, 128.2.1 n.24
75-128 .... 129.4.3 n.26, 129.4.7 n.162
75-145 .... 125.6 n.4, 128.2.3 n.39
75-176 .... 126.8.5 n.83
75-177 .... 131.4.2 n.27
75-336 .... 137.5.2 n.16
75-350 .... 129.2.2 n.6, 129.4.3 n.50
75-351 .... 128.3.2 n.6
75-364 .... 137.3 n.12
75-365 .... 137.5.2 n.16
75-367 .... 137.5.2 n.16
75-401 .... 135.7.2 n.23
75-408 .... 126.8.5 n.79
75-415 .... 124.3.2 n.20
75-439 .... 132.7.3 n.32
75-440 .... 129.4.3 ns. 29, 37
75-505 ..... 126.3.3 n.39, 126.8.2 ns. 23, 27, 126.8.3 ns. 57, 63
75-506 .... 124.3.2 n.21
75-507 .... 123.4 n.11
75-550 .... 132.6.3 n.29
75-551 .... 123.2.2 n.6, 123.2.3 n.10
76-15 .... 129.2.2 n.2
76-102 .... 125.6 n.4, 126.8.2 n.26
76-113 .... 127.4.4 n.25
76-114 .... 137.7.3 n.24
76-155 .... 129.2.2 n.2, 129.2.3 n.29
76-156 .... 121.6.3 n.22, 121.7.2 n.21
76-157 .... 123.4 n.11
76-165 .... 130.5.5 n.43
76-166 .... 129.4.2 ns. 8, 21

[References are to paragraphs (¶) and notes (n.).]

REV. RUL.

76-178 .... 126.7.4 n.47
76-199 .... 129.2.3 n.32, 129.3.2 n.8
76-234 .... 135.7.2 n.22
76-235 .... 126.4.4 n.64, 131.5 n.11
76-236 .... 130.6 n.3
76-274 .... 127.4.8 n.58
76-275 .... 122.5 n.14
76-303 .... 125.11.1 n.1, 129.2.2 n.14
76-304 .... 125.6 n.12, 126.3.2 n.33, 126.5.1 n.8
76-312 .... 137.4.2 n.19
76-349 .... 129.7.1 n.12
76-358 .... 130.6 n.3
76-360 .... 124.3.1 ns. 7, 9
76-367 .... 137.4.2 n.20
76-368 .... 128.2.1 n.10
76-369 .... 131.2 n.13
76-380 .... 126.8.2 n.40
76-421 .... 127.4.4 n.25
76-470 .... 132.5 n.6
76-471 .... 132.5 n.8
76-472 .... 135.4.10 ns. 116, 117
76-490 .... 124.3.4 n.53
76-498 .... 131.3.3 n.53, 131.5 n.12
76-501 .... 125.6 ns. 4, 5, 126.8.2 n.26
76-502 .... 128.2.1 n.20
76-503 .... 129.4.3 n.63
76-542 .... 131.4.3 n.49
76-546 .... 130.3.3 n.25
76-547 .... 121.6.2 ns. 11, 12
77-30 .... 129.4.3 n.58
77-48 .... 122.3.1 n.5, 122.3.6 n.31
77-95 .... 126.8.2 n.11
77-97 .... 130.5.4 n.41
77-99 .... 122.5 n.14
77-130 .... 129.3.3 & ns. 43, 45
77-139 .... 126.8.5 n.89
77-157 .... 126.8.5 n.84
77-170 .... 129.4.3 n.52
77-180 .... 135.7.3 n.47
77-181 .... 127.7 n.4
77-183 .... 126.8.2 n.30, 126.8.2 n.39
77-194 .... 128.2.2 n.32
77-195 ..... 135.4.10 n.100, 135.4.10 n.101, 136.4.1 n.5
77-202 .... 130.6 n.3
77-221 .... 135.7.3 n.36
77-222 .... 126.8.5 n.87
77-232 .... 130.2 n.1
77-274 .... 131.2 n.9

REV. RUL.

77-287 .... 135.3.7 n.64
77-299 .... 121.1 n.25, 124.1 n.9
77-314 .... 123.6.1 n.9, 131.4.3 n.77
77-345 .... 129.5.2 n.13
77-346 .... 129.4.3 n.45
77-358 .... 124.3.2 n.18
77-372 .... 121.4.5 n.50
77-374 .... 130.4 n.6
77-378 .... 122.5 ns. 13, 15
77-385 .... 130.5.2 n.21
77-404 .... 129.3.3 n.14, 129.4.4 n.93
77-423 .... 123.4 n.10
77-443 .... 131.3.2 n.27, 131.6.1 n.11
77-444 .... 129.4.3 n.83
77-460 .... 128.2.1 ns. 5, 16, 17
77-461 .... 131.3.2 n.40
78-15 .... 126.3.2 n.33
78-16 .... 126.5.5 n.80
78-27 .... 123.5.2 n.22
78-125 .... 131.3.2 n.36
78-137 .... 127.7 n.3
78-151 .... 126.8.5 n.94
78-152 .... 130.3.1 n.8, 130.3.2 n.17
78-168 .... 124.3.1 n.6
78-242 .... 131.4.5 ns. 91–93
78-255 .... 121.8.3 n.22, 130.4 n.6, 130.6 n.12
78-271 .... 131.4.3 n.45
78-283 .... 130.6 n.3
78-323 .... 137.9 n.6
78-362 .... 121.1 n.19
78-366 .... 130.2 n.4
78-367 .... 135.1.2 n.29
78-378 .... 135.7.3 ns. 41, 43
78-399 .... 126.8.5 n.103
78-409 .... 126.6.2 n.37
78-431 .... 135.7.3 n.39
78-445 .... 130.4 n.10
79-7 .... 126.4.4 n.62
79-14 .... 129.5.2 n.6
79-35 .... 126.8.2 n.26
79-47 .... 124.3.4 n.54
79-54 .... 124.2 n.6, 124.3.1 n.6
79-63 .... 128.2.3 ns. 35, 40, 42
79-86 .... 129.4.3 n.83
79-94 .... 126.3.5 n.62
79-105 .... 123.4 n.3
79-109 .... 126.6.2 n.38
79-117 .... 127.4.4 n.28
79-118 .... 123.6.2 ns. 23, 31

TABLE OF IRS RELEASES

[References are to paragraphs (¶) and notes (n.).]

REV. RUL.

79-129 .... 127.4.2 n.13, 128.2.1 n.21
79-154 .... 128.2.1 n.14
79-159 .... 130.2 n.10
79-160 .... 132.2.1 n.8
79-177 .... 126.5.4 n.74
79-190 .... 126.8.5 n.96
79-211 .... 132.6.2 n.10
79-219 .... 132.4 n.23
79-224 .... 129.3.3 n.15
79-243 .... 122.3.1 n.6
79-252 .... 131.3.2 n.36
79-301 .... 126.8.5 n.81
79-302 .... 125.11.4 ns. 67, 69, 131.4.1
n.10, 131.5 ns. 4, 7
79-303 .... 127.5 n.4
79-312 .... 123.6.1 n.4, 123.6.2 n.30
79-317 .... 132.6.4 n.40
79-327 .... 121.6.3 n.23
79-353 .... 126.5.5 n.89, 126.6.3 n.64
79-354 .... 129.2.2 n.4
79-359 .... 130.6 n.3
79-363 .... 121.4.3 n.25, 123.6.1 n.9
79-372 .... 125.11.4 n.60
79-373 .... 128.3.4 n.19
79-383 .... 129.2.3 n.19
79-384 .... 121.3.2 n.14, 121.4.2 n.15,
121.4.4 n.39
79-397 .... 125.6 n.4, 126.8.2 n.26
79-421 .... 121.6.2 n.16
79-429 .... 127.7 n.4
79-432 .... 135.2.1 n.4
80-66 .... 130.3.3 n.26
80-80 .... 126.7.4 n.41, 127.4.4 n.26,
131.4.2 n.37, 132.6.3 n.22, 135.4.10
n.111
80-123 .... 130.5.2 n.22
80-142 .... 125.11.4 ns. 63, 64
80-148 .... 129.6.4 n.24
80-158 .... 126.8.5 n.89
80-159 .... 129.5.2 n.8
80-186 .... 135.4.7 n.82
80-196 .... 121.4.5 n.44
80-209 .... 134.2.1 n.6
80-224 .... 123.5.2 n.24
80-241 .... 123.4 n.11
80-242 .... 127.5 n.6
80-250 .... 131.3.2 n.37
80-255 ..... 122.3.5 ns. 24, 26, 126.5.4 n.76,
126.6.4 n.67
80-261 .... 124.3.3 n.39

REV. RUL.

80-271 .... 121.8.1 n.7
80-329 .... 135.1.2 n.46
80-336 .... 126.4.4 n.64
80-346 .... 126.6.5 n.91
80-347 .... 137.3 n.9
81-7 .... 124.3.3 n.49
81-15 .... 126.6.5 ns. 88, 90
81-31 .... 121.2 n.6, 122.3.5 n.22, 125.6
n.11
81-51 .... 126.6.3 n.64
81-54 .... 121.2 n.3, 122.3.1 n.8
81-85 .... 123.5.1 n.10
81-110 .... 121.1 n.19
81-118 .... 132.6.3 n.20
81-128 .... 127.4.2 n.15
81-146 .... 125.11.3 n.31
81-154 .... 131.3.2 n.36
81-165 .... 129.5.2 n.8
81-166 .... 122.3.1 n.5, 128.2.1 n.24
81-170 .... 135.6.7 n.104
81-179 .... 135.6.2 n.14
81-182 .... 126.8.2 n.26
81-183 .... 131.4.1 n.10, 131.5 n.4
81-184 .... 125.11.4 n.68, 131.4.1 n.10
81-220 .... 135.6.3 n.36
81-221 .... 126.6.2 n.44
81-227 .... 125.11.2 n.28
81-228 ..... 135.4.6 n.80, 137.4.2 ns. 20, 22
81-230 .... 135.3.8 n.78
81-236 .... 135.6.2 n.14
81-237 .... 137.3 n.12
81-253 .... 135.3.4 n.40
81-256 .... 131.3.2 n.36
81-263 .... 132.4 n.22
81-264 .... 121.1 n.22, 121.2 n.3
81-285 .... 135.6.5 n.64
81-286 .... 121.1 n.25
81-287 .... 131.3.2 n.37
81-302 .... 132.4 ns. 7, 9
81-303 .... 134.2.7 n.89
81-308 .... 135.6.9 n.145
82-5 .... 125.6 n.4, 127.2 n.14
82-6 .... 130.6 n.7
82-13 .... 127.8 ns. 1, 3, 8, 9
82-24 .... 126.7.5 n.52
82-25 .... 129.4.3 n.32
82-35 .... 135.6.9 n.139
82-63 .... 128.2.2 n.28
82-82 .... 131.6.2 ns. 23, 33, 37, 132.7.1
n.4

[References are to paragraphs (¶) and notes (n.).]

REV. RUL.

82-83	129.6.3 n.11
82-85	127.4.8 ns. 51, 55
82-98	121.5 n.8
82-104	135.6.7 n.104
82-105	130.3.1 n.2
82-120	137.5.4 n.57
82-140	135.6.3 n.36
82-141	127.8 n.5
82-143	121.5 n.10
82-145	127.4.8 n.58
82-156	128.2.3 n.35, 129.3.3 n.28, 129.4.3 ns. 53, 87
82-193	134.2.3 ns. 44, 52
82-199	126.8.5 n.74
82-216	121.9 ns. 2, 5
83-15	132.6.4 n.37, 137.4.4 n.36
83-20	130.5.1 n.10
83-24	131.3.2 n.36
83-26	129.2.3 n.40, 129.4.5 n.128
83-30	131.3.2 n.47
83-35	121.7.2 n.21, 121.7.4 n.39
83-44	127.2 n.13
83-45	130.5.1 n.10
83-54	131.4.1 n.4, 131.4.3 n.50, 131.6.1 n.12
83-71	135.6.7 n.104
83-81	131.6.3 n.42, 135.6.7 n.102
83-96	135.6.7 n.96
83-103	137.4.4 n.36
83-107	129.3.3 n.26
83-108	124.3.3 n.49
83-115	135.6.7 n.112
83-120	135.4.3 ns. 34, 35
83-147	127.4.5 n.30, 127.4.8 n.63
83-148	127.4.8 n.60
83-158	130.5.5 n.42
83-178	123.4 n.11
83-180	124.1 n.8
84-11	132.2.2 n.10
84-25	121.3.2 n.12, 131.4.3 n.84, 132.3 n.9
84-38	137.4.2 n.23
84-42	126.6.2 n.16, 131.4.3 ns. 57, 58
84-75	131.3.2 n.35
84-76	126.4.2 n.25
84-97	130.5.5 n.42
84-105	129.2.3 n.41
84-119	135.6.7 n.104

REV. RUL.

84-130	127.4.3 n.21
84-147	135.4.9 n.93
84-179	127.4.6 n.42
85-23	130.5.5 n.42
85-24	124.2 n.12, 124.3.3 n.47
85-35	129.4.3 n.39
85-66	135.6.9 n.126
85-88	121.6.2 n.19
85-92	135.6.7 n.104
86-38	132.4 n.21
86-39	121.6.2 n.9, 128.3.3 n.14
86-41	121.3.3 n.29, 121.4.5 n.57
86-44	130.2 n.2
86-54	137.5.4 n.52
86-85	135.6.7 n.104
86-117	132.4 n.16
87-122	135.6.4 n.42
87-142	135.6.7 n.104
88-59	135.6.7 n.104
88-78	135.6.9 ns. 121, 131
88-82	130.5.3 n.31
88-85	126.3.3 n.39, 126.8.2 n.11, 126.8.2 ns. 23, 40, 126.8.3 ns. 57, 63, 126.8.5 ns. 74, 79, 81, 83, 84, 87, 89, 90, 94–97
88-89	135.6.7 n.104
88-90	129.4.3 n.92
89-3	121.2 n.3, 133.2.6 n.38, 133.5 n.11
89-4	135.6.9 n.124, 137.5.4 n.51
89-22	135.6.9 n.129
89-30	135.6.7 n.114
89-31	130.3.1 n.8, 130.3.2 n.21
89-32	137.5.3 n.43
89-58	135.6.7 n.104
89-89	129.4.5 n.121
90-2	132.6.4 n.41
90-3	129.7.2 n.20
90-8	131.3.2 n.38
90-21	126.4.2 n.21, 127.8 n.7
90-45	121.7.4 n.33
90-49	135.6.7 n.104
90-101	134.2.7 ns. 89, 90
90-110	121.7.6 n.89
91-24	135.6.7 n.104
92-12	135.6.7 n.104
92-22	126.8.5 n.71
92-26	133.2.5 n.34

TABLE OF IRS RELEASES

[References are to paragraphs (¶) and notes (n.).]

REVENUE PROCEDURES

REV. PROC.
64-19 .... 129.7.2 n.20, 133.3.4 n.66
65-19 .... 135.1.2 n.49
69-18 .... 137.4.2 n.19
81-14 .... 135.6.6 n.78
81-27 .... 131.3.2 n.37, 137.5.3 n.39
85-13 .... 137.3 n.18

REV. PROC.
85-46 .... 121.3.4 n.37
88-50 .... 137.9 n.8
92-1 .... 137.9 n.8
92-3 .... 124.3.4 n.54, 137.9 n.8
92-9 .... 134.2.2 n.10, 134.2.3 n.53

ANNOUNCEMENTS

ANN.
83-43 .... 135.6.2 n.17

GENERAL COUNSEL'S MEMORANDA

GCM
27242 .... 125.6 n.10

IRS NOTICES

NOTICE
89-4 .... 129.4.5 n.118
89-60 .... 135.4.10 n.97

NOTICE
90-46 .... 129.4.5 n.118

MIMEOGRAPHS

MIM.
3361 .... 137.3 n.12

TREASURY DECISIONS

TD
2450 .... 125.10 n.2, 129.1 n.3
7612 .... 131.3.2 n.21

TD
8395 .... 136.2.8 n.88, 136.4.3 ns. 35, 52,
                                  63, 136.4.6 n.118

Index

Index

[References are to paragraphs (¶).]

A

Acceptance
gift transfers, defective, 122.2

Accountant's fees
administrative expenses deduction, 131.3.2

Accounts receivable
gift property, 121.3.2

Actuarial valuation
generally, 135.4.10, 135.7.4
gross estate, 125.5, 125.7
claims against estate, 131.4.2
retained reversionary interests, 125.5

Adjusted basis
generation-skipping transfers, 133.4

Adjusted taxable estate (ATE), 132.4

Administration expenses, estates
stock redemptions to pay, 126.4.2

Administration expenses deduction, estates
community property, 131.4.5
generally, 120.3, 131.1, 131.3.1
nonprobate property, 131.3.3
defined, 131.3.3
local law, 131.3.3
restriction of expenses, 131.3.3
tax liens, effect of, 137.6.2
nonresident aliens, 134.2.4
probate property, 131.3.2
attorney's fees, 131.3.2
benefit of beneficiaries, expenses incurred for, 131.3.2
executor's commissions, 131.3.2
interest, 131.3.2
miscellaneous expenses, 131.3.2
protracted administration, 131.3.2
sale of estate assets, expenses of, 131.3.2
tax liens, effect of, 137.6.2

"property subject to claims" limitation, 131.6.3
state law, 131.3.2, 131.3.3, 131.6.1
taxes as administration expenses, 131.6.2

Agents
beneficial ownership of property, 125.2
estate tax return, filing of, 137.2
gifts through
annual per-donee exclusion, 124.2
indirect gifts, 121.1
gift tax return, filing of, 137.2
gross estate, rights and powers of decedent's agent, 126.3.3

Agricultural property
valuation, special use election, 135.6
See also: Farmers and ranchers—special use valuation election

Aliens. *See*: Nonresident aliens; Resident aliens

Alimony
retained life estate, trusts through, 126.6.2

Alternate valuation date. *See*: Valuation date—alternate date for estate tax purposes

Amateur sports
charitable bequests to organizations fostering competition, 130.2
gift tax liability for contributions toward fostering of competition, 121.8

Animals
prevention of cruelty to
charitable bequests to organizations dedicated to, 130.2
gift tax liability for contributions for, 121.8

Annual per-donee exclusion
amounts excluded, 124.1
bonds, 124.3.4

[References are to paragraphs (¶).]

Annual per-donee exclusion *(cont'd)*
  child support, 124.1
  community property, 123.1
  computation of, 124.1
  contract rights to future payments, 124.3.4
    outright gifts vs. sequential temporal interests, 124.3.4
  debt discharges, effect of annual partial, 120.1
  demand trusts, 124.3.3
    assets not convertible into cash, 124.3.3
    Crummey powers, harmony of exclusion with, 124.3.3
    minor beneficiaries, 124.3.3
  donee identification, 124.2
    agents or intermediaries, 124.2
    beneficiaries of trusts, 124.2
    charitable organizations, 124.2
    corporate donees, 124.2
    divided interests, 124.2
    generally, 124.1
    jointly held property, 124.2
    number of permissible exclusions determined by, 124.2
    organizational vs. individual donees, 124.2
    partnerships, 124.2
    reciprocal trusts, 124.2
    shareholders, 124.2
    trusts, 124.2
    veil-piercing approach, 124.2
  estate planning, limitations for, 124.1
  future interests exception, 124.3
    class gifts, 124.3.2
    closely held corporation stock, 124.3.1
    contract rights to future payments, 124.3.4
    definition of future interests, 124.3.1
    generally, 124.1, 124.3.1
    history, 124.3.1
    interests in income exclusion, 124.3.2
    marketability, 124.3.1
    present enjoyment of property, right to, 124.3.1
    present excludable interests distinguished, 124.1, 124.3.1
    spendthrift clauses, 124.3.1, 124.3.2
  generally, 120.2.1, 120.2.2, 121.1, 124.1, 132.1
  gift tax return, filing of, 137.2

history, 124.1
income interests in trusts, 124.3.2
  actuarial computation, effect of, 124.3.2
  discretionary distributions, 124.3.2
  external standard, rights to distributions determined by, 124.3.2
  fiduciary administrative powers, 124.3.2
  invasion of principal, effect of power of, 124.3.2
  nonproductive property, 124.3.2
installment gifts, 124.1
life insurance policies, 124.3.4
marital deduction, possible effect on, 129.1
minors, gifts to, 124.4
  custodianship statutes, state, 124.4.3
  demand trusts, 124.3.3
  generally, 124.1, 124.4.1
  guardians, 124.3.3
  state law, 124.4.1–124.4.3
  statutory trusts, 124.4.2
nonresident aliens, 134.2.2
notes, 124.3.4
present excludable interests distinguished from future interests, 124.1, 124.3.1, 124.3.2
principal issues of application, 124.1
promissory notes, 124.3.4
purpose of, 124.1, 124.3.1
split-gift election, effect of, 120.2.1, 123.5.1, 124.1

Annuities
  See also: Survivorship annuities
  estate freeze rules for qualified annuity interests, 136.4.3
  gift property, 121.3.2, 123.3.3
  gross estate transfers, effect of, 126.6.2
  guaranteed, 130.5.3
  marital deduction, 123.3.3
  powers of appointment, 128.5.2
    proceeds subject to power in surviving spouse, 129.4.4
  private, 135.4.10
  QTIP transfers, 123.3.3, 129.4.5
  valuation, 126.8.1, 126.8.3, 135.4.9, 135.4.10

Antenuptial agreements. *See*: Prenuptial agreements

INDEX

[References are to paragraphs (¶).]

Antiques
valuation, 135.4.8

Apportionment of estate tax
appointive assets, 128.5.3
apportionment statutes, 137.8
charitable bequests, 130.6, 137.8
common law rule, 137.8
constitutional issues, 120.1.2, 125.11.1, 129.1
decedent's intent, 129.5.2, 137.8
effect on tax, 137.8
equitable apportionment, 137.8
generally, 137.8
marital deduction and, 137.8
QTIP transfers, 137.8
state law, 120.1.2, 129.5.2, 137.8
will provisions, 137.8

Appraisers
administrative expenses deduction, 131.3.2
expert witnesses in valuation matters, 135.5.1

Appreciated property
appreciation between gift and death dates, estate and gift taxes, 120.2.2, 126.4.1, 126.4.2

Armed forces. *See*: Military personnel

Arm's-length standard
estate freezes, 136.1
gift tax donative intent distinguished, 121.4.5
valuation of property, 135.1.2, 135.2.1

Art, works of
contributions for encouragement of charitable bequests, 130.2, 130.5.1
gift tax deductions, 121.8.1
defined in terms of copyright, 130.5.1
estate freeze valuation, 136.1
gross estate inclusion of property owned by decedent at death, 125.1, 125.7
valuation
blockage discount, 135.3.3
generally, 135.4.8
gross estate inclusion purposes, 125.7

Assets
gross estate claims, contingent, defeasible, and speculative assets, 125.7

nonprobate
administrative expenses deduction, 131.3.3
personal liability for estate tax, 137.7.3
tax liens, 137.6.2
passive, 137.5.2
probate
See also: Probate property
administrative expenses deduction, 131.3.2
marital deduction, 129.2.3
personal liability for estate tax, 137.7.3
tax liens, 137.6.2
rent-free use of, as gift property, 121.3.4
valuation of, 135.4.5

Assignment of income
gifts of property, 121.3.5

Attorney's fees. *See*: Legal expenses

Auctions
valuation of property, 135.1.2

Audits
estate tax returns, 137.3, 137.9

Avoidance of tax. *See*: Tax avoidance

B

Bank accounts
joint. *See*: Joint bank accounts
nonresident aliens, taxation of, 134.2.3

Bank account trusts
gift transfers
relinquished power of revocation, 122.3.4
revocable, 122.3.4

Bankruptcy
as forced sale, 135.1.2
valuation of property, 135.1.2

Barter equation method of valuation, 135.2.5

Basis
See also: Date-of-death basis
gift property, generally, 120.3
income in respect of decedents, 120.3
inherited property, 120.3, 128.5.4
powers of appointment, 128.5.4
QTIP property, 129.4.5
special use election, 135.6.10

Below-market loans
gift property, 121.3.4

[References are to paragraphs (¶).]

Beneficial ownership
joint bank accounts, 122.3.2
property owned by decedent at death,
125.2

**Beneficiaries of charitable bequest
deduction**, 130.2, 136.4.7

Beneficiary of trusts and estates
defined, 136.2.10
minors. *See*: Minors
nonresident aliens, 134.2.3
property owned by decedent at death,
125.1

Bequests
charitable bequests, 130.1–130.3, 130.5,
130.6, 137.8
See also: Charitable bequest deduction
charitable pledges, 130.3.4
conditional
marital deduction valuation, 129.5.3
terminable interests, 129.3.3
contingent bequests, 130.4
direct skip compared, 133.1
income, value of bequest as, 120.3
nonresident aliens, 134.2.4
split-interest charitable/private transfers,
130.5
in trust, 130.2
zero-tax bequests, 129.6.2

Bonds
annual per-donee exclusion, 124.3.4
closely held business interests, payment
of deferred estate tax on, 137.5.3
flower bonds
defined, 137.4.2
payment of estate tax with, 137.4.2
valuation, 135.4.6
stock exchange trading, 135.4.2
valuation, 135.4.2, 135.4.6, 137.4.2
See also: Securities—valuation

Book value
closely held corporation stock, 135.4.3

Brokerage accounts
joint tenancies in other property
distinguished, 122.3.2
revocable transfers, 122.3.2
survivorship feature, 125.11.4

Burden of proof
expatriation, tax-motivated, 134.4
transferor of property included in gross
estate, identification of, 126.3.1

valuation of property, 135.1.1

Business purpose
donative intent distinguished, 121.4.4,
121.4.5

Buy-sell agreements
bona fide business exception, 135.3.10
effective date, 135.3.10
estate freeze valuation rules, 135.3.10,
136.3.3
modified right or restriction, 135.3.10
options under, 135.3.10
pre-1990 authorities, 135.3.10
bona fide business arrangement or
testamentary device, 135.3.10
freedom to dispose during life,
135.3.10
local law, 135.3.10
obligation to sell at formula price,
135.3.10
right of first refusal, 135.3.10
rights and restrictions, 135.3.10
valuation of property, effect on, 135.3.10

C

Calendar year
gift tax, 120.2.1

Call options
valuation, 135.4.7

Call rights
estate freeze valuation, 136.1, 136.2.2,
136.2.4, 136.2.5

Cancellation of debt. *See*: Debt discharges

Capital assets
gift property, holding period of, 120.3
holding period, 120.3

Capital call rights
estate freeze valuation, 136.1

Capitalization of income
generally, 135.2.3
real property, 135.4.1

Carryover basis
gifts made within three years of death,
126.4.2
inherited property, 120.3
property acquired by gift, 120.3

Cash equivalency
vs. fair market value, 135.1.2
valuation of property, 135.1.2

INDEX

[References are to paragraphs (¶).]

Casualty losses
community property, 131.4.5
deductibility, 131.8
defined, 131.8
estate tax deduction, 131.4.5, 131.8
  income tax deduction vs., 131.8
  nonresident aliens, 134.2.4

Charitable bequest deduction
apportionment of estate tax, 130.6
charges against charitable bequests,
  130.6
contingent bequests, 130.4
  charitable remainder trusts, 130.4
  cy pres doctrine, 130.4
  "negligible" standard, 130.4
death taxes, 130.6
estate tax apportionment and, 137.8
foreign death taxes, 132.7.3
generally, 130.1
history, 130.1
noncharitable purposes
  charitable lead trusts, 130.5.3
  transfers subject to invasion for, 130.4
nonresident aliens, 134.2.4
principal issues under statutory
  provisions, 130.1
private and charitable purposes, split
  interest transfers involving both,
  130.5
qualified beneficiaries, 130.2
  amateur sports competition,
    organizations fostering, 130.2
  art, organizations operated for
    encouragement of, 130.2, 130.5.1
  charitable organizations, 130.2
  educational organizations, 130.2
  foreign governments, 130.2
  fraternal orders, 130.2
  governmental agencies, 130.2
  literary organizations, 130.2
  prevention of cruelty to children or
    animals, organizations dedicated
    to, 130.2
  religious organizations, 130.2
  scientific organizations, 130.2
  testator's intentions, 130.2
  trusts, qualified, 130.2
  veterans' organizations, 130.2
qualified reformations, 130.5.6, 130.5.7
qualifying transfers, 130.3
  charitable pledges, 130.3.4

compromise payments, 130.3.2
defined, 130.3.1
disclaimers, 130.3.3
generally, 130.3.1
settlements of will contests, 130.3.2
will contests, 130.3.2
reformable interests, 130.5.6
  pre-1979 will or trust, 130.5.7
split interests (transfers for both private
  and charitable purposes), 130.5
  charitable lead trusts, 130.5.3
  charitable remainder trusts, 130.5.1,
    130.5.2
  conservation interests, 130.5.5
  cooperative housing corporations,
    130.5.5
  decedent's death, interests
    extinguished by, 130.5.1
  definition of split interests, 130.5.1
  farms, 130.5.5
  generally, 130.5.1
  gross estate, relation of interests to,
    130.5.1
  guaranteed annuities, 130.5.3
  personal residences, 130.5.5
  pooled income funds, 130.5.1, 130.5.2
  reformation rule, 130.5.6, 130.5.7
  restrictions, 130.5.1
  "same property" rule, 130.5.1
  transition rules, 130.5.7
  trust transfers before October 10,
    1969, 130.5.7
  undivided interests, 130.5.4
  wills executed before October 10,
    1969, 130.5.7
state tax, 130.6
statutory provisions, 130.1
tax liens, effect of
  estate tax, 137.6.2
  gift tax, 137.6.3
valuation, 130.5.3, 130.5.6, 135.1.2,
  135.4.10
  alternate date, 135.7.5
  estate freeze rules, 136.4.7

Charitable contributions
art, works of, 121.8.1, 135.4.8
death taxes, state and foreign, 131.7
donative intent, 121.4.1
foreign death taxes, 131.7
gift tax deductions, 121.1, 121.8
  conditional gifts, 121.8.3

[References are to paragraphs (¶).]

Charitable contributions *(cont'd)*
gift tax deductions *(cont'd)*
generally, 121.8.1
gift requirement, 121.8.1
noncharitable purposes, gifts subject to invasion for, 121.8.3
qualifying organizations, 121.8.1
split-interest gifts, 121.8.2
music manuscripts, 135.4.8
nonresident aliens, 134.2.2, 134.2.4
state death taxes, 131.7
valuation, 135.1.2

Charitable organizations
See also: Charitable contributions
annual per-donee exclusion, 124.2
charitable bequests, qualified beneficiaries of, 130.2
nonresident aliens, contributions by, 134.2.4
foreign, 130.2, 131.7
gift tax deductions for contributions to. *See*: Charitable contributions—gift tax deductions
gift tax liability, 121.1
qualified retirement plans, 126.8.5
restrictions, 130.2

Charitable pledges
charitable bequest deduction, 130.3.4
claims against estate, 131.4.4
nonresident aliens, 134.2.4

Charitable trusts
lead trusts, 130.5.3
advantages of, 130.5.3
estate freeze valuation rules, 136.4.7
guaranteed annuities, 130.5.3
income tax consequences, 130.5.3
noncharitable interests, 130.5.3
private foundation rules, 130.5.3
unitrust interests, 130.5.3
remainder annuity and unitrusts, 123.3.3, 129.4.6, 130.4, 130.5.1, 130.5.2
defined, 130.5.2
estate freeze valuation rules, 136.4.7
generation-skipping transfers, 133.2.3, 133.2.8

Checks
gift property, 121.3.2

Children
community property gifts to, 123.2.1, 123.2.2

prevention of cruelty to
charitable bequests to organizations dedicated to, 130.2
gift tax liability for contributions for, 121.8

Child support
annual per-donee exclusion, 124.1
gift tax transfers
donative intent, 121.4.3
marital property settlements, 123.6.1, 123.6.2
lifetime transfers subject to retained right to receive income, 126.6.2

Claims
gross estate
See also: Claims against estate, deductions for
contingent claims, 125.7
defeasible claims, 125.7
expectancies or hopes vs., 125.7
generally, 125.1, 125.7
speculative claims, 125.7
tax liens, effect of, 137.6.2
unliquidated claims, 125.7

Claims against estate, deductions for, 131.4
actuarial valuation, 131.4.2
community property, 131.4.5
contract claims, 131.4.3
bona fide contract requirement, 131.4.3
charitable pledges, 131.4.4
completed gifts, 131.4.3
contractual origin, 131.4.3
employment agreements, 131.4.3
full consideration requirement, 131.4.3
guarantees, 131.4.3
judicial decrees, 131.4.3
loan agreements, 131.4.3
marriage, separation, and divorce, 131.4.3
mortgages, 131.4.3, 131.5
prenuptial agreement, 131.4.3
quasi-testamentary arrangements, 131.4.3
related parties, 131.4.3
support agreements, 131.4.3
debts, secured and unsecured, 131.5
decedent's debts, defined, 131.4.1
generally, 131.1, 131.4.1

[References are to paragraphs (¶).]

indebtedness in respect of property, 131.5
joint and several liability, 131.4.1
local jurisdiction, 131.4.1
major issues concerning, 131.4.1
nonrecourse debts, 131.4.1, 131.5
nonresident aliens, 134.2.4
postmortem events, 131.4.2
  date-of-death issue, 131.4.2
  divorce and remarriage, 131.4.2
  estoppel, waiver, and fraud doctrines, effect of, 131.4.2
  local statutes, 131.4.2
  statute of limitations, 131.4.2
  taxes, 131.6.2
"property subject to claims" limitation, 131.6.3
state law, 131.4.1, 131.4.2, 131.6.1
statutory provisions, 131.4.1
test for deductibility, 131.4.1
timing, 131.1
tort claims, 131.4.3
unpaid taxes, 131.6.2
widow's allowance, nondeductibility of, 131.4.1

Class gifts
annual per-donee exclusion, 124.3.2

Clifford trusts
principles of, 125.3

Closely held corporations
buy-sell agreements. *See*: Buy-sell agreements
estate freeze valuation of interests in, 136.2
  See also: Estate freezes—corporations and partnerships, valuation of interests in
estate tax on interests in, elective extension of time for payment of, 137.5
  See also: Estate tax payment—closely held business interests, elective extension of time for
gift tax liability, 121.1
valuation of stock, 135.2.2, 135.4.3
  book value, 135.4.3
  estate freezes, 136.2
  factors relevant to, 135.4.3
  goodwill factor, 135.4.3

Collection of tax
liens
  See also: Tax liens
  collection upon threat of, 137.6.1
  estate and gift taxes, 137.6
  generally, 137.6.1

Common disaster terminable interest exception, 129.4.2
marital deduction, effect on, 129.4.2
proof of survival of spouse, 129.4.2
purpose, 129.4.2
six-month survivorship terminable interest exception as alternative or concurrent condition, 129.4.2
time period unlimited, 129.4.2
unified credit, effect on, 129.4.2

Common law
community property law and, 120.2.2, 123.1, 123.5.1, 125.10, 129.1
funeral expenses, 131.2
gift, concept of, 121.4.1, 122.2
powers of appointment, 128.1
split-gift election, 123.5.1
terminable interest rule, 129.3.1

Community property
claims against estate, 131.4.5
  administration expenses, 131.4.5
  casualty losses, 131.4.5
  funeral expenses, 131.4.5
closely held business interests, eligibility for extension of payment of estate tax on, 137.5.2
common law and
  generally, 120.2.2, 125.10, 129.1
  geographical disparities, 123.1, 123.5.1, 125.10, 129.1
  gift tax issues, 123.1
funeral expenses, 131.4.5
gift tax
  children donees, 123.2.1, 123.2.2
  conversion into separate property, 123.1, 123.2.1
  earned income, 123.2.1, 123.2.3
  generally, 123.1, 123.2.1
  life insurance, 122.3.6
  marital property settlements, 123.6.1
  separate annual per-donee exclusions, 123.1
  split-gift election, 123.5.1
  spouse donees, 123.2.1, 123.2.3

[References are to paragraphs (¶).]

Community property *(cont'd)*
gift tax *(cont'd)*
third-party (nonspousal) donees,
123.2.1, 123.2.2
vested interest theory, 123.2.1
gross estate, 120.1.2, 120.2.2, 125.10
claims against estate, 131.4.5
funeral expenses, 131.2, 131.4.5
retained life estate, community income
from separate property, 126.6.2
life insurance
gift transfers, 122.3.6
gross estate, 127.5
marital deduction, 123.3.5, 125.10, 129.1,
129.3.1, 129.5.3
pre-1982 decedents, 129.7.1
nonresident aliens, 134.2.4
qualified retirement plans, 126.8.5

Compensation
uncompensated services
as gift property, 121.3.6
gross estate inclusion of postmortem
payment, 125.7

Compromise payments
charitable bequest deduction, 130.3.2

Conditional gifts to charity
gift tax deductions, 121.8.3

Conservation
deduction for qualified conservation
contribution, 130.5.5
preservation of land areas, deduction
for, 130.5.5
protection of natural habitats, deduction
for, 130.5.5

Constitutional issues
direct taxation, 120.1.2, 125.11.1
estate tax, 120.1.2, 129.1
allocation and apportionment, 120.1.2,
125.11.1, 129.1
Direct Tax Clause of Constitution,
120.1.2, 125.11.1
Due Process Clause and, 120.1.2
joint tenancies with right of
survivorship, 125.11.1
retroactivity, 120.1.2
generation-skipping transfer tax, 120.2.3
gift tax, 120.1.2
marital deduction, 129.1
transfer of property by decedent, 120.1.2
wealth, regulation of transfer of, 120.1.2
state law and, 120.1.2

Construction of buildings
"replacement or reproduction cost"
valuation method, 135.2.4

Constructive distributions
generation-skipping transfers, 133.2.7

Constructive receipt
property transferred by decedent during
life, 126.3.4
qualified retirement plans, 126.8.5

Contingent interests
gift property, 121.3.3
charitable contributions, 121.8.3
legal fees, gross estate inclusion, 125.7
retained life estate, 126.6.4

Contracts
claims against estate, 131.4.3
periodic payment obligations, gift
property, 121.3.2
valuation, 135.4.5
alternate date of, 135.7.3

Contributions. *See*: Charitable
contributions; Political activities and
contributions

Contributions to capital
estate freeze rules, as transfer under,
136.2.3

Controlled corporations
gift tax liability, 121.1
life insurance incidents of ownership
held by, 127.4.8
retained right to vote stock
amount of stock included, 126.6.5
control, defined, 126.6.5
direct vs. indirect voting, 126.6.5
generally, 126.3.3, 126.6.5
rationale, 126.6.5
release within three years of death,
126.6.5

Conversion rights
estate freeze valuation, 136.2.2, 136.2.4,
136.2.5

Cooperatives
housing corporations
charitable bequest of remainder in,
130.5.5

Copyrights
art work defined in terms of, 130.5.12
marital deduction, 129.3.2, 129.3.3
nonresident aliens, 134.2.3
valuation, 134.4.5

INDEX

[References are to paragraphs (¶).]

Corporate capital structure
estate freeze rules for changes in, 136.2.3

Corporations
See also: Closely held corporations; Controlled corporations; Family corporations; Securities; Stock
annual per-donee exclusion, 124.2
estate freeze valuation of interests in, 136.2, 136.3
See also: Estate freezes
gift tax liability, 120.2.1, 121.1
life insurance incidents of ownership held by, 127.4.8
passive assets, 137.5.2
special use election, 135.6.8
valuation of property. *See*: Estate freezes —corporations and partnerships, valuation of interests in; Securities —valuation; Stock—valuation; Valuation

Courts. *See*: Federal circuit courts; Litigation; Tax Court; Tax litigation

Covenants not to compete
valuation, 135.4.5

Credits. *See*: Personal credits

***Crummey* powers**
annual per-donee exclusion, harmony with, 124.3.3
demand trusts, 124.3.3
statutory trusts for minors, 124.4.3

Curtesy
See also: Dower
gross estate, 125.1, 125.9
release or promised release of, donative intent, 121.4.2
statutory interest in lieu of, 125.1
taxable estate, 125.9

Custodianships for minors
See also: Guardians
annual per-donee exclusion, 124.4.3
lifetime transfers subject to retained powers, 126.5.1
powers of appointment of parent over custodial property, 128.2.1
retained life estate, 126.6.2
state statutes, 124.4.3

Cy pres doctrine
contingent charitable bequests, 130.4

D

Date-of-death basis
claims against estate, deductions for, 131.4.2
generally, 120.3
marital deduction, 129.2.2, 129.5.1
spousal joint tenancies, 125.11.3
surviving spouse's property share, 129.2.2, 129.5.1

Deathbed transfers, 126.1, 126.2
See also: Gifts made within three years of death

Death benefits
employee, gross estate, 125.6
gift tax property, 121.2, 121.3.3, 122.3.5
gross estate, 125.6
vested interests vs. expectancies, gross estate, 125.6

Death taxes. *See*: Estate tax; State death taxes

Debt
See also: Debt discharges
gross estate, deduction for mortgage secured by includable property, 131.1, 131.5
nonresident aliens, taxation of, 134.2.3

Debt discharges
gifts as, 121.1
annual per-donee exclusion, effect of partial annual discharge, 121.1
donative intent, 121.4.3
transfer requirement, 121.2
intrafamily transactions, 121.1
support obligations, marital, 121.4.3
testamentary cancellation, gross estate, 125.5

Debt instruments
valuation
instruments not traded in securities market, 135.4.6
instruments traded in securities market, 135.4.2

Decedents. *See*: Deductions in respect of decedents; Estates, decedents'; Estate tax; Property owned by decedent at death, gross estate inclusion; Property transferred by decedent during life, gross estate inclusion; Income in respect of decedents (IRD); Wealth, transfer of

Deductions. *See*: Charitable bequest deduction; Deductions in respect of decedents; Marital deduction; Personal deductions

Deductions in respect of decedents, 120.3

Defeasible interests
gift property, 121.3.3

Defective transfers. *See*: Transfers, gift—defective

Deficiencies in taxes
estate tax
closely held business interests, 137.5.3
flower bonds used in payment of, 137.4.2
tax liens, 137.6.2

Delivery
gift transfers, defective, 122.2

Demand loans, 121.3.4

Demand trusts
annual per-donee exclusion, 124.3.3
Crummey powers, 124.3.3
minors and guardians, 124.3.3
noncash assets, 124.3.3
outright gifts compared, 124.3.3
powers of appointment, 124.3.3

Devises. *See*: Bequests

Direct skips in generation-skipping transfers, 120.2.3
See also: Generation-skipping transfers
defined, 120.2.3, 133.1, 133.2.5
generally, 120.2.3, 133.1
incomplete gifts, 133.2.5
nonresident aliens, 134.2.6
orphans' exception, 133.2.5
returns, 133.6.2
taxable amount, 133.3.2
taxable terminations contrasted, 133.2.6
types, 133.2.5

Disabled
See also: Incompetents
special use valuation for farms and real property, alternative requirements for disabled decedents, 135.6.5

Discharge of indebtedness. *See*: Debt discharges

Disclaimers and renunciations of property interests
charitable bequests, 130.3.3
estate freeze rules, 136.2.3

estate tax rules, effect on application of, 121.7.1
fiduciary power, exercise as nonacceptance, 121.7.5
generally, 121.7.1
generation-skipping transfer tax rules, effect on application of, 121.7.1, 133.2.10
gift tax rules, effect on application of, 121.7.1
gross estate, 125.12, 126.3.2
irrevocability, 121.7.1, 121.7.2
marital deduction, effect of qualified disclaimer on, 129.2.3
merged interests, 121.7.5
nonacceptance of benefits, 121.7.1, 121.7.5
surviving spouse exception, 121.7.6
no-transfer rationale, 121.7.1
partial disclaimer, 121.7.5
passage of interest without action by disclaimant, 121.7.1, 121.7.6
powers of appointment
estate tax, 128.3.5
gift tax, 121.7.5
preemption, 121.7.7
pre-1976 rules, 121.7.1
qualified disclaimer, defined, 121.7.1, 121.7.2, 125.12, 126.3.2
receipt of title as nonacceptance, 121.7.5
severable interests, 121.7.5
state law, 121.7.1, 121.7.5–121.7.7, 129.2.2
surviving spouse exception
generally, 129.2.3
nonacceptance of benefits, 121.7.6
writing requirement, 121.7.3
time limit, 121.7.1, 121.7.4
installment transfers, 121.7.4
second disclaimer, 121.7.4
transfers treated as, disqualified, 121.7.6
undivided portion of interest, 121.7.5
uniform federal standard, goal of, 121.7.1
writing requirement, 121.7.1, 121.7.3
surviving spouse or child exception, 121.7.3

Discount coupons
valuation of property affected by discounts, 135.3

INDEX

[References are to paragraphs (¶).]

See also: Valuation—discounts and premiums

Distributions, corporate
valuation date, 135.7.2

Distributions, trusts and estates
demand trusts, 124.3.3
estate freezes
distribution right, defined, 136.2.2, 136.2.4
extraordinary payment right, defined, 136.2.2
junior equity interest, defined, 136.2.2
generation-skipping transfers, 120.2.3, 133.1, 133.2.7
See also: Taxable distributions, generation-skipping transfers
valuation date, 135.7.2, 135.7.3

Dividends
valuation date, 135.7.2

Divorce
See also: Alimony; Marital property settlements; Marital separation; Support obligations, marital
claims against estate, 131.4.2, 131.4.3
gift transfers
adequate or full consideration, 123.6.1, 123.6.2
contemplation of divorce, effect of, 123.6.1, 123.6.2
exemption from gift tax, conditions for, 123.6.1, 123.6.2
generally, 123.6.1
marital property settlements, 123.6.1, 123.6.2
life insurance beneficiaries, 127.4.7
lifetime transfers by decedent, 126.3.4
marital deduction, 123.6.3, 129.2.2
split-gift elections, 123.5.3

Domicile treaties, 134.2.7

Donative intent, gift tax
arm's length transactions distinguished, 121.4.5
business purpose distinguished, 121.4.4, 121.4.5
charitable contributions, 121.4.1
common law concept of gift, 121.4.1, 122.2
curtesy, release or promised release of, 121.4.2
defective transfers, 122.2

dower, release or promised release of, 121.4.2
family transactions, 121.4.5
gambling, inapplicability to, 121.4.5
generally, 121.4.1
interspousal transfers, 121.4.2
intrafamily transfers, 121.4.5
legal obligations, payments to discharge, 121.4.4
local law, 121.4.3
marital property settlements, 123.6.1
nonmonetary consideration, transfers for, 121.4.2
ordinary course of business, transfers made in, 121.4.5
promise of marriage, 121.4.2
support obligations, payments to discharge, 121.4.3
tort claims, 121.4.4

Donors, gift tax
agents or intermediaries, 121.1
charitable organizations, 121.1
controlled entities, gifts involving, 121.1
corporations, 120.2.1, 121.1
creditor-donor, 121.1
discharge of donee's debts, 121.1
grantor trusts, 121.1
incompetents, 122.2
indirect gifts, 121.1
individuals, 121.1
ostensible intermediate recipients, gifts involving, 121.1
partnerships, 121.1
related entities, gifts involving, 121.1
shareholders, 121.1

Double taxation
avoidance of, estate freeze rules, 136.2.12, 136.4.4
estate freeze rules for adjustments to mitigate
corporations and partnerships, interests in, 136.2.12
trust, transfers in, 136.4.4
foreign held U.S. property, 132.7.1, 132.7.4
lifetime transfers, 126.3.6
powers of appointment, life estate with, 128.2.4
QTIP transfers, 129.4.5
tax treaties, prevention through, 132.7.4

Dower
See also: Curtesy
claims against decedent's estate, 125.9
gross estate, 125.1, 125.9, 129.2.3
marital deduction, 125.9, 129.2.3, 129.3.3
no consideration rule, 125.9, 126.3.4
release of
  donative intent, 121.4.2
  inter vivos transfers in exchange for, 125.9
  promised, 121.4.2
retained rights, property transfers subject to, 125.9
statutory interest in lieu of, 125.1
taxable estate, 125.9

E

Earned income
community property, transfers of, 123.2.1, 123.2.3

Easements
conservation contribution, deduction for, 130.5.5

Educational expenses
generation-skipping transfer exemption, 133.2.13
gift tax exemption, 121.5
  direct payments, 121.5
  generally, 132.1
  income tax exclusion, relation to, 121.5
  part-time students, 121.5
  qualifying educational organizations, 121.5
  tuition payments, 121.5

Educational organizations
charitable bequests, qualified beneficiaries of, 130.2
nonresident aliens, contributions by, 134.2.4
contributions to, gift tax deductions for, 121.8
gift tax exemption, definition of organization for purposes of, 121.5
qualified retirement plans, 126.8.5

Employee benefits
See also: Death benefits; Survivorship annuities—employee benefit plans
gross estate, transfer of property included in, 126.3.2

powers of appointment, effect on benefit plans, 128.5.2

Employee Stock Ownership Plans (ESOPs)
estate tax liability, assumption of, 135.7.3

Employment contracts
claims against estate, 131.4.3
valuation, 135.4.5

Encumbered property. *See*: Property—encumbered

Endowment policies
power of appointment in surviving spouse, proceeds subject to, 129.4.4
survivorship annuities, 126.8.2

Estate freezes
arm's length standard, 136.1
art works, 136.1
buy-sell agreements, 135.3.10, 136.3.3
control, 136.2.2, 136.3.4
corporations and partnerships, valuation of interests in, 136.2
amount of transfer tax inclusion, 136.2.9
applicable family member, defined, 136.2.2
applicable retained interests, 136.2.2, 136.2.4, 136.2.5, 136.2.8, 136.2.10
call rights, 136.1, 136.2.2, 136.2.4, 136.2.5
capital call rights, 136.1
capital structure, changes in, 136.2.3
ceiling on transfer tax inclusion, 136.2.9
contribution to capital as transfer, 136.2.3
control, defined, 136.2.2, 136.3.4
conversion rights, 136.2.2, 136.2.4, 136.2.5
definitions, 136.2.2
delinquent payment, election to treat receipt as taxable event, 136.2.9
disclaimers, 136.2.3
distribution rights, 136.2.2, 136.2.4, 136.2.7
election to treat nonqualified distribution right as qualified payment, 136.2.7
election to treat qualified payment as nonqualified payment, 136.2.6
election to treat receipt of delinquent payment as taxable event, 136.2.9

INDEX

[References are to paragraphs (¶).]

extraordinary payment rights, 136.2.2, 136.2.4, 136.2.5

family interest percentage in junior equity, 136.2.8

family member, defined, 136.2.2, 136.3.4

generally, 136.2.1

indirect holdings and transfers, 136.2.10

junior equity interests, 136.2.1, 136.2.2, 136.2.8

liquidation rights, 136.2.2, 136.2.4, 136.2.5, 136.3.1–136.3.3

lookback rule, 136.2.7, 136.2.9

member of family, defined, 136.2.2, 136.3.4

minimum valuation rule, 136.2.8

nongeneral power of appointment, exercise of, 136.2.3

nonqualified distribution right, election to treat qualified payment as, 136.2.7

nonqualified payment, election to treat qualified payment as, 136.2.6

proportional transfers, 136.2.3

put rights, 136.1, 136.2.2, 136.2.4, 136.2.5

qualified payments, 136.2.1, 136.2.4–136.2.7

quoted securities, 136.2.3

recapitalization as transfer, 136.2.3

redemption as transfer, 136.2.3

same class transferred and retained interests, 136.2.3

Section 2701, transfers subject to, 136.2.3

senior interests, 136.2.1

split interests, 136.2.3

statute of limitations, 136.2.11

subtraction method, 136.2.8

taxable event, significance of, 136.2.9

valuation of qualified payments, 136.2.5

voting rights, 136.1, 136.2.2, 136.3.1, 136.3.2

zero value for applicable retained interests, 136.2.4

defined, 136.1

family member, defined, 136.2.2, 136.3.4

generally, 136.1

gift tax, applicability to, 136.2.1

history, 136.1

lapsing rights and restrictions, 136.3

control, defined, 136.3.4

disregarded restrictions, 136.3.3

generally, 136.3.1

liquidation right, 136.3.1–136.3.3

members of family, defined, 136.3.4

prelapse value, 136.3.2

taxable transfer, lapse of rights treated as, 136.3.2

valuation of constructive transfer, 136.3.2

voting right, 136.3.1, 136.3.2

method, 136.1

nominal transfer of interests, possibility of use for, 136.1

options, 135.3.10, 136.3.3

preferred stock freeze, 136.1

real property, 136.1

restrictions, disregarded, 136.3.3

statutes of limitations

corporations and partnerships, interests in, 136.2.11

trust, transfers in, 136.4.8

statutory provisions, 136.1

stock, 136.1–136.3

transfer tax concerns, 136.1

trust, transfers in, 136.4

annuity interests, 136.4.3

charitable beneficiaries, 136.4.7

concurrent acquisition of term interest and remainder, 136.4.2

double taxation, adjustments to mitigate, 136.4.4

generally, 136.4.1

gift of retained interest, 136.4.4

grantor retained income trust (GRIT), 136.4.1

gross estate inclusion or retained interest, 136.4.4

incomplete transfers, 136.4.5

nonproductive tangible property, 136.4.3

personal residence trusts, 136.4.6

pooled income funds, 136.4.7

qualified interests, 136.4.3

qualified personal residence trust (QPRT), 136.4.6

remainder interests, 136.4.2, 136.4.3

retained interests, 136.4.3, 136.4.4

Section 2702(a), interests subject to, 136.4.2

statute of limitations, 136.4.8

Estate freezes *(cont'd)*
  trust, transfers in *(cont'd)*
    term interests, 136.4.2
    unitrust interests, 136.4.3
    valuation of retained interests, 136.4.3
  undervaluation with, 136.1

Estate planning
  See also: Estate freezes; Estate tax;
    Generation-skipping transfer (GST)
    tax; Generation-skipping transfers;
    Gift tax; Property owned by
    decedent at death, gross estate
    inclusion; Property transferred by
    decedent during life, gross estate
    inclusion; Transfers, gift; Wealth,
    transfer of
  annual per-donee exclusion, limitation
    on use of, 124.1, 124.3.1
  lifetime transfers, 126.1
  marital deduction, 129.6.1

Estates, decedents'. *See*: Estate freezes;
  Estate planning; Estate tax; Gross
  estate; Wealth, transfer of

Estate tax
  See also: Estate freezes; Estate tax
    computation; Estate tax payment;
    Estate tax returns; Tax liens—estate
    tax
  administration expenses deduction. *See*:
    Administration expenses deduction,
    estates
  allocation and apportionment
    appointive assets, payment from,
      128.5.3
    apportionment statutes, 137.8
    charitable bequests, 130.6, 137.8
    common law rule, 137.8
    constitutional issues, 120.1.2, 125.11.1,
      129.1
    decedent's intent, 129.5.2, 137.8
    effect on tax, 137.8
    equitable apportionment, 137.8
    generally, 137.8
    marital deduction and, 137.8
    QTIP transfers, 137.8
    state law, 120.1.2, 125.9.2, 137.8
    will provisions, 137.8
  basis of property subject to, 120.3
  buy-sell agreements, effect of, 135.3.10
  charitable deduction. *See*: Charitable
    bequest deduction

claims against estate, deductibility. *See*:
  Claims against estate, deductions for
constitutionality of, 120.1.2
contemplation-of-death provision and,
  126.4.1
date-of-death basis of property subject
  to, 120.3
deferred payment, 126.4.2
disclaimer of property interest, effect of,
  121.7.1
double deductions, disallowance of, 120.3
expatriation, tax-motivated, 134.1, 134.4
funeral expenses deduction, 131.2
generally, 120.1.1, 120.1.2, 120.2.2, 126.1,
  132.1
generation-skipping transfer (GST) tax,
  similarity of, 133.1, 133.6.5
generation-skipping transfers,
  inapplicability to, 120.1.1
gifts causa mortis, 122.2
gift tax and
  appreciation between gift and death
    dates, 120.2.2, 126.4.1, 126.4.2
  differences, 133.1
  procedural rules, 137.1
  qualified retirement plans, 126.8.5
  unified system, 120.1.1, 122.4.1,
    126.3.6, 126.4.1, 132.1
gross estate. *See*: Gross estate
history, 120.1.1, 126.2
holding period of property subject to,
  120.3
income tax, relationship to, 120.3
  decedent's property, valuation of,
    125.7
  procedural rules in common with,
    137.1
life insurance. *See*: Life insurance, gross
  estate inclusion
life insurance beneficiary's liability,
  127.4.9
lifetime transfers, 126.1–126.8
  See also Lifetime transfers
marital deduction. *See*: Marital
  deduction
nonresident aliens, 134.1, 134.2.1,
  134.2.3–134.2.5
  See also: Nonresident aliens—estate
    tax computation; Nonresident
    aliens—estate tax deductions;
    Nonresident aliens—gross estate
options and, 135.3.10

INDEX

personal liability for, 137.7
  amount of liability, 137.7.3
  application by executor for amount
    due, 137.7.4
  assumptions by ESOPs, 137.7.3
  discharge from liability, 137.7.4
  executor's liability, 137.7.3
  faulty gift tax return, effect of, 137.7.4
  generally, 137.7.1, 137.7.3
  IRS notice or failure to notify of
    amount due, 137.7.4
  nonprobate property, 137.7.3
  parties subject to, 137.7.1, 137.7.3
  priority of U.S. claims, 137.7.3
  probate property, 137.7.3
  state law, effect of, 137.7.3
  transferee liability, 137.7.3
  unpaid taxes, 137.7.1, 137.7.3
powers of appointment, 128.1
See also: Powers of appointment
procedural rules
  apportionment of tax burden, 137.8
  generally, 137.1, 137.9
  miscellaneous rules, 137.9
  payment of taxes, 137.4.2–137.4.4,
    137.5
  personal liability for tax, 137.7.1,
    137.7.3, 137.7.4
  tax liens, 137.6.1, 137.6.2
  tax returns, 137.3
property. *See*: Property owned by
  decedent at death, gross estate
  inclusion; Property transferred by
  decedent during life, gross estate
  inclusion
property-transfer rationale, applicability
  of, 122.3.5
purpose of, 133.1
qualified domestic trust (QDI),
  additional tax on, 129.2.5
quasi-testamentary lifetime transfers,
  126.1
rates, 120.1.1, 120.2.2
  cumulative, 120.2.2
  single rate schedule, 120.2.2
specially treated taxpayers, 134.1
split-gift election, effect of, 123.5.1
stock redemptions to pay, 126.4.2
taxable estate. *See*: Gross estate; Taxable
  estate
unified credit, 120.1.1

U.S. possessions, U.S. citizens resident
  in, 134.1, 134.3
valuation of property, 135.1–135.7
See also: Valuation
  accuracy-related penalty for errors,
    137.9
  special use valuation for farms and
    business real property. *See*: Real
    property valuation—special use
    election

Estate tax computation, 132.3
See also: Unified wealth transfer tax
  system
credit for federal estate tax on prior
  transfers, 132.6
  definitions, 132.6.2
  first limitation, 132.6.4
  generally, 132.6.1
  limitations on credit, 132.6.4
  marital deduction, 132.6.3
  multiple transfers, 132.6.4
  purpose, 132.6.1
  second limitation, 132.6.4
  simultaneous deaths, 132.6.3
  "transfer" of "property," 132.6.2
  valuation of transferred property,
    132.6.3
credit for foreign death taxes, 132.7
  double taxation, possibility of, 132.7.1,
    132.7.4
  first limitation (foreign death tax),
    132.7.3
  foreign country defined for purposes
    of, 132.7.1
  generally, 132.7.1
  limitations on credit, 132.7.3
  second limitation (U.S. estate tax),
    132.7.3
  situs rules, 132.7.2
  third limitation (charitable bequests),
    132.7.3
  treaty provisions, 132.7.4
credit for pre-1977 gift taxes, 132.5
  first limitation, 132.5
  gift includabie in gross estate, 132.5
  payment of gift tax, 132.5
  second limitation, 132.5
  two or more qualifying gifts, 132.5
credit for state death taxes, 132.4
  "actual payment" requirement, 132.4
  basic estate tax, defined, 132.4

[References are to paragraphs (¶).]

Estate tax computation *(cont'd)*
  credit for state death taxes *(cont'd)*
    creditable taxes, 132.4
    generally, 132.1
    persons other than decedent, 132.4
    purpose and history, 132.4
    refunds, 132.4
    state jurisdiction to impose tax, 132.4
    timing considerations, 132.4
    waiver of credit, 132.4
  nonresident aliens, 134.2.5
  no taxable gifts in decedent's lifetime, 132.3
  post-1976 gifts included in gross estate, 132.3
  post-1976 taxable gifts not included in gross estate, 132.3
  pre-1977 taxable gifts, 132.3
  unified credit, 132.3
  unified wealth-transfer tax system, 132.1

Estate tax liens. *See*: Tax liens—estate tax

Estate tax payment
  cash payment, 137.4.2
  check or money order, payment with, 137.4.2
  closely held business interests, elective extension of time for, 137.5
    acceleration of payment, 137.5.1, 137.5.4
    additional deferral at discretion of IRS, 137.5.3
    advance liquidation of unpaid tax, 137.5.4
    aggregation of interests, 137.5.2
    belated elections, 137.5.2
    bond to secure payment, 137.5.3
    conduct of business requirement, 137.5.2
    deferral period, 137.5.1
    deficiencies and overpayments, 137.5.3
    disposition-withdrawal rule, 137.5.4
    due date of installments, 137.5.3
    effect of election, 137.5.3
    eligibility, 137.5.1, 137.5.2
    failure to pay on time, 137.5.4
    farm property, 137.5.1
    features of election, 137.5.1
    forms of interests eligible, 137.5.2
    4 percent interest rate, 137.5.3
    generally, 137.5.1
    initial interest-only period, 137.5.3
    installment payments, 137.5.1, 137.5.3
    interest on, 137.5.1
    interest on deferred tax, 137.5.3
    numerical test, 137.5.2
    overpayments of deficiency installments, 137.5.3
    passive assets, effect of, 137.5.2
    property transferred within three years of death, 137.5.2
    protective elections, 137.5.2
    real property, business, 137.5.1
    tax eligible for deferral, 137.5.3
    tax liens to secure, 137.5.3
    termination of deferral, 137.5.1, 137.5.4
    35 percent test, 137.5.2
    20 percent requirement, 137.5.2
    undistributed estate income, 137.5.4
  discretionary extension of time, 137.4.3
    application for, 137.4.3
    examples of reasonable cause, 137.4.3
    interest on deferred tax, 137.4.3
    reasonable cause substitute for undue hardship, 137.4.3
    10 year limit, 137.4.3
    12 month extension, 137.4.3
  extensions of time
    closely held business interests, elective extension for, 137.5
    discretionary, 137.4.3
    generally, 137.4.2
    reversionary and remainder interests, 137.4.4
  flower bonds, payment with, 137.4.2
  generally, 137.4.2
  method of payment, 137.4.2
  reversionary and remainder interests, extensions of time for, 137.4.4
    gross estate inclusion requirement, 137.4.4
    interest on deferred tax, 137.4.4
    reasonable cause, 137.4.4
  time for filing, 137.4.2
    extensions, 137.4.2–137.4.4, 137.5

Estate tax returns
  accuracy-related penalty for errors, 137.9
  audit procedures, 137.3, 137.9
  date-of-death value, significance of, 137.3
  election against will, filing prior to, 129.3.3

INDEX

executor, filing by, 137.3
filing requirement
  alternate valuation date election,
    135.7.6
  generally, 137.3, 137.9
  special use election, 135.6.6
  valuation date, 137.3
generally, 137.3
nonresident aliens, 137.3
parties required to file, 137.3
qualified domestic trust election, 129.2.5
statute of limitations, 137.9
surviving spouse election against will,
  129.3.3
time for filing, 137.3
  extensions, 137.3

Estate trusts, 129.4.1, 129.4.7

Estoppel
claims against estate, 131.4.2

Expatriation, tax-motivated
burden of proof against, 134.4
death within 10 years, 134.4
generally, 134.1, 134.4
intangible property, 134.4
situs of property in U.S., 134.4
unified credit, 134.4

Expert witnesses
valuation issues, 135.5.1

F

Fair market value
See also: Valuation—governing standard
annuities, 135.4.10
arm's length standard, 135.1.2, 135.2.1
basis computations, property acquired
  from decedent, 135.6.10
bonds traded on stock exchange, 135.4.2
cash sale value, 135.1.2
defined, 135.1.2
"fair value" vs., 135.1.2
forced sales, 135.1.2
freedom from compulsion, 135.1.2
generally, 135.1.2
hindsight, 135.1.2
historical cost, 135.2.1
hypothetical parties, 135.1.2
knowledge of facts, 135.1.2
lack of marketability discount, 135.1.2
life estates, 135.4.10
nature of market and, 135.1.2

real property, 135.4.1
relevant facts, consideration of, 135.1.2
remainder interests, 135.4.10
reversionary interests, 135.4.10
securities traded on stock exchange,
  135.4.2
selling expenses, significance of, 135.1.2
special use valuation for farms and
  business real property, 135.6.1
split interests in property, 135.4.10
taxes, effect of, 135.3.8
"willing buyer, willing seller" standard,
  135.1.2
willing parties, assumption of, 135.1.2

Family
See also: Family corporations; Family
  partnerships; Intrafamily
  transactions; Related taxpayers
estate freezes, family members defined
  for purposes of, 136.2.2, 136.3.4

Family corporations
estate freeze valuation of interests in,
  136.2, 136.3
  See also: Estate freezes
farms, valuation of. *See*: Real property
  valuation—special use election
life insurance incidents of ownership
  held by, 127.4.8
stock, gross estate inclusion upon
  decedent's death, 125.7

Family partnerships
estate freeze valuation of interests in,
  136.2, 136.3
  See also: Estate freezes
gift tax, donative intent and, 121.4.5
gross estate inclusion, partnership
  interests, 125.8
life insurance incidents of ownership
  held by, 127.4.8

Farmers and ranchers
charitable bequest of remainder in farm,
  130.5.5
farming purposes, defined, 135.6.2
farms, defined, 135.6.2
special use valuation election
  See also: Real property valuation—
    special use election
  capitalization of cash rentals for
    comparable land, 135.6.7
  definitions of farm and farming
    purposes, 135.6.2

[References are to paragraphs (¶).]

Farmers and ranchers *(cont'd)*
special use valuation election *(cont'd)*
fifty percent test, 135.6.4
generally, 135.6.1
ownership, qualified use, and material
participation for five of eight
years, 135.6.5
qualified use text, 135.6.2
woodlands as farm, 135.6.2
valuation of farms. *See*: Farmers and
ranchers—special use valuation
election; Real property valuation—
special use election

Federal circuit courts
valuation issues, role in, 135.5.2

Fiduciaries
annual per-donee exclusion, fiduciary
administrative powers and, 124.3.2
estate tax return, filing of, 137.3
gift tax payment, 137.4.1
gift tax return, filing of, 137.2
life insurance, incidents of ownership
held in fiduciary capacity, 127.4.6
lifetime transfers subject to retained
powers, 126.5.1, 126.5.2
personal liability for gift and estate
taxes, 137.7
See also: Personal liability—estate tax;
Personal liability—gift tax

Films
valuation, 135.4.8

Fines and penalties
estate tax returns, accuracy-related
penalty for valuation errors, 137.9
gift tax returns, accuracy-related penalty
for valuation errors, 137.9
overvaluation of property, 135.5.3

Flower bonds
defined, 137.4.2
payment of estate tax with, 137.4.2
state law on time of purchase, 137.4.2
valuation, 135.4.6

Foreclosure
as forced sale, 135.1.2
valuation of property, 135.1.2

Foreign corporations
securities issued by, 134.2.3

Foreign death taxes
charitable bequests, 132.7.3
charitable transfers, 131.7

credit for, 132.7
double taxation, possibility of, 132.7.1,
132.7.4
first limitation (foreign death tax),
132.7.3
foreign country defined for purposes
of, 132.7.1
generally, 132.7.1
limitations on credit, 132.7.3
second limitation (U.S. estate tax),
132.7.3
situs rules, 132.7.2
third limitation (charitable bequests),
132.7.3
treaty provisions, 132.7.4
generally, 132.1, 132.7
tax treaties, effect of, 132.7.1, 132.7.4

Foreign governments
charitable bequests, qualified
beneficiaries of, 130.2
double taxation, prevention through tax
treaties, 132.7.1, 132.7.4

Foreign law
death taxes
See also: Foreign death taxes
charitable transfers, 131.7
estate tax credit, 132.1, 132.7
estate tax deductions
charitable bequests, 130.2
death taxes, 131.6.2, 131.7

Former citizens and residents of U.S.
tax-motivated expatriates, 134.1, 134.4

Fourteenth Amendment
citizenship determined under, 134.2.1

Franchises
nonresident aliens, 134.2.3
valuation, 135.4.5

Fraternal societies
charitable bequests, qualified
beneficiaries of, 130.2
nonresident aliens, contributions by,
134.2.4
contributions for charitable purposes,
gift tax deductions for, 121.8

Fraud
claims against estate, 131.4.2

Funeral expenses deduction
aggregate limit, 131.2
allowable under local law, 131.2
common law, 131.2

INDEX

community property, 131.2, 131.4.5
definition of funeral expenses, 131.2
generally, 131.1
nonresident aliens, 134.2.4
payment requirement, 131.2
"property subject to claims" limitation, 131.6.3
reasonable expenditures, 131.2
reimbursement, effect of, 131.2
scope of expenses covered, 131.2
Social Security Administration payments, reducing effect of, 131.2
state law, 131.2, 131.4.5, 131.6.1
Veterans Administration payments, reducing effect of, 131.2

Fungible assets, 135.2.3

Future income
gift property, 121.3.5

Future interests
See also: Remainder interests
annual per-donee exclusion, 124.1, 124.3
See also: Annual per-donee exclusion
—future interests exception
gift property, 121.3.3
gross estate, 125.4

G

Gambling
business purpose vs. donative intent, 121.4.5

Generation-skipping transfers
See also: Generation-skipping transfer (GST) tax; Generation-skipping trusts
bequests compared, 133.1
charitable interests, 133.2.8
direct skips, taxable, 120.2.3, 133.1, 133.2.5
defined, 133.2.5
incomplete gifts, 133.2.5
orphans' exception, 133.2.5, 133.2.6
returns, 133.6.2
taxable amount, 133.3.2
taxable terminations contrasted, 133.2.6
types, 133.2.5
disclaimers, effect of, 121.7.1, 133.2.10
educational (tuition) expense payment exemption, 132.2.13
estate tax, inapplicability of, 120.1.1
forms of, 120.2.3, 133.1, 133.2.1
generally, 120.1.1, 120.2.3, 133.2.1
generation assignments, 133.2.3
earlier transfer to same generation, 133.2.9
entities (tax-exempt, charitable or governmental), 133.2.3
lineal descendants of grandparent of transferor's spouse or former spouse, 133.2.3
lineal descendants of transferor's grandparent, 133.2.3
marital relationships, 133.2.3
nonrelated individuals by blood or marriage, 133.2.3
overlapping relationships, 133.2.3
reassignments, 133.2.9
gift tax, inapplicability of, 120.1.1
GST tax. *See*: Generation-skipping transfer (GST) tax
income tax basis, adjustments to, 133.4
addition to basis, 133.4
fair market value basis, effect of taxable termination at death on, 133.4
medical expense payment exemption, 132.2.13
multiple grantors and separate shares, 132.2.11
multiple skips, 133.2.9
earlier transfer to same generation, 133.2.9
reassignment of generations following transfer, 133.2.9
non-skip persons, classification of, 133.2.3
outright gifts compared, 133.1
permissible current recipients of income or principal, 133.2.8
pooled income fund, 133.2.8
property held in trust, interest in, 133.2.8
QTIP election, 133.2.2
rights other than future rights, 133.2.8
separate shares due to multiple grantors, 132.2.11
skip person, 133.2.1, 133.2.4
taxable distributions, 120.2.3, 133.1, 133.2.7
constructive distributions, 133.2.7
defined, 133.2.7
returns, 133.6.2
taxable amount, 133.3.2

[References are to paragraphs (¶).]

Generation-skipping transfers *(cont'd)*
taxable terminations, 120.2.3, 133.1, 133.2.6
  defined, 133.2.6
  direct skips contrasted, 133.2.6
  income tax basis, effect on, 133.4
  recomputation of inclusion ratio after, 133.3.4
  taxable amount, 133.3.2
  taxable distributions, 133.6.2
transferor
  defined, 133.2.2
  generally, 133.2.1, 133.2.2
tuition expense payment exemption, 132.2.13
types, 120.2.3, 133.1, 133.2.1

Generation-skipping transfer (GST) tax
See also: Generation-skipping transfers; Generation-skipping trusts
allocation of GST exemption, 133.3.3
  death of transferor, at and after, 133.3.3
  late allocations, 133.3.4
  lifetime transfers subject to retained rights triggering estate tax inclusion, 133.3.3
  procedures for, 133.3.3
  QTIP transfers, special rule for, 133.3.3
  subsequent transfers, effect on, 133.3.3
  transferor's lifetime, during, 133.3.3
amount taxable, 133.3.2
applicable rate, 133.1, 133.3.4
  charitable beneficiaries, special rules for trusts with, 133.3.4
  death taxes, reduction for, 133.3.4
  defined, 133.3.4
  existing trusts, transfers to, 133.3.4
  generally, 133.3.1
  inclusion ratio, 133.3.4
  late allocations of GST exemption, 133.3.4
  recomputation of inclusion ratio after taxable termination, 133.3.4
  valuations of property, 133.3.4
  zero ratio for certain lifetime gifts, 133.3.4
avoidance of, interest intended for use in, 133.2.8
computation of, 133.3
  allocation of GST exemption, 133.3.3

applicable rate, 133.3.4
credit for state GST taxes, 133.3.5
generally, 133.3.1
taxable amount, 133.3.2
constitutionality, 120.2.3
credits
  state GST taxes, 133.3.5
  unified, 120.2.3
delay of, interest intended for use in, 133.2.8
disclaimers, effect of, 121.7.1, 133.2.10
effective dates, 133.5
  direct skips to grandchildren, pre-1990, 133.5
  gifts from September 26, 1985 through October 22, 1986, 133.5
  incompetent individuals, 133.5
  irrevocable trusts, on September 25, 1985, 133.5
  post–October 22, 1986 transfers, 133.5
  pre-1987 death of decedent, 133.5
estate tax, similarity to, 133.1, 133.6.5
  procedural rules in common with, 137.1
exemptions, 133.1, 133.3.3
expatriation, tax-motivated, 134.1, 134.4
generally, 120.1.1, 120.2.3, 133.1
gift tax, similarity to, 133.1, 133.6.5
  procedural rules in common with, 137.1
history, 120.1.1, 120.2.3, 133.1
  1986 rules, 120.2.3, 133.1
  1976 rules, 120.2.3, 133.1
installment payments of, 133.6.3
liability for, 133.6.1
nonresident aliens, 134.1, 134.2.1, 134.2.6
options and, 135.3.10
procedural rules, 133.6
  See also: Estate tax—procedural rules; Gift tax—procedural rules
  estate tax rules, applicability of, 133.6.5
  generally, 137.1
  gift tax rules, applicability of, 133.6.5
  installment payments of tax, 133.6.3
  liability for tax, 133.6.1
  returns, 133.6.2
  stock redemptions to pay tax, 133.6.4
purpose of, 133.1
rate of tax, 133.1, 133.3.4
  generally, 133.3.1
returns, 133.3.3, 133.3.4, 133.6.2

INDEX

specially treated taxpayers, 134.1
state GST taxes, credit for, 133.3.5
stock redemptions to pay, 133.6.4
taxable amount, 133.3.2
   consideration paid by transferee,
      133.3.2
   direct skips, 133.3.2
   generally, 133.3.1
   taxable distributions, 133.3.2
   taxable terminations, 133.3.2
   tax-exclusive vs. tax-inclusive basis,
      133.3.2
   transfers subject to, 120.2.3, 133.1,
      133.2.5–133.2.7
U.S. possessions, U.S. citizens resident
   in, 134.1, 134.3

**Generation-skipping transfer (GST) tax
   returns**, 133.3.3, 133.3.4, 133.6.2

Generation-skipping trusts
See also: Generation-skipping transfers;
   Generation-skipping transfer (GST)
   tax
arrangements with effect of, 120.2.3,
   133.2.12
charitable beneficiaries, special rules for
   trusts with, 133.3.4
direct skips, 133.2.5
existing trusts, transfers to, 133.3.4
generally, 120.2.3
interests in property held in trust,
   133.2.8
irrevocable on September 25, 1985, 133.5
life insurance policy as equivalent,
   133.2.12
multiple grantors, effect of, 133.2.11
separate shares as separate trusts,
   133.2.11
as skip persons, 132.2.4
transfers to existing trusts,
   recomputation of applicable rate
   upon, 133.3.4
trustee identity, 133.2.12
trust equivalents, 120.2.3, 133.2.12

Gifts
See also: Donative intent; Gift tax;
   Property, gift; Split-gift election;
   Transfers, gift
basis of property acquired, 120.3
causa mortis. *See*: Gifts causa mortis
charitable contributions, 121.8

See also: Charitable contributions—gift
   tax deductions
community property, 123.2
   See also: Community property—gift
   tax
completed, claims against estate and,
   131.4.3
defined, 120.2.1, 121.4.1
discharge-of-debt principle, 121.1
exclusion from gross income, 120.3
holding period, 120.3
as income, 120.3
indirect gifts, 121.1
marital deduction, 129.2.3
marital deduction. *See*: Marital
   deduction
to minors, 124.4
   demand trusts, 124.3.3
   outright gifts, 124.4.1
   state custodianship statutes, 124.4.3
   statutory trusts, 124.4.2
nonproperty benefits not qualified as,
   137.2
property. *See*: Property, gift
services vs. property, 121.3.6
transfer requirement, 121.2
trusts, making gifts through, 121.1

Gifts causa mortis
See also: Gifts made within three years
   of death
defective transfers, 122.2
estate tax, 122.2
gift tax, 122.2, 122.3.1
gross estate inclusion, 122.2
revocable transfers, 122.3.1

Gifts made within three years of death
appreciation between gift and death
   dates, 120.2.2, 120.4.2, 126.4.1
bona fide sales, 126.4.2
carryover basis, 126.4.2
controlled corporations, releases of
   retained right to vote stock of,
   126.6.5
deathbed transfers, description as, 126.1,
   126.2
deferred payment of estate taxes, 126.4.2
generally, 126.2, 126.4.1, 126.4.2
gifts causa mortis, 122.2
gifts "in contemplation" of death, pre-
   1977, 126.4.1, 126.4.4
   circumstantial evidence, 126.4.4

[References are to paragraphs (¶).]

Gifts made within three years of death
(cont'd)
gifts "in contemplation" of death, pre-
1977 *(cont'd)*
decedent's motives, 126.4.4
defined, 126.4.4
statutory presumptions, 126.4.4
valuation, 126.4.4
gift tax, pre-1977, 126.4.1
gift tax returns, transfers not requiring,
126.4.2
gross estate, generally, 126.1, 126.4.1
gross-up of gift tax paid, 126.4.1, 126.4.3
split-gift election, 126.4.3
income tax basis, 126.4.2
life insurance, 127.6, 127.8
decedents's life, transfers of policy on,
127.8
gift tax, 127.8
lives of other persons, transfers of
policies on, 127.8
payment of premiums on previously
transferred policy, 127.8
purchase of policy within three-year
period, 127.8
post-1981 decedents, 126.4.1, 126.4.2
redemptions to pay death taxes and
estate expenses, 126.4.2
releases
controlled corporations, retained right
to vote stock of, 126.6.5
reversionary interests, 126.7.6
right to receive income or designate
income beneficiary, 126.6.9
tainted interests and powers, 126.3.5,
126.5.7
retained interest and powers, transfers
of, 126.4.2
sales for full consideration, 126.4.2
special use valuation, 126.4.2
statutory provisions, 126.1, 126.2
tainted interests and powers, 126.3.5,
126.5.7
tax liens, 126.4.2
three-year inclusionary rule, 126.4.2
unified rate schedule and unified credit,
126.4.1, 126.4.2
Gifts of Securities to Minors Act, 126.6.2

Gift tax
See also: Gift tax computation; Gift tax
payments; Gift tax returns; Split-gift
election
basis of gift property, 120.3
blockage discount, 135.3.3
charitable, religious, public, and similar
purposes. *See*: Charitable
contributions—gift tax deductions
community property, 123.1
constitutionality of, 120.1.2
contemplation-of-death provision and,
126.4.1
defective transfers. *See*: Transfers gift—
defective
definition of gift, 120.2.1
disclaimer of property interest, effect of,
121.7.1
donative intent. *See*: Donative intent, gift
tax
donors. *See*: Donors, gift tax
educational expenses, exemption of,
121.5
See also: Education expenses—gift tax
exemption
estate freezes, applicability of, 136.2.1
estate tax and
appreciation between gift and death
dates, 120.2.2, 126.4.1, 126.4.2
differences, 133.1
procedural rules, 137.1
qualified retirement plans, 126.8.5
unified system, 120.1.1, 122.4.1,
126.3.6, 126.4.1, 132.1
expatriation, tax-motivated, 134.1, 134.4
generally, 120.1.1, 120.2.1, 132.1
generation-skipping transfer (GST) tax,
similarity of, 133.1, 133.6.5
generation-skipping transfers,
inapplicability to, 120.1.1
gifts causa mortis, 122.2
gross-up of gift tax paid, 126.4.1, 126.4.3
history, 120.1.1
holding period of gifts, 120.3
income tax, relationship to, 120.3
educational and medical expense
exemptions, 121.5
procedural rules in common with,
137.1
incomplete transfers. *See*: Transfers gift
—nonbeneficial powers reserved
indirect gifts, 121.1

INDEX

[References are to paragraphs (¶).]

individuals, imposition upon, 121.1
life insurance, 127.8
medical expenses, exemption of, 121.5
nonresident aliens, 134.1, 134.2.1, 134.2.2
  See also: Nonresident aliens—gift tax
options and, 135.3.10
personal liability for, 137.7
  amount of liability, 137.7.2
  death of donor, unpaid taxes upon, 137.7.2
  donee liability, 137.7.2
  generally, 137.7.1, 137.7.2
  parties subject to, 137.7.1, 137.7.2
  transferee liability, 137.7.2
  unpaid taxes, 137.7.1, 137.7.2
political contributions, 121.9
powers of appointment, 121.6.1
procedural rules
  generally, 137.1, 137.9
  miscellaneous rules, 137.9
  payment of taxes, 137.4.1
  personal liability for tax, 137.7.1, 137.7.2, 137.7.4
  tax liens, 137.6.1, 137.6.3
  tax returns, 137.2
property. *See*: Property, gift
property-transfer rationale, applicability of, 122.3.5
purpose of, 133.1
rates, 120.1.1, 120.2.1
  cumulative, 120.2.1, 120.2.2
  single rate schedule, 120.2.2
revocable transfers. *See*: Transfers gift—revocable
shareholder-imputation principle, 121.1
specially treated taxpayers, 134.1
state gift taxes, 132.4
total amount of gifts in calendar year, determination of, 120.2.1
transfer requirement, 121.1
  See also: Transfers, gift
unified credit, 120.1.1
U.S. possessions, U.S. citizens resident in, 134.1, 134.3
valuation of property, 135.1–135.6, 136.2.1
  See also: Valuation
  accuracy-related penalty for errors, 137.9

Gift tax computation, 132.2
  See also: Unified wealth transfer tax system
  annual determination, 132.2.1
  errors in treatment of prior gifts, 132.2.2
  generally, 132.2.1
  prior gifts, 132.2.1
    errors in treatment of, 132.2.2
  unified credit, 132.2.1, 132.2.2
  unified wealth-transfer tax system, 132.1
  valuation errors, 132.2.2
Gift tax liens. *See*: Tax liens—gift tax
Gift tax payment
  executor or estate, decedent's tax payable by, 137.4.1
  generally, 137.4.1
  interest on postponed payments, 137.4.1
  joint and several liability, 137.4.1
  parties liable, 137.4.1
  split gifts, 137.4.1
  tax lien, secured by, 137.4.1
  time for payment, 137.4.1
    extensions, 137.4.1
Gift tax returns
  absence or nonresidence, filing by agent in event of, 137.2
  accuracy-related penalty for errors, 137.9
  agent or fiduciary, filing by, 137.2
  death of donor, filing by fiduciary in event of, 137.2
  filing requirement, 137.2, 137.9
  generally, 137.2
  illness, filing by agent in event of, 137.2
  incompetency, filing by agent in event of, 137.2
  minors, filing by guardian in event of, 137.2
  parties required to file, 137.2
  split-gift election, 123.5.3
  statute of limitations, 137.2, 137.9
  time for filing, 137.2
    extensions, 137.2
  transfers not requiring, 126.4.2
Going concern value of intangible assets
  defined, 135.4.5
  valuation, 135.4.5
Goodwill
  closely held corporations, 135.4.3
  defined, 135.4.5
  gross estate inclusion, 125.7
  nonresident aliens, 134.2.3

[References are to paragraphs (¶).]

Goodwill *(cont'd)*
unincorporated business interest,
valuation of, 135.4.4
valuation, 135.4.4, 135.4.5

Governmental agencies
charitable bequests, qualified
beneficiaries of, 130.2

Governmental units
generation-skipping transfers, 133.2.3

Government obligations
valuation, 135.4.6

Grandchildren. *See*: Generation-skipping
transfer (GST) tax; Generation-
skipping transfers; Generation-
skipping trusts; Skip person

Grandfather rule
wealth, transfers of, 120.1.2

Grantor retained income trust (GRIT)
estate freeze rules for, 136.4.1

Grantor trusts
generally, 122.3.1
gift tax consequences of, 121.1, 121.3.3
GRIT (grantor retained income trust),
estate freeze rules for, 136.4.1

GRIT (grantor retained income trust)
estate freeze rules for, 136.4.1

Gross estate
See also: Property owned by decedent at
death, gross estate inclusion;
Property transferred by decedent
during life, gross estate inclusion
adjusted gross estate, defined, 137.5.2
assets included in, 120.2.2
community property, 120.1.2, 120.2.2
deductions
administration expenses, 131.1, 131.3,
131.4.5
casualty losses, 131.1, 131.4.5, 131.8
charitable transfers, death taxes on,
131.7
claims against estate, 131.1, 131.4,
131.4.5, 131.6.3
debts secured by includable property,
131.5
decedent's vs. beneficiary's affairs,
131.1
foreign death taxes, 131.7
funeral expenses, 131.1, 131.2, 131.4.5
generally, 131.1, 131.6.1

income tax deductions, relationship to,
131.1, 131.6.4, 131.8
jurisdiction of state court, 131.1
limitations, 131.6
local law, allowable under, 131.6.1
mortgages secured by includable
property, 131.1, 131.5
nonresident aliens, 134.2.4
probate vs. nonprobate assets, 131.1
"property subject to claims" limitation,
131.6.3
state death taxes, 131.7
taxes, 131.6.2, 131.6.4, 131.7
timing, 131.1
defined, 120.2.2
generally, 120.2.2
gifts causa mortis, 122.2
income in respect of decedent, 120.3,
125.8
life insurance. *See*: Life insurance, gross
estate inclusion
lifetime transfers, 126.1
marital deduction, 129.1, 129.2.1, 129.2.4
See also: Marital deduction
nonresident aliens, 134.2.3–134.2.5
probate and nonprobate assets,
includable, 131.1
See also: Probate property
split-gift election, effect of, 123.5.1
transfers subject to nonbeneficial powers
to alter or amend, 122.4.1

Gross income
gifts, 120.3
inherited property, 120.3

Gross-up of gift tax paid, 126.4.1, 126.4.3

GST tax. *See*: Generation-skipping transfer
(GST) tax

Guaranteed annuities, 130.5.3

Guarantees
claims against estate, 131.4.3

Guardians
demand trusts, annual per-donee
exclusion, 124.3.3
gift tax return of minor or incompetent,
filing of, 137.2
outright gifts to minors through, 124.4.1
state custodianship statutes, 124.4.3
statutory trusts for minors, 124.4.2

INDEX

H

Heirlooms
valuation, 135.1.2

High-income levels. *See*: Estate tax; Wealth, transfer of

Holding period
gift property, 120.3
inherited property, 120.3

I

Illness. *See*: Medical and dental expenses; Personal injury or sickness

Imputed gifts, 121.1

Income
earned
gift property, 121.3.5
gift property, 121.3.5
unearned, as gift property, 121.3.5

Income in respect of decedents (IRD)
basis, 120.3
generally, 120.3
gross estate, 120.3, 125.7, 125.8

Income tax
barter equation method of valuation, 135.2.5
estate tax, relationship to, 120.3
decedent's property, valuation of, 125.7
estate tax and income tax deduction compared, 131.1, 131.6.4, 131.8
procedural rules in common with, 137.1
generation-skipping transfers, effect on income tax basis of, 133.4
gift tax, relationship to, 120.3
procedural rules in common with, 137.1
gross estate appointive assets, income tax basis of, 128.5.4
procedural rules, generally, 137.1, 137.9
valuation
See also: Valuation
generally, 135.1.1
special use election, income tax consequences of, 135.6.10

Incompetents
generation-skipping transfer (GST) tax, effective date exception, 133.5
gift tax return, filing of, 137.2

gift transfers by
defective, 122.2
under guardian's authority, 122.2
revocable, 122.3.2
joint bank account owners, 122.3.2
marital property settlements, incompetent spouse and, 123.6.2

Incomplete transfers. *See*: Transfers, gift— nonbeneficial powers reserved

Indebtedness. *See*: Debt; Debt discharges

Indirect gifts, 121.1
controlled or related entities, gifts involving, 121.1
discharge of donee's debts, 121.1
ostensible intermediate recipients, gifts involving, 121.1

Individual
gift tax liability, 121.1

Individual retirement plans (IRAs)
gross estate exclusion, 126.8.5

Inheritance taxes. *See*: Estate tax; State death taxes

Inherited property
See also: Estate tax; Gift tax; State death taxes; Wealth, transfer of
basis, 120.3, 128.5.4
holding period, 120.3
QTIP transfers, effect of, 129.4.5
valuation, 135.1.1
See also: Valuation
will contests, settlements of, 130.3.2

Injury. *See*: Medical and dental expenses; Personal injury or sickness

Installment payments
closely held business interests, payment of deferred estate tax on, 137.5.1, 137.5.3
generation-skipping transfer (GST) tax, 133.6.3

Installment sales
gross estate transfers, effect on payments of, 126.6.2

Insurance
See also: Life insurance; Life insurance, gross estate inclusion
annuities under gross estate
life insurance distinguished, 126.8.4
survivorship annuities, 126.8.1
medical, gift tax exemption, 121.5

Insurance *(cont'd)*
settlement options, gross estate, 126.3.2

Intangible assets
expatriates, tax-motivated, 134.4
nonresident aliens
estate tax, 134.2.3
gift tax exception for, 134.2.2
valuation, 135.4.5
formula method, 135.4.5
residual method, 135.4.5

Interest
on deferred tax
estate tax, 137.4.2–137.4.4, 137.5
gift tax, 137.4.1

Intermediaries. *See*: Agents; Fiduciaries;
Guardians

Internal Revenue Service
estate tax, advance rulings on, 137.9

Inter vivos transfers. *See*: Gifts made
within three years of death; Lifetime
transfers; Property transferred by
decedent during life, gross estate
inclusion; Survivorship annuities;
Transfers subject to power to revoke,
alter, amend, or terminate transferee's
enjoyment; Transfers subject to
retained reversionary interests;
Transfers subject to retained right to
receive income or designate income
beneficiary

Inter vivos trusts
estate freeze valuation rules, 136.4.1

Intrafamily transactions
See also: Estate tax; Wealth, transfer of
bona fide transfers, 121.4.5
debt discharges, 121.1
estate freeze valuation rules. *See*: Estate
freezes

Inventories
valuation, 135.4.5

IRD. *See*: Income in respect of decedents

J

Joint and mutual wills
terminable interests, 129.3.3

Joint and survivor annuities
QTIP transfers, 123.3.3, 129.4.5

Joint bank accounts
gift transfers
beneficial ownership, 122.3.2
deposits as nontaxable revocable
transfers, 122.3.2
incompetent joint owners, 122.3.2
joint tenancies in other property
distinguished, 122.3.2
revocable, 122.3.2
gross estate, 125.11.1–125.11.4
survivorship feature, 125.11.4
withdrawals, right to, 122.3.2

Jointly held property
See also: Joint bank accounts; Joint
tenancies; Tenancies by the entirety;
Tenancies in common
annual per-donee exclusion, 124.2
gross estate, 125.11.1–125.11.4
marital deduction, 129.2.3
marital property settlements, 123.6.1,
123.6.2

Joint returns
split-gift election, 123.5.1

Joint tenancies
closely held business interests, eligibility
for extension of payment of estate
tax on, 137.5.2
direct taxation, constitutionality, 125.11.1
gift transfers
annual per-donee exclusion, 124.2
brokerage accounts distinguished,
122.3.2
excess consideration by one party,
123.4
generally, 122.3.3, 123.4
joint bank accounts distinguished,
122.3.2
marital deduction, 123.4
personal property, 123.4
prior contributions, 122.3.3
real property, 123.4
revocable, 122.3.3
right of severance, 122.3.3, 123.4
right of survivorship, 122.3.3, 123.3.2,
123.4
spousal tenancies, 122.3.3, 123.4
termination of tenancy, 122.3.3, 123.4
gross estate, generally, 125.1, 125.11.1,
125.11.2
history, 125.11.1
marital deduction, 123.4, 125.11.3

INDEX

[References are to paragraphs (¶).]

nonspousal
  assumption of liabilities by survivor,
      125.11.4
  consideration received from decedent,
      125.11.4
  exceptions to inclusionary principle,
      125.11.4
  generally, 125.11.2, 125.11.4
  gross estate inclusion, 125.11.4
  post-acquisition contributions, 125.11.4
  property acquired by gift, devise,
      bequest, or inheritance, 125.11.4
  qualifying contributions, 125.11.4
  survivor's original contributions
      exclusion, 125.11.4
  valuation, 125.11.4
right of severance, 125.11.1–125.11.3
with right of survivorship
  current law, 125.11.2
  defined, 125.11.1
  generally, 122.3.3, 123.3.2, 125.1,
      125.11.1
  history and rationale, 125.11.1
  joint and mutual wills, 129.3.3
  joint tenants, defined, 125.11.2
  nonspousal, 125.11.4
  scope of property encompassed by,
      125.11.2
  spousal, 125.11.3
  survivorship, defined, 125.11.2
  valuation, 125.11.1
spousal
  date-of-death stepped-up basis,
      125.11.3
  generally, 125.11.3
  gift transfers, 122.3.3, 123.4
  gross estate inclusion, 125.1
  marital deduction, 122.3.3
  one-half interest vs. proportionate
      contribution, 125.11.3
  qualified joint interests, 125.11.3
  quasi-testamentary transfers, 125.11.3
  sole joint tenants, 125.11.4

Joint ventures
  valuation, 135.4.4

K

Key person
  loss of, effect on value of stock, 135.3.5

L

Land and farmland .
  valuation, special use election, 135.6
  See also: Farmers and ranchers—
      special use valuation election

Legacies. *See*: Bequests; Estate tax;
      Inherited property; State death taxes

Legal expenses
  estate administration expenses
      deduction, 131.3.2
  local law, 131.3.2
  will contests, 131.3.2

Legal obligations, transfers to discharge,
      121.4.4

Letter rulings
  estate tax, advance rulings on, 137.9

Liens. *See*: Tax liens

Life estates
  charitable remainder trusts with life
      estate in surviving spouse, 129.4.6
  gross estate, generally, 125.1, 125.5
  with powers of appointment
      See also: Life estates with power of
          appointment in surviving spouse
      in donee spouse, 123.3.3
      double taxation, 128.2.4
      in surviving spouse, 129.4.3
  QTIP transfers, 129.4.5
  retained. *See*: Transfers subject to
      retained right to receive income or
      designate income beneficiary
  valuation, 135.1.2, 135.4.10
      actual life expectancy, 135.4.10
      events other than death, probability of,
          135.4.10
      interest factor, 135.4.10
      marketability, 135.4.10

**Life estates with power of appointment in
      surviving spouse**, 129.4.3
  beneficiary of trust vs. legal life tenant
      of underlying property, 129.4.3
  conflicting powers, 129.4.3
  inter vivos transfers, 129.4.3
  marital deduction as related to surviving
      spouse's estate, 129.4.3
  others, powers in, 129.4.3
  QTIP transfers vs., 129.4.3
  right to income, 129.4.3
  allocations between income and
      corpus, 129.4.3

[References are to paragraphs (¶).]

Life estates with power of appointment in surviving spouse *(cont'd)*
right to income *(cont'd)*
annual-interval condition, 129.4.3
degree of spouse's enjoyment, 129.4.3
income, defined, 129.4.3
periodic payments, 129.4.3
specific portions of interests, 129.4.3
definition of specific portion, 129.4.3
fractional shares, 129.4.3
spouse's power of appointment, 129.4.3
combined powers, 129.4.3
exercisable by spouse alone and in all events, 129.4.3
inconsistency in governing instruments, 129.4.3
proof of, 129.4.3
state law, 129.4.3
survivorship conditions, 129.4.3

Life insurance
on decedent's life, 125.6, 127.1–127.5
See also: Life insurance, gross estate inclusion
generation-skipping trust, life insurance policy as, 133.2.12
gift transfers
beneficiary designation, 122.3.6
community property, 122.3.6
completion of, 122.3.6
installment transfers, 122.3.6
payment of premiums, 122.3.6
reversionary interests retained, 122.3.6
right to change beneficiary, 122.3.6
within three years of death, 127.8
gross estate. *See*: Life insurance, gross estate inclusion
valuation, 125.4.4, 125.4.8, 127.7, 135.4.9

Life insurance contracts
annual per-donee exclusion, 124.3.4

Life insurance, gross estate inclusion
accidental death, 127.2
amounts includable, 127.4.2, 127.7
defined, 127.7
valuation, 127.7
beneficiary liability for estate tax, 127.4.9
community funds, insurance purchased with, 127.5
conversion into separate property, 127.5
state law, 127.5
conditions for inclusion, 127.1

contingent rights, 127.4.3
corporations or other entities, incidents of ownership held by
control, defined, 127.4.8
corporation not beneficiary, 127.4.8
proceeds not payable to corporation, 127.4.8
proceeds payable to corporation, 127.4.8
valuation, 127.4.8
decedent-ownership rule, 127.1, 127.4
estate-benefit rule, 127.1, 127.3
executor
amounts receivable by, 127.1, 127.3
defined, 127.2
fiduciary powers, 127.4.6
flight insurance, 127.4.3
fraternal beneficial societies, death benefits paid by, 127.2
generally, 125.1, 125.6, 127.1, 127.2
gifts made within three years of death, 127.6, 127.8
See also: Gifts made within three years of death—life insurance
history, 127.1
incidents of ownership, 127.4
contingent rights, 127.4.3
controlled corporations, 127.4.8
corporations, 127.4.8
definition, possible, 127.4.2
economic benefits vs., 127.4.2
family corporations and partnerships, 127.4.8
fiduciary capacity, 127.4.6
generally, 127.4.1, 127.4.2
joint powers, 127.4.5
ostensible vs. legally enforceable rights, 127.4.7
partnerships, 127.4.8
reversionary interests, 127.4.4
rights of, 127.4.2, 127.4.3
state law, 127.4.2, 127.4.7
trusts, 127.4.8
valuation, 127.4.8
insurance, defined for purposes of, 127.2
insurance-annuity combination, 127.2
joint powers, 127.4.5
adverse effects, 127.4.5
veto powers, 127.4.5
legally enforceable vs. ostensible rights, 127.4.7
divorce decrees, 127.4.7

INDEX

marital deduction, 127.4.9
beneficiary's estate tax liability and, 127.4.9
property passing from decedent, 129.2.3
mutual benefit societies, death benefits paid by, 127.2
nonresident aliens, 134.2.3
ostensible vs. legally enforceable rights, 127.4.7
other persons, insurance on life of, 127.6
powers of appointment, 127.6, 128.5.2
    proceeds subject to power in surviving spouse, 129.4.4
premium payment test, 127.1
regulated insurance company contracts, 127.2
requirements for inclusion, 127.2
reversionary interests, 127.4.4
    defined, 127.4.4
    valuation, 5 percent rule, 127.4.4
revocable trusts, 127.6
scope of insurance, 127.2
    risk-shifting and risk-distribution, 127.2
split-dollar arrangements, 127.4.8
survivorship annuities distinguished, 125.8.4
transfers subject to power to revoke, alter, amend, or terminate transferee's enjoyment, 127.6
transfers subject to retained reversionary interests, 127.6
transfers subject to retained right to receive income or designate income beneficiary, 127.6
valuation, 127.4.4, 127.4.8, 127.7
    generally, 135.4.9
    replacement value approach, 127.7
    terminal reserve method, 127.7
wrongful death recoveries distinguished, 127.2

Lifetime transfers
See also: Gifts made within three years of death; Property transferred by decedent during life, gross estate inclusion; Survivorship annuities; Transfers subject to power to revoke, alter, amend, or terminate transferee's enjoyment; Transfers subject to retained reversionary interests; Transfers subject to

retained right to receive income or designate income beneficiary
current law, 126.2
double taxation, 126.3.6
estate tax, 126.1
generally, 126.1
generation-skipping transfers, 133.1, 133.3.3
gross estate inclusion, generally, 126.1, 126.3
marital deduction, 129.2.3
nonresident aliens, 134.2.5
state death taxes, 132.4
state gift taxes, 132.4
statutory provisions for, 126.1

Liquidation rights
defined, 136.3.2
estate freeze valuation, 136.2.2, 136.2.4, 136.2.5
lapse of rights, 136.3.1–136.3.3

Liquidations, complete
estate freeze rules
    lapsing rights and restrictions, 136.3
    right to force liquidation, 136.2.2, 136.2.4, 136.2.5, 136.3.1–136.3.3

Literary organizations
charitable bequests, qualified beneficiaries of, 130.2
contributions to, gift tax deductions for, 121.8

Literary works
valuation, 135.4.8

Litigation. *See*: Tax litigation

Loans
See also: Below-market loans
gift property
    demand loans, 121.3.4
    interest-free loans, 121.3.4

Lookback rules
estate freeze valuation, 136.2.7, 136.2.9

Losses. *See*: Casualty losses

Lump-sum distributions
qualified retirement plans, 126.8.5

M

Manuscripts
valuation, 135.4.8

Marginal tax rates
phase-out of lower marginal rates, 132.1

[References are to paragraphs (¶).]

Marital deduction
  amount deductible, 129.2.1
  annual per-donee exclusion, possible
    effect of, 129.1
  apportionment of estate tax, 137.8
  common disaster terminable interest
    provision, effect of, 129.4.2
  common law and, 129.1
  community property, 123.3.5, 125.10,
    129.1, 129.3.1, 129.5.3
  constitutional issues, 129.1
  current law, 129.6
  denial of, 129.2.4, 129.2.5
  dower, 125.9
  economic source, attribution to, 129.1
  encumbrances and obligations, effect of,
    129.5.3
  estate tax
    apportionment of tax, 137.8
    generally, 129.1
    prior transfers, credit on, 129.1
    tax-free transfer of assets between
      spouses, 129.1, 129.6.1
    tax liens, effect of, 137.6.2
  50 percent ceiling, pre-1982, 123.3.1,
    129.3.1, 129.6.1, 129.6.4
  generally, 120.2.2, 129.1
  gift tax
    alien spouses, 123.3.4
    generally, 120.2.1, 123.1, 123.2.3
    history, 120.2.1, 123.1
    joint tenancies, 123.4
    pre-1982 restrictions on deduction,
      123.3.5
    split-gift election vs., 123.5.1, 123.5.2
    tax liens, effect of, 137.6.3
    tenancies by the entirety, 123.4
  gross estate inclusion, 129.1, 129.2.1,
    129.2.4
  nonresident alien surviving spouse,
    129.2.5
  history, 120.2.2, 129.1, 129.6.1
  joint tenancies, 123.4, 125.11.3
  life insurance beneficiary's estate tax
    liability and, 127.4.9
  limited, 129.7
    community property, 129.7.1
    generally, 129.1, 129.7.1
    maximum marital deduction formula
      clauses, 129.7.2
    minimum allowance, 129.7.1
    percentage limit, 123.3.5

  percentage limit/adjusted gross estate,
    129.7.1
  pre-1982 restrictions, 123.3.5
  wills and trusts, transitional exemption
    for, 129.6.4
  marital property settlements, 123.6.3
  maximum marital deduction formula
    clauses, pre-1982, 129.7
    equalization clauses, 129.7.2
    fractional share clauses, 129.7.2
    overfunding, 129.7.2
    pecuniary clauses, 129.7.2
    wills and trusts, pre-1982 transitional
      exemption for, 129.6.4
    wording, 129.7.2
  medium-sized estates, 129.1
  minimum deduction, 123.3.1
  minimum exemption of $250,000, 129.1
  mortgaged property, 129.5.3
  nonresident alien decedent, 134.2.2,
    134.2.4
  nonresident alien surviving spouses
    disqualification of certain, 129.2.5
    generally, 129.2.5, 134.2.4
    qualified domestic trust (QDI), 129.2.5
  post-1981 decedents, 129.6
  powers of appointment, 128.2.4
  pre-1982 decedents, 123.3.5, 129.7
  property interests qualifying for
    deduction, 129.2
    disclaimers, 129.2.3
    inclusion in gross estate, 129.2.4
    jointly held property, 129.2.3
    life insurance, 129.2.3
    lifetime gifts, 129.2.3
    noncitizen spouses, disqualification of
      certain, 129.2.5
    powers of appointment, 129.2.3
    probate property, 129.2.3
    property "passing" from decedent,
      129.2.1, 129.2.3, 129.2.4
    surviving spouse, 129.2.2
    threshold requirements, 129.2.1
  purpose of, 123.3.1
  small estates, 129.1
  state death taxes, 129.5.2, 129.6.2
  surviving spouse, 123.6.3, 129.2.1, 129.2.2
    common disaster terminable interest
      provision, effect of, 129.4.2
    date-of-death status, 129.2.2
    divorce, effect of, 123.6.3, 129.2.2
    entire property passing to, 129.3.3

[References are to paragraphs (¶).]

lavish expenditures by, effect of, 129.1
life estates with power of appointment
  in, 129.4.3
nonresident aliens, 129.2.5
order of deaths of spouses, 129.2.2
QTIP transfers, 129.4.5
qualified disclaimer by, 129.2.3
remarriage of, 129.1
simultaneous deaths of spouses,
  129.2.2
six-month survivorship terminable
  interest provision, effect of,
  129.4.2
state law, 129.2.2
status as, 129.2.2
valuation of interests passing to, 129.5
terminable interests. *See*: Terminable
  interests
unlimited, 129.6
  divorce, effect on, 123.6.3
  equalization provisions, 129.6.3
  generally, 123.3.1, 129.1, 129.6.1
  graduated rates, effects of, 129.6.3
  net worth amounts, 129.6.2
  time value of money, effects of,
    129.6.3
  unified credit, 129.1, 129.6.2
  wills and trusts, transitional exemption
    for, 129.6.4
valuation, 129.5
  alternate date, 135.7.5
  date-of-death, as of, 129.5.1
  death taxes, 129.5.2
  encumbrances and obligations, 129.5.3
  generally, 129.1, 129.5.1
will contests, 129.2.3
  See also: Will contests—marital
    deduction
wills, elections against, 129.2.3
  See also: Wills, elections against—
    marital deduction
zero-tax bequest, impact of other
  transfers on, 129.6.2

Marital deduction trusts
  See also: Life estates with power of
    appointment in surviving spouse
  generally, 129.4.3
  transitional exemption for, 129.6.4

Marital property settlements
  See also: Alimony

gift tax exemption
  agreements vs. judgments, 123.6.1,
    123.6.2
  child support, 123.6.1, 123.6.2
  community property, 123.6.1
  consideration requirement, 123.6.1,
    123.6.2
  contemplation of divorce, settlements
    in, 123.6.1, 123.6.2
  divorce decrees, 123.6.1, 123.6.2
  donative intent, absence of, 123.6.1
  generally, 123.6.1, 123.6.2
  incompetent spouse, 123.6.2
  involuntary vs. voluntary settlements,
    123.6.1
  jointly-owned property, 123.6.1, 123.6.2
  judicial decree of absolute divorce,
    123.6.1, 123.6.2
  nonobligatory support payments,
    123.6.1, 123.6.2
  prenuptial agreements, 123.6.1, 123.6.2
  property rights, 123.6.1, 123.6.2
  support payments, 123.6.1, 123.6.2
  three-year time period requirement,
    123.6.2
  valuation, 123.6.2
  writing requirement, 123.6.2
gross estate, 126.3.4
marital deduction, effect of unlimited,
  123.6.3

Marital separation
  See also: Alimony; Child support;
    Divorce; Support obligations,
    marital
  agreements for, 123.6.1, 123.6.2
  claims against estate, 131.4.3

Market
  concept of, for purposes of valuation,
    135.1.2

Market discount
  blockage discount, 135.3.3
  control premiums, 135.3.4
  estate freeze rules for valuation of
    qualified payments, 136.2.5
  governmental restrictions, 135.3.7
  lack of diversification, 135.3.6
  lack of marketability discount, 135.3.2
  loss of key person, effect of, 135.3.5
  minority discounts, 135.3.4
  taxes, consideration of, 135.3.8
  valuation of property affected by, 135.3

FEDERAL TAXATION OF INCOME, ESTATES AND GIFTS

Market discount *(cont'd)*
  valuation of property affected by *(cont'd)*
    See also: Valuation—control premiums
      and minority discounts; Valuation
      —discounts and premiums

Marriage, promise of, 121.4.2

Married couples
  See also: Community property; Joint
    tenancies; Marital deduction;
    Spouses; Tenancies by the entirety
  claims against estate, 131.4.3
  generation-skipping transfers, effect of
    marital relationship on, 133.2.3
  interspousal transfers, 121.4.2
  split gifts to third persons. *See*: Split-gift
    election

Medical and dental expenses
  generation-skipping transfer exemption,
    133.2.13
  gift tax exemption, 121.5
    amount unlimited, 121.5
    direct payments, 121.5
    generally, 132.1
    income tax exclusion, relation to, 121.5
    insurance payments, 121.5
    medical care defined for purposes of,
      121.5
  insurance, gift tax exemption, 121.5
  medical care, defined, 121.5

Memorabilia
  valuation, 135.4.8

Military personnel
  qualified retirement plans, 126.8.5
  soldiers dying in action, estate tax
    computation, 125.6, 132.8
    basic estate tax vs. additional estate
      tax, 132.8

Minors
  See also: Children; Child support;
    Custodianships for minors;
    Grandchildren
  annual per-donee exclusion, 124.3.3,
    124.4
    See also: Annual per-donee exclusion
      —minors, gifts to
  custodianship statutes, state, 124.4.3
  demand trusts, 124.3.3
  gift tax return, filing of, 137.2
  gift transfers by, defective, 122.2
  guardians, 124.3.3, 124.4.1–124.4.3

outright gifts to, 124.4.1
  present interest, 124.4.1
property owned by decedent at death,
  125.1
retained life estate, gifts through, 126.6.2
statutory trusts, 124.4.2
  annual per-donee exclusion, 124.4.2
  constructive vs. unitary present
    interests, 124.4.2
  Crummey powers, 124.4.3
  discretionary distributions, 124.4.2
  distributions of unexpended items at
    age 21, 124.4.2
  donee death before age 21, 124.4.2
  expenditures of property and income
    by or for donee before age 21,
    124.4.2
  post-21 income, 124.4.2
  powers of appointment, 124.4.2
  property and income requirement,
    124.4.2
  trustee powers, 124.4.2

Model Gifts of Securities to Minors Act,
  124.4.3

Mortgaged property
  gross estate, 125.4
  marital deduction, 129.5.3
  taxable estate, 125.4
  valuation
    generally, 135.1.2, 135.3.9

Mortgages
  claims against estate, 131.4.3, 131.6.3
  foreclosures
    See also: Foreclosure
    valuation of property, 135.1.2
  gross estate, deduction for mortgage
    secured by includable property,
    131.1, 131.5
  nonresident aliens, 134.2.3, 134.2.4

Motion pictures
  valuation, 135.4.8

Musical compositions
  valuation, 135.4.8

Mutual benefit societies
  life insurance, death benefits paid as,
    127.2

Mutual funds
  valuation, 135.4.2

Mutual wills
  terminable interests, 129.3.3

INDEX

[References are to paragraphs (¶).]

N

Natural habitats, deduction for protection of, 130.5.5

Natural person as skip person, 133.2.4

Nominees
See also: Agents
beneficial ownership of property, 125.2

Nonbeneficial powers reserved. *See*:
Transfers, gift—nonbeneficial powers
reserved; Transfers subject to power to
revoke, alter, amend, or terminate
transferee's enjoyment—nonbeneficial
powers

Noncompetition contracts
valuation, 135.4.5

Nonprofit organizations. *See*: Tax-exempt
organizations

Nonresident aliens
decedent, 134.2.1
defined, 134.2.1
domicile, acquisition of, 134.2.1
estate tax computation
adjusted taxable gifts, 134.2.5
generally, 134.1, 134.2.5
lifetime gifts, 134.2.5
pre-1977 gifts, 134.2.5
prior transfers, 134.2.5
state death taxes, 134.2.5
tax treaties, 134.2.7
unified credit, 134.2.5
unified rates schedule, 134.2.5
estate tax deductions
charitable contributions, 134.2.4
determination of, 134.2.4
expenses, losses, indebtedness, and
taxes, 134.2.4
marital deduction, 134.1, 134.2.4
estate tax returns, filing of, 137.3
expatriates, tax-motivated, 134.1, 134.4
foreign death taxes, 132.7.2
generation-skipping transfer (GST) tax,
134.1, 134.2.1, 134.2.6, 134.2.7
gift tax
annual per-donee exclusion, 134.2.2
charitable contributions, 134.2.2
domicile requirement, 134.2.1
exceptions for nonresident aliens,
134.2.2
generally, 134.1
intangible property exception, 134.2.2

marital deduction, 134.2.2
real or tangible personal property in
U.S., 134.2.2
returns, filing of, 137.2
situs of property, 134.2.2
split-gift election, 134.2.2
tax treaties, 134.2.7
unified credit, 134.2.2
unified rate schedule, 134.2.2
gross estate
bank deposits, 134.2.3
beneficial interests in trusts, 134.2.3
community property, 134.2.4
corporate stock, 134.2.3
debt obligations, 134.2.3
determination of, 134.2.3
domicile requirement, 134.2.1
generally, 134.1
intangibles, 134.2.3
life insurance, 134.2.3
partnership interests, 134.2.3
real property, 134.2.3
securities issued by foreign
corporations, 134.2.3
situs of property in U.S., 134.2.3
tangible personal property, 134.2.3
worldwide, 134.2.3, 134.2.4
surviving spouse, 129.2.5
See also: Qualified trusts—qualified
domestic trust (QDI)
certain disqualifications, 129.2.5
credit allowed, 129.2.5
denial of marital deduction, 129.2.5
qualified domestic trust, generally,
129.2.5
taxation, generally, 134.1, 134.2.1
tax-motivated expatriates as, 134.1, 134.4
tax treaties, effect of, 134.2.7
domicile treaties, 134.2.7
situs treaties, 134.2.7
taxes covered, 134.2.7

Notes
annual per-donee exclusion, 124.3.4
gift property, 121.3.2
valuation, 135.4.6

O

Options
buy-sell agreements and, 135.3.10,
136.3.3
call, 135.4.7

Options *(cont'd)*
  estate freeze valuation rules, 135.3.10,
    136.3.3
  put, 135.4.7
  valuation of property, 135.3.10, 135.4.7

Overpayments of tax
  excessive deficiencies, 137.5.3

Ownership
  joint bank accounts, beneficial ownership
    of, 122.3.2
  property owned by decedent at death
    beneficial ownership of, 125.2
    dominion and control as ownership,
      125.3
    future interests, 125.4
    partial and divided interests, 125.4
    substantial-ownership rationale, 125.3
  special use election for real property and
    farms, ownership requirement for,
    135.6.5

P

Partnerships
  See also: Family partnerships
  estate freeze valuation of interests in,
    136.2, 136.3
    See also: Estate freezes
  gift tax liability, 121.1
    annual per-donee exclusion, 124.2
  interests
    closely held business interests,
      eligibility for extension of
      payment of estate tax on, 137.5.2
    nonresident aliens, owned by, 134.2.3
    valuation, 135.4.4, 135.4.5
  life insurance incidents of ownership
    held by, 127.4.8
  passive assets, 137.5.2
  special use election, 135.6.8
  valuation of interests in, 135.4.4, 135.4.5
    estate freeze valuation, 136.2, 136.3

Passive assets, 137.5.2

Patents
  marital deduction, 129.3.2, 129.3.3
  nonresident aliens, 134.2.3
  valuation, 135.4.5

Periodic payments
  gift property, 121.3.2

Personal credits
  estate tax on prior transfers, 132.6

  foreign death taxes, 132.1, 132.7
  nonresident alien surviving spouse,
    129.2.5
  pre-1977 gift taxes, 132.6
  state death taxes, 132.1, 132.4
  state GST taxes, 133.3.5
  unified. *See*: Unified credit; Unified
    wealth transfer tax system

Personal deductions
  estates
    See also: Administration expenses
      deduction, estates; Charitable
      bequest deduction; Claims against
      estate, deductions for; Gross
      estate—deductions; Marital
      deduction
    casualty losses, 131.8
    double deductions, disallowance of,
      120.3
    funeral expenses, 131.2
    generally, 131.1
    nonresident aliens, 134.2.4

Personal injury or sickness
  gift tax return, filing by agent of, 137.2

Personal liability
  estate tax, 137.7
    amount of liability, 137.7.3
    application by executor for amount
      due, 137.7.4
    assumptions by ESOPs, 137.7.3
    discharge from liability, 137.7.4
    executor's liability, 137.7.3
    faulty gift tax return, effect of, 137.7.4
    generally, 137.7.1, 137.7.3
    nonprobate property, 137.7.3
    parties liable, 137.7.1, 137.7.3
    priority of U.S. claims, 137.7.3
    probate property, 137.7.3
    state law, effect of, 137.7.3
    tax litigation, 137.9
    transferee liability, 137.7.3
    unpaid taxes, 137.7.1, 137.7.3
  gift tax, 137.7
    amount of liability, 137.7.2
    death of donor, unpaid taxes upon,
      137.7.2
    donee liability, 137.7.2
    generally, 137.7.1, 137.7.2
    parties liable, 137.7.1, 137.7.2
    transferee liability, 137.7.2
    unpaid taxes, 137.7.1, 137.7.2

INDEX

[References are to paragraphs (¶).]

Personal residence
charitable bequest of remainder in, 130.5.5
estate freeze rules, transfers in trust, 136.4.6
retained life estate, transfer through, 126.6.2

Personal residence trusts
defined, 136.4.6
estate freeze rules, 136.4.6
personal residence defined for purpose of, 136.4.6
qualified (QPRT), 136.4.6

Political activities and contributions
annual per-donee exclusion, 124.2
gift tax exemption, 121.9
retroactive application, 121.9

Pooled income funds
charitable bequests, 130.5.1, 130.5.2, 136.4.7
defined, 130.5.2
generation-skipping transfers, charitable interests, 133.2.8

Possessions, U.S. *See*: United States possessions

Powers of appointment
adverse interest rule, 128.2.3
affected property, 128.2.1
annuities, 129.4.4
appointive assets
estate tax payment from, 128.5.3
income tax basis of, 128.5.4
ascertainable standard limitation, 128.2.2
common law, 128.1
current law, 128.1
custodial property, parent's power over, 128.2.1
decedent's death, powers held upon, 128.3.2
defined, 121.6.1, 128.1, 128.2.1
by American Law Institute (ALI), 128.1
demand trusts, 124.3.3
disclaimer of power
estate tax, 128.3.5
gift tax, 121.6.2, 121.7.5
donor superiority rule, 128.2.3
employee benefit plans, 128.5.2
endowment contracts, 129.4.4

estate tax
appointive assets, payment from, 128.5.3
dominion and control of property preserved by retained powers, 125.3, 125.7
evolution of estate tax rules, 128.1
exercised vs. unexercised powers, 125.3, 125.7, 128.3.1
generally, 128.1
general power, 128.2
joint powers, 128.2.3
nongeneral and successive powers, 128.5
taxable events, 128.3
exercise of powers
death, exercisable at, 128.3.2
estate tax, 125.3, 128.1, 128.3.1, 128.3.3
gift tax, 121.6.2
pre-1942 power, 128.4
five-and-five powers
estate tax, 128.1, 128.3.1, 128.3.4
gift tax, 121.6.2
generally, 121.6.1, 128.1
general power of appointment, 128.1, 128.2
defined, 121.6.1, 128.1, 128.2.1, 130.3.3
exercise vs. nonexercise of, 128.1
introduction, 128.2.1
nongeneral power vs., 128.1
outright ownership, treatment as, 128.1
state law, 128.2.1
gift tax
appointment of cotrustees as release, 121.6.2
definition of power, 121.6.1, 121.6.2
disclaimer of power, 121.6.2
exercise of powers, 121.6.1, 121.6.2
five-and-five powers, 121.6.2
generally, 121.6.1
general powers, 121.6.1, 121.6.2
lapse of powers, 121.6.2
marital deduction, 123.3.2
nongeneral (special) powers, 121.6.3
parallel estate tax rules, 121.6.1
partial release of powers, 121.6.2
post-1942 powers, 121.6.1, 121.6.2
pre-1942 powers, 121.6.4
release of powers, 121.6.1, 121.6.2
renunciation of power, 121.6.2
split-gift elections, 123.5.2

Powers of appointment *(cont'd)*
gross estate inclusion, 128.1, 128.3.1, 128.3.2
history, 128.1, 128.4
joint powers, 128.2.3
lapsed powers
estate tax, 128.3.4
gift tax, 121.6.2
life insurance, 127.6, 129.4.4
marital deduction, 128.2.4
general powers, 129.2.3
retained powers, 123.3.2, 129.4.3, 129.4.4
taxability of powers and, 128.2.4
minors
demand trusts, 124.3.3
statutory trusts, 124.4.3
nongeneral (special) power
estate freeze rules for exercise of, 136.2.3
estate tax, 128.1, 128.5.1
general power vs., 128.1
gift tax, 121.6.3
overlap with other provisions, 128.5.2
ownership theory, 128.1
permissible appointees, 128.2.1
post-1942 powers
estate tax, 128.1–128.3, 128.5
gift tax, 121.6.1, 121.6.2
pre-1942 powers
estate tax, 128.4
gift tax, 121.6.4
property owned or transferred by decedent, effect on, 128.5.2
pro rata rule, 128.2.3
QTIP transfers, 129.4.5
qualifying uses, 128.2.2
quasi-testamentary release or exercise, 128.3.3
release of powers
estate tax, 128.3.2–128.3.4
gift tax, 121.6.1, 121.6.2
partial, 121.6.2
pre-1942 power, 128.4
renunciation of power
estate tax, 128.3.5
gift tax, 121.6.2
reverse powers, 128.5.2
rights not qualifying as, 128.2.1
rule against perpetuities, 128.5.1
state law, 121.6.2, 128.1, 128.2.1, 128.5.1
successive powers, 128.5.1

surviving spouse, life estates with power of appointment in, 129.4.3
See also: Life estates with power of appointment in surviving spouse
surviving spouse, proceeds of life insurance, endowment, and annuity contracts subject to power of appointment in, 129.4.4
taxable events, 128.3
time of creation, 128.4
transfer of property by gift, 121.6.1
unexercised powers, 125.3, 128.1
wrongful death recoveries, 125.6, 128.2.1
Powers of Appointment Act of 1951, 128.1
Preferred stock
estate freeze valuation, 136.1, 136.2.5
present value, 136.2.5
Premium coupons
valuation of property affected by, 135.3
valuation of property affected by premiums
See also: Valuation—discounts and premiums
Prenuptial agreements
claims against estate, 131.4.3
marital property settlements, 123.6.1, 123.6.2
powers of appointment, effect of, 123.5.2
split-gift election, 123.5.2
Present value
preferred stock, 136.2.5
Preservation and conservation of land areas, deduction for, 130.5.5
Private annuities
See also: Survivorship annuities
valuation, 135.4.10
Private foundations
charitable lead trusts treated as, 130.5.3
Probate property
See also: Gross estate
administration expenses, deductibility, 131.3.2
attorney's fees, 131.3.2
benefit of beneficiaries, expenses incurred for, 131.3.2
common disaster provision as avoidance of probate, 129.4.2
executor, defined, 131.3.2
executor's commissions, 131.3.2
interest, 131.3.2

jurisdiction of state court, 131.1

marital deduction, 129.2.3

miscellaneous expenses, 131.3.2

nonprobate assets vs., 131.1

personal liability for estate tax, 137.7.3

"property subject to claims" limitation, 131.6.3

protracted administration, 131.3.2

sale of estate assets, expenses of, 131.3.2

six-month survivorship provision as avoidance of probate, 129.4.2

tax liens, coverage in, 137.6.2

unpaid estate taxes, liability for, 137.7.3

Promises

gift property, 121.3.2

  enforceable or irrevocable vs. unenforceable promises, 121.3.2

  marriage, promise of, 121.4.2

gratuitous promise as completed gift, 132.3

Promissory notes

annual per-donee exclusion, 124.3.4

gift property, 121.3.2

Property

See also: Assets; Community property; Inherited property; Jointly held property; Property, gift; Property owned by decedent at death, gross estate inclusion; Property transferred by decedent during life, gross estate inclusion; Real property; Sale of property; Valuation

encumbered

  valuation of property, effect on, 135.3.9

Property, gift

acceptance by donee, 122.2

accounts receivable, 121.3.2

annuities, 121.3.2

assignment of income, 121.3.5

basis, 120.3

characteristics of, 122.2

checks, 121.3.2

competent donor, 122.2

contingent interests, 121.3.3

death benefits, 121.2, 121.3.3

defeasible interests, 121.3.3

defined, 121.3.1

delivery, actual or symbolic, 122.2

disclaimers of interest in property. *See*: Disclaimers and renunciations of property interests

donative intent. *See*: Donative intent, gift tax

earned income, 121.3.5

future interests, 121.3.3

generally, 121.3.1

gifts causa mortis, 122.2

holding period, 120.3

income, 121.3.5

interest-free loans, 121.3.4

loans

  below-market, 121.3.4

  demand, 121.3.4

  interest-free, 121.3.4

to nonprofit organizations, 121.9

notes, 121.3.2

periodic payment obligations, 121.3.2

to political organizations, 121.9

promises, enforceable or irrevocable, 121.3.2

promissory notes, 121.3.2

rent-free use of assets, 121.3.4

vs. services, gift, 121.3.6

uncompensated services, 121.3.6

unearned income, 121.3.5

valuation, 121.3.2, 121.3.3, 123.5.1, 123.6.2, 135.1–135.5

  See also: Valuation

Property owned by decedent at death, gross estate inclusion

actuarial value, 125.5, 125.7

art, works of, 125.1, 125.7

beneficial ownership, 125.2

beneficiaries of decedent, benefits to, 125.1

cash, 125.1

children of decedent, benefits to, 125.1

claims, 125.1, 125.7

Clifford trusts, 125.3

community property, 120.1.2, 120.2.2, 125.10

compensation for services of decedent, postmortem, 125.7

competing claims, 125.7

complete ownership, 125.3

contingent claims and assets, 125.7

death benefits, 125.6

debt discharge upon death, 125.5

defeasible claims and assets, 125.7

[References are to paragraphs (¶).]

**Property owned by decedent at death,
gross estate inclusion** *(cont'd)*
disclaimers, 125.12
divided interests, 125.4
dominion and control as ownership of
property, 125.3
dower, curtesy, and statutory substitutes,
125.1, 125.9
employee death benefits, 125.6
expectancy and hope distinguished from
property, 125.6, 125.7
family corporation stock, 125.7
family partnership interests, 125.8
future interests, 125.4
generally, 125.1
goodwill, business, 125.7
income in respect of decedents, 120.3,
125.7, 125.8
interests created at death, 125.6
interests terminating at death, 125.5
joint bank accounts, 125.11.1–125.11.4
joint tenancies with right of survivorship,
125.1, 125.11
See also: Joint tenancies
current law, 125.11.2
history and rationale, 125.11.1
nonspousal, 125.11.4
qualified joint interests of husband
and wife, 125.11.3
legal fees, contingent, 125.7
life insurance proceeds, 125.1, 125.6
See also: Life insurance, gross estate
inclusion
mortgaged property, 125.1, 125.4
options, 125.7
outright ownership vs. life tenancy, 125.5
ownership of property, 125.3, 125.4
partial interests, 125.4
partnership interests, 125.8
powers of appointment. *See*: Powers of
appointment
property and interest therein, concept of,
125.1
quasi-testamentary transfers of jointly
held property, 125.11.3
real estate, 125.1, 125.7
record ownership of property, 125.2
remainder interests, 125.7
reserved right to income, 125.5
speculative claims and assets, 125.7
spouse of decedent, benefits to, 125.1
state law, 125.2, 125.6

statutory provisions for, 125.1
stock and securities, 125.1, 125.7
substantial-ownership rationale, 125.3
tenancies by the entirety, 125.1,
125.11.1–125.11.3
tenancies in common, 125.11.1–125.11.3
testamentary debt cancellations, 125.5
time of death, significance of, 125.1,
125.5
tort claims, 125.6
unincorporated business interests, 125.1
unliquidated claims and assets, 125.7
valuation, 125.1, 125.5, 125.7
income tax vs. estate tax, 125.7
wrongful death recoveries, 125.6, 127.2

**Property transferred by decedent during
life, gross estate inclusion**
annuities. *See*: Survivorship annuities
bona fide dispute settlements, 126.3.2
bona fide sale exemptions, 126.3.4
tainted interests and powers, 126.3.5
common problems, 126.1
control, issue of, 126.1
current law, legislative evolution of,
126.2
deathbed transfers. *See*: Gifts made
within three years of death
decedent as transferor, 126.3.1
disclaimers, qualified, 126.3.2
disputes, settlements of, 126.3.2
divorce and separation agreements,
126.3.4
double taxation of lifetime transfers,
126.3.6
employee benefits, 126.3.2
estate tax, generally, 126.1
generally, 125.1, 126.1, 126.3
history, 126.2
insurance settlement options, 126.3.2
legally enforceable rights and powers,
126.3.3
agents of transferor, 126.3.3
controlled corporation voting rights,
126.3.3
inferences from conduct, 126.3.3
possession or enjoyment, retention of,
126.3.3
terminology, difficulties of, 126.3.3
life of transferor as measuring stick,
126.3.7
marital property settlements, 126.3.4

INDEX

[References are to paragraphs (¶).]

marital support obligations, 126.3.4
property, defined, 126.3.2
quasi-testamentary character of, 126.1
renunciation or waiver, 126.3.2
retained life estate. *See*: Transfers subject
    to retained right to receive income
    or designate income beneficiary
retained powers affecting transferee's
    enjoyment. *See*: Transfers subject to
    power to revoke, alter, amend, or
    terminate transferee's enjoyment
retained reversionary interests. *See*:
    Transfers subject to retained
    reversionary interests
rights and powers, legally enforceable,
    126.3.3
sales and other transfers for
    consideration, 126.3.4
    annuities, 126.3.4
    constructive receipt, 126.3.4
    interrelated gifts, 126.3.4
    partial consideration principle, 126.3.4
    sale, defined, 126.3.4
    widow's election wills, 126.3.4
settlements of disputes, 126.3.2
split-gift election, 123.5.3
statutory provisions, 126.1
tainted interests and powers, dispositions
    of, 126.3.5, 126.5.7
transfer of property, defined, 126.3.1
transferor, identification of, 126.3.1
    bona fide dispute settlements, 126.3.2
    burden of proof, 126.3.1
    decedent as transferor, 126.3.1
    reciprocal trust doctrine, 126.3.1
transferor's life as measuring stick,
    126.3.7
waiver or renunciation, 126.3.2
widow's election wills, 126.3.4

Proprietorships
closely held business interests, eligibility
    for extension of payment of estate
    tax on, 137.5.2
valuation, 135.4.4

Public organizations. *See*: Charitable
    organizations; Tax-exempt
    organizations

Put options
valuation, 135.4.7

Put rights
estate freeze valuation, 136.1, 136.2.2,
    136.2.4, 136.2.5

Q

QTIP transfers
annuities, 123.3.3, 129.4.5
basis, 129.4.5
charitable-spousal bequests, as
    alternative to, 129.4.6
defined, 123.3.3, 129.3.1
double deductions, 129.4.5
election by executor, 129.4.5
estate tax apportionment and, 137.8
generally, 129.3.1, 129.3.3, 129.4.3,
    129.4.5
generation-skipping transfer rules and,
    133.2.2, 133.3.3
gift transfers
    irrevocable QTIP election, 123.3.3
    joint and survivor annuity, rules for,
        123.3.3
    lifetime transfers, 129.4.5
    terminable interests, 123.3.3
history, 129.4.5
inheritance, effect of delay, 129.4.5
invalidity under local law, 129.4.5
marital deduction trusts distinguished,
    129.4.3
non-trust, 129.4.5
overlap with statutory provisions, 129.4.5
payment of gift or estate tax from,
    129.4.5
powers of appointment, 129.4.5
prohibition of powers, 129.4.5
property passing from decedent, 129.4.5
purpose and result of election, 129.3.1
qualification as, 129.4.5
specific portion rule, 129.4.5
state law, 129.4.5
surviving spouse's right to income,
    129.4.5
    periodic payments, annual or more
        frequent, 129.4.5
    remarriage, 129.4.5
    subsequent transfers, 129.4.5
taxation of surviving spouse, 129.4.5
types, 129.4.5

Qualified personal residence trust (QPRT)
defined, 136.4.6
estate freeze valuation rules, 136.4.6

Qualified retirement plans
gift transfers, 122.3.5
gross estate exclusion, 126.8.5
amounts payable to executor, 126.8.5
armed forces, 126.8.5
charitable organizations, 126.8.5
community property, 126.8.5
complementary gift tax rules, 126.8.5
constructive receipt, 126.8.5
decedent's contributions, 126.8.5
individual retirement accounts (IRAs), 126.8.5
lump sum distributions, 126.8.5
military personnel, 126.8.5
nonemployee decedents, 126.8.5
qualification requirements, 126.8.5
powers of appointment, effect of, 128.5.2
survivorship annuities, 126.8.5

Qualified terminable interest property transfers. *See* QTIP transfers

Qualified trusts
qualified domestic trust (QDI)
additional estate tax on, 129.2.5
noncitizen surviving spouse and marital deduction, 129.2.5
requirements of, 129.2.5
qualified personal residence trust (QPRT)
defined, 135.4.6
estate freeze valuation rules, 135.4.6

R

Railroad Retirement Act of 1937, 126.8.2

Rate of tax. *See*: Tax rates

Real property
See also: Real property valuation
conservation contribution, deduction for, 130.5.5
gross estate inclusion of property owned by decedent at death, 125.1, 125.7
joint tenancies, 123.4
nonresident aliens
estate tax, 134.2.3
gift tax on transfers by, 134.2.2
tenancies by the entirety, 123.4

Real property valuation
blockage discount, 135.3.3
capitalization of income method, 135.2.3, 135.4.1
comparable sales method, 135.2.2, 135.4.1
comparative sales method, 135.2.2, 135.4.1
estates freezes, 136.1
fair market value criterion, 135.4.1
generally, 135.4.1
gross estate inclusion purposes, 125.7
property taxes, effect of, 135.3.8, 135.4.1
special use election, 135.6
acquisition by qualified heir, 135.6.3
additional estate tax, 135.6.9
capitalized-rents-for-comparable-land-value method, 135.6.7
combining individuals, 135.6.5
combining properties, 135.6.5
corporations, qualified real property held by, 135.6.8
disabled decedents, alternative time period for, 135.6.5
disposition of property, 135.6.9
election of, 135.6.6
estate tax payment, extension of time for, 137.5.1
estate tax return filing, 135.6.6, 137.3
fifty percent test, 135.6.4
five out of eight years, ownership, qualified use, and material participation for, 135.6.5
generally, 120.3, 135.6.1
income tax consequences of, 135.6.10
liability and lien to secure payment of tax, 135.6.9
lifetime transfers, 126.4.2
material participation, 135.6.5
methods of valuation of qualified real property, 135.6.7
multiple factor method, 135.6.7
ownership, qualified use, and material participation for five of eight years, 135.6.5
partnerships, qualified real property held by, 135.6.8
qualified real property, defined, 135.6.1
qualified use test, 135.6.2
recapture of tax benefits, 135.6.9
relaxed participation rule, 135.6.5
retired decedents, alternative time period for, 135.6.5
termination of qualified use, 135.6.9
time requirements, meeting, 135.6.5

INDEX

trusts, qualified real property held by, 135.6.8

twenty five percent test, 135.6.5

Recapitalizations (Type E reorganizations)
estate freeze rules, as transfer under, 136.2.3

Recapture
special use election termination, recapture of tax benefits upon, 135.6.9

Reciprocal trusts
annual per-donee exclusion, 124.2
gross estate, 126.3.1
interrelated requirement, uncrossing of trusts and, 126.3.1

Redemptions
death taxes, for payment of, 126.4.2
estate freeze rules, as transfer under, 136.2.3
generation-skipping transfer tax, for payment of, 133.6.4

Related taxpayers
See also: Family; Intrafamily transactions
claims against estate by, 131.4.3
gift tax liability, 121.1
donative intent, 121.4.5

Religious organizations
charitable bequests, qualified beneficiaries of, 130.2
nonresident aliens, contributions by, 134.2.4
contributions to, gift tax deductions for, 121.8
qualified retirement plans, 126.8.5

Remainder interests
estate tax payment, extensions of time for, 136.4.4
gift property, 121.3.3
gross estate, 125.7
valuation, 135.4.10
actual life expectancy, 135.4.10
estate freeze rules, 136.4.2, 136.4.3
events other than death, probability of, 135.4.10
interest factor, 135.4.10
marketability, 135.4.10

Remainder trusts, charitable
annuity trusts, 123.3.3, 129.4.6, 130.4, 130.5.1, 130.5.2
defined, 130.5.2

generation-skipping transfers, 133.2.3
unitrusts, 130.5.1, 130.5.2
defined, 130.5.2
generation-skipping transfers, 133.2.3

Rental payments
future income, 121.3.5
gift property, 121.3.4
income, 121.3.5

Rental property
valuation, 135.4.1

Renunciations. *See*: Disclaimers and renunciations of property interests

Reorganizations, corporate
gift transfer, diminished stock value as, 121.2

Residence. *See*: Personal residence

Resident aliens
spouse
gifts to, 123.3.4
marital deduction, 123.3.1, 123.3.4
split-gift election, eligibility for, 123.5.3
taxation, generally, 134.2.1

Retired decedents
special use valuation for farms and real property, alternative requirements for, 135.6.5

Retirement plans. *See*: Individual retirement plans (IRAs); Qualified retirement plans

Returns. *See*: Tax returns

Revenue Act of 1916, 128.1

Revenue Act of 1918, 128.1, 130.1

Revenue Act of 1941, 128.4

Revenue Act of 1942, 128.1

Reversionary interests
estate freeze valuation, 136.4.3
estate tax payment, extensions of time for, 136.4.4
life insurance policy, gift transfers of, 122.3.6
valuation, 135.4.10

Revised Uniform Gifts to Minors Act, 124.4.3

Revocable trusts
See also: Grantor trusts; Transfers, gift—revocable; Transfers subject to power to revoke, alter, amend, or terminate transferee's enjoyment

[References are to paragraphs (¶).]

Revocable trusts *(cont'd)*
defined, 122.3.1
generally, 126.5.1
life insurance, 127.6

S

Sale of property
buy-sell agreements, 135.3.10
forced sales, 135.1.2
gross estate, 123.3, 126.3.4
expenses of sales of estate assets,
131.3.2

Scientific organizations
charitable bequests, qualified
beneficiaries of, 130.2
contributions to, gift tax deductions for,
121.8

Securities
foreign corporations, issued by, 134.2.3
valuation
See also: Stock—valuation; Valuation
—control premiums and minority
discounts
adjustments, 135.4.2
bid and asked prices, 135.4.2
generally, 135.1.2, 135.2.2, 135.3
mutual funds, 135.4.2
over-the-counter market, 135.4.2
redemption price rule, 135.4.2
selling prices, 135.4.2
stock exchange trading, 135.4.2

Securities accounts
revocable transfers, 122.3.2

**Securities and Exchange Commission
(SEC)**
cost of registration with, governmental
restrictions and, 135.3.7

Securities Exchange Act, 135.3.7

Separate maintenance. *See*: Alimony; Child
support; Support obligations, marital

Separation. *See*: Marital separation

Separation agreements
claims against estate, 131.4.3
generally, 123.6.1, 123.6.2

Services
uncompensated
as gift property, 121.3.6
gross estate inclusion of postmortem
compensation, 125.7

Shareholders
annual per-donee exclusion, 124.2
gift tax liability, 121.1

Simultaneous death of spouses
marital deduction, 129.2.2

**Six-month survivorship terminable interest
exception**, 129.4.2
common disaster terminable interest
exception as alternative or
concurrent condition, 129.4.2
computation of six-month period, 129.4.2
month, defined, 129.4.2
purpose, 129.4.2
state law, 129.4.2
survivorship conditions, effect of certain,
129.4.2
unified credit, effect on, 129.4.2

Skip person
See also: Generation-skipping transfers
defined, 133.2.1
entity other than trust as, 133.2.4
generally, 133.2.4
natural person as, 133.2.4
trust as, 133.2.4

Social Security Act, 125.6

Social Security Administration
funeral expense payments by, effect on
deduction of, 131.2

Soldiers dying in action
estate tax computation, 125.6, 132.8
basic estate tax vs. additional estate
tax, 132.8

Special use election. *See*: Real property
valuation—special use election

Spendthrift trusts, 122.5, 124.3.1, 124.3.2

Split-gift election
advantages, 123.5.1
annual per-donee exclusion, effect on,
120.2.1, 123.5.1, 124.1
ascertainable interests, 123.5.2
charitable contributions of, gift tax
deduction for, 121.8.2
community property and common law
disparities, reduction of, 123.5.1
consent requirement, 123.5.2, 123.5.3
death of spouse, effect of, 123.5.3
disqualified gifts, 123.5.2
divorce, effect of, 123.5.3
earlier or later year elections, 123.5.3
estate tax rates and, 123.5.1

INDEX

50-50 requirement, 123.5.1

filing of gift tax returns, 123.5.3

generally, 120.2.1, 123.1, 123.5.1

generally, 132.1

geographical equalization objective, 123.1

gifts made within three years of death, 126.4.3

gift tax payment, joint and several liability for, 137.4.1

gift tax return, filing of, 137.2

gross estate, 123.5.1

history, 123.5.1

indirect unequal division, possibility of, 123.1

joint and several liability, 123.5.3

lower bracket of progressive rates, utilization of, 123.5.1

marital deduction vs., 123.5.1, 123.5.2

nonresident aliens, 134.2.2

powers of appointment, 123.5.2

prenuptial agreements, 123.5.2

purpose of, 123.1, 123.5.1

qualifying gifts, 123.5.2

remarriage, effect of, 123.5.2, 123.5.3

residency requirement, 123.5.3

revocation of consent, 123.5.3

severable interests, 123.5.2

unified credit, 123.5.1

valuation, 123.5.1

Split interests

valuation, 135.4.10

  actual life expectancy, 135.4.10

  estate freeze rules, 136.2.3

  events other than death, probability of, 135.4.10

  interest factor, 135.4.10

  marketability, 135.4.10

Sports

charitable bequests to organizations fostering amateur competition, 130.2

gift tax liability for contributions toward fostering of amateur competition, 121.8

Spouses

See also: Community property; Jointly held property; Joint returns; Marital deduction; Married couples; Surviving spouse

community property gifts to, 123.2.1, 123.2.3

estate freeze valuation rules, 136.2.2, 136.3.4

See also: Estate freezes

gifts to, generally, 123.1

interspousal transfers, 121.4.2

nonresident alien spouse, marital deduction, 129.2.5

resident alien spouse, marital deduction, 123.3.1, 123.3.4

State death taxes

charitable bequests, 130.6

charitable transfers, 131.7

estate tax credit, 132.4

  "actual payment" requirement, 132.4

  basic estate tax, defined, 132.4

  creditable taxes, 132.4

  generally, 132.1

  nonresident aliens, 134.2.5

  persons other than decedent, 132.4

  purpose and history, 132.4

  refunds, 132.4

  state jurisdiction to impose tax, 132.4

  timing considerations, 132.4

  waiver of credit, 132.4

estate tax deductions, 131.6.2

  charitable transfers, 131.7

funeral expenses, deductibility, 131.2

generally, 120.1.2, 120.2.2

generation-skipping transfer (GST) tax, reduction of rate of, 133.3.4

marital deduction, 129.5.2, 129.6.2

state gift taxes compared, 132.4

stock redemptions to pay, 126.4.2

State generation-skipping transfer (GST) tax, credit for, 133.3.5

State gift taxes, 132.4

State law

charitable bequest deduction, 130.6

claims against estate

  absence of local decree, 131.6.1

  administration expenses, 131.3.2, 131.3.3, 131.6.1

  allowable claims, 131.6.1

  funeral expenses, 131.2, 131.4.5, 131.6.1

  generally, 131.4.1, 131.4.2, 131.6.1

  independent federal standard, 131.6.1

  local decree, effect of, 131.6.1

constitutional issues, 120.1.2

custodianship statutes affecting minors, annual per-donee exclusion, 124.4.3

[References are to paragraphs (¶).]

State law *(cont'd)*
disclaimers of property interests, 121.7.1,
121.7.5–121.7.7
estate tax apportionment, 120.1.2,
129.5.2, 137.8
flower bonds, time of purchase of,
137.4.2
gift transfers, defective, 122.2
gross estate
administration expenses (legal fees),
131.3.2
generally, 125.2
lifetime transfers subject to retained
powers, 126.5.1
probate jurisdiction, 131.1
life insurance
community funds, purchase with, 127.5
incidents of ownership, 127.4.2, 127.4.7
marital deduction, 129.2.2
disclaimers, 129.2.3
election against will, 129.2.3
joint and mutual wills, 129.3.3
marital deduction trusts, 129.4.3
powers to consume, 129.3.3
six-month survivorship provision,
129.4.2
widow's allowance, 129.3.3
will contests, 129.2.3
minors, annual per-donee exclusion,
124.4.1–124.4.3
powers of appointment, 121.6.2, 128.1,
128.2.1, 128.5.1
QTIP transfers, 129.4.5
wealth, regulation of transfer of, 120.1.2
wrongful death recoveries, 125.6

Statutes of limitations
claims against estate, 131.4.2
estate freezes
corporations and partnerships,
interests in, 136.2.11
trust, transfers in, 136.4.8
estate tax returns, 137.9
gift tax returns, 137.2, 137.9
gift transfer, lapse of statute on debt
enforcement as, 121.2
gross estate omission, assessments of
taxes, 125.4
special use election, assessment of tax
upon termination of, 135.6.9

Stepped-up basis
spousal joint tenancies, 125.11.3

Stock
See also: Redemptions; Securities
closely held business interests, eligibility
for extension of payment of estate
tax on, 137.5.2
discount. See: Market discount
estate freezes, 136.1–136.3
See also: Estate freezes
nonresident aliens, estate tax on stock
transferred by, 134.2.3
valuation
See also: Valuation—control premiums
and minority discounts
blockage discount, 135.3.3
closely held corporation stock, 135.4.3
control premiums, 135.3.4
discounts, effect of, 135.3
generally, 135.1.2, 135.2.2
governmental restrictions, 135.3.7
gross estate inclusion purposes, 125.7
lack of diversification, 135.3.6
lack of marketability, 135.3.2
loss of key person, effect of, 135.3.5
minority discounts, 135.3.4
private restrictions, 135.3.9
taxes, consideration of, 135.3.8

Students
See also: Educational expenses
educational expenses, gift tax exemption
for, 121.5
part-time students, 121.5

Support obligations, marital
See also: Alimony; Child support
discharge of, 121.4.3
gift tax transfers
donative intent, 121.4.3, 121.5.1
immunity, 121.4.3
marital property settlements, 123.6.1,
123.6.2
gross estate, 126.3.4
claims against estate, 131.4.3
retained life estate, 126.6.2
support allowance for surviving
spouse, 129.3.3

Surviving spouse
See also: Curtesy; Dower; Life estates
with power of appointment in
surviving spouse; Marital deduction
—surviving spouse; Wills, elections
against

[References are to paragraphs (¶).]

charitable remainder trusts with life
estate in, 129.4.6
disclaimer of property interest,
exceptions to rules for
nonacceptance of benefits exception,
121.7.3
writing requirement exception, 121.7.3
generally, 123.6.3, 129.2.1, 129.2.2
gift-at-death rationale, 121.3.3
joint interests with right of survivorship,
125.11.1, 125.11.3
nonresident alien, 129.2.5
See also: Nonresident aliens—surviving
spouse
powers of appointment in
life estates, 129.4.3
life insurance, endowment, and
annuity contract proceeds, 129.4.4
property owned by decedent at death,
generally, 125.1
QTIP transfers, 129.4.5
support (widow's) allowance, 129.3.3

Survivorship annuities
See also: Annuities
amounts includable, 126.8.1, 126.8.3
broad inclusionary rule, 126.8.1
decedent's contributions, 126.3.4
partial consideration rule, 126.3.4
annuities covered, 126.8.1, 126.8.2
annuity, defined, 126.8.2, 126.8.5
other payment, defined, 126.8.2
combined contracts, 126.8.2
contingencies, 126.8.2
contracts and agreements included,
126.8.2
decedent's contribution, 126.8.3
decedent's rights, 126.8.2
duration of, 126.8.2
employee benefit plans, 126.3.2, 126.8.5
endowment contracts, 126.8.2
forfeiture, possibility of, 126.8.2
generally, 126.2, 126.8.1
gross estate, generally, 126.1, 126.8.1,
126.8.3
history, 126.8.1
insurance-annuity combination, 127.2
insurance contracts, 126.8.1
joint payments, 126.8.2
life insurance distinguished, 126.8.4
postemployment benefits, 126.8.2

qualified retirement plans, 126.8.2,
126.8.5
See also: Qualified retirement plans—
gross estate exclusion
armed forces, 126.8.5
charitable organizations, 126.8.5
qualification requirements, 126.8.5
qualified retirement plans, benefits
under, 126.3.2, 126.8.5
statutory provisions, 126.1, 126.2, 126.8.1
survivorship requirement, 126.8.2
transfers subject to retained right to
receive income, 126.6.2
valuation of annuity or other payment,
126.8.1, 126.8.3

Survivorship terminable interest exception.
See: Six-month survivorship terminable
interest exception

T

Tainted interests and powers
lifetime transfers, 126.3.5, 126.5.4,
126.5.7

Tangible property
business assets, valuation of, 135.4.5
estate freeze rules for nonproductive
property, 136.4.3
nonresident aliens
estate tax, 134.2.3
gift tax on transfers by, 134.2.2

**Taxable distributions, generation-skipping
transfers**, 120.2.3, 133.1, 133.2.7
constructive distributions, 133.2.7
defined, 133.2.7
nonresident aliens, 134.2.6
returns, 133.6.2
taxable amount, 133.3.2

Taxable estate
See also: Gross estate
adjusted (ATE), 132.4
defined, 120.2.2
double deductions, disallowance of, 120.3
dower, curtesy, and statutory substitutes,
125.9
generally, 120.2.2
marital deduction, 129.1
See also: Marital deduction
mortgaged property, 125.4
reduction by deductions, 131.1

[References are to paragraphs (¶).]

Taxable terminations, generation-skipping transfers, 120.2.3, 133.1, 133.2.6
defined, 133.2.6
direct skips contrasted, 133.2.6
income tax basis, effect on, 133.4
nonresident aliens, 134.2.6
recomputation of inclusion ratio after, 133.3.4
returns, 133.6.2
taxable amount, 133.3.2

Taxation, double. *See*: Double taxation

Tax avoidance
expatriation, tax-motivated, 134.1, 134.4
generation-skipping transfer (GST) tax, 133.2.8

Tax Court
valuation issues, role in, 135.5.2
expert witnesses, 135.5.1, 135.5.2

Taxes, generally
valuation of property, effect on, 135.3.8

Taxes, unpaid
claims against estate, 131.6.2
tax liens to secure payment, 137.6

Tax-exempt organizations
See also: Charitable contributions
annual per-donee exclusion, 124.2
generation-skipping transfers, 133.2.3
gift tax liability, 121.1, 121.9
nonresident aliens, contributions by, 134.2.4
qualified retirement plans, 126.8.5

Tax liability
See also: Personal liability
estate tax, 137.7
generation-skipping transfer (GST) tax, 133.6.1
gift tax
corporations, 120.2.1, 121.1
generally, 120.2.1, 121.1, 132.1, 137.7
revocable trusts, 122.3.1

Tax liens
collection of tax with, 137.6.1
estate tax
administration expenses, effect of, 137.6.2
charitable bequest deduction, 137.6.2
claims against estate, effect of, 137.6.2
collection upon threat of lien, 137.6.1
deficiencies, determination of, 137.6.2
elective extensions, 137.5.3

generally, 137.6.1, 137.6.2
gifts made within three years of death, 126.4.2
marital deduction, 137.6.2
nonprobate and probate property, coverage of, 137.6.2
nontax law, 137.6.1
other liens compared, 137.6.1
property covered, 137.6.2
protected liens, 137.6.2
release of lien, 137.6.2, 137.6.3
statutory provisions, 137.6.1, 137.6.2
successors in interest, 137.6.2
superpriority claimants, 137.6.3
time period, 137.6.1
validity of underlying claim, 137.6.1
generally, 137.6.1
gift tax
charitable bequest deduction, 137.6.3
closely held business interests, secured deferred payment of estate tax on, 137.5.3
collection upon threat of lien, 137.6.1
generally, 137.4.1, 137.6.1, 137.6.3
marital deduction, 137.6.3
nontax law, 137.6.1
other liens compared, 137.6.1
property subject to, 137.6.3
release of lien, 137.6.3
statutory provisions, 137.6.1
superpriority claimants, 137.6.3
time period, 137.6.1, 137.6.3
transferred property, inclusion of, 137.6.3
validity of underlying claim, 137.6.1
mechanic's liens, priority of, 137.6.3
sales, valuation of property and, 135.1.2
special use election recapture, lien to secure payment of tax, 135.6.9

Tax litigation
estate tax liability, 137.9
valuation issues, 135.5.2
special use election, 135.6.6

Taxpayers
citizenship, determination of, 134.2.1
expatriates, tax-motivated, 134.1, 134.4
nonresident aliens, 134.1, 134.2
tax-motivated expatriates, 134.1, 134.4
in United States possessions, 134.1, 134.3

Tax payments
estate tax, 137.4.2

INDEX

[References are to paragraphs (¶).]

See also: Estate tax payment
   extensions, 137.4.3, 137.4.4
gift tax, 137.4.1
   See also: Gift tax payment
tax liens to secure, 137.6

Tax rates
estate tax, 120.1.1, 120.2.2, 132.1
generation-skipping transfer (GST) tax,
   133.1, 133.3.4
gift tax, 120.1.1, 120.2.1, 132.1
marginal, 132.1
marital deduction, effect of graduated
   rates on, 129.6.3
unified system, 120.1.1, 122.4.1, 126.3.6,
   126.4.1, 132.1

Tax returns
See also: Estate tax returns; Gift tax
   returns
generation-skipping transfer (GST) tax,
   133.3.3, 133.3.4, 133.6.2

Tax treaties
death taxes, 132.7.4
domicile treaties, 134.2.7
double taxation, prevention of, 132.7.1,
   132.7.4
foreign income, 132.7.4
foreign-source income, 132.7.4
nonresident aliens, effect on taxation of,
   134.2.7
   domicile treaties, 134.2.7
   situs treaties, 134.2.7
   taxes covered, 134.2.7
situs treaties, 134.2.7

Technical Changes Act of 1949, 126.7.7

Tenancies by the entirety
closely held business interests, eligibility
   for extension of payment of estate
   tax on, 137.5.2
defined, 125.11.1
gift transfers
   annual per-donee exclusion, 124.2
   excess consideration by one party,
      123.4
   generally, 123.4
   marital deduction, 123.4
   personal property, 123.4
   real property, 123.4
   right of severance, 123.4
   right of survivorship, 123.4
   spousal tenancies, 123.4
   termination of tenancy, 123.4

gross estate, 125.11.1–125.11.3
gross estate inclusion, 125.1

Tenancies in common
art works, 130.5.4
closely held business interests, eligibility
   for extension of payment of estate
   tax on, 137.5.2
gift transfers
   annual per-donee exclusion, 124.2
gross estate, 125.11.1–125.11.3

Terminable interests
See also: Life estates with power of
      appointment in surviving spouse;
      Marital deduction; Six-month
      survivorship terminable interest
      exception
acquisition by executor of, 129.3.5
conditional bequests, 129.3.3
deductible, 129.4
   annuity proceeds subject to power of
      appointment in surviving spouse,
      129.4.4
   charitable remainder trusts with life
      estate in surviving spouse, 129.4.6
   common disaster exception, 129.4.2
   endowment proceeds subject to power
      of appointment in surviving
      spouse, 129.4.4
   estate trusts, 129.4.1, 129.4.7
   generally, 129.4.1
   life estate with power of appointment
      in surviving spouse, 129.4.3
   life insurance proceeds subject to
      power of appointment in surviving
      spouse, 129.4.4
   QTIP transfers, 129.3.1, 129.3.3,
      129.4.3, 129.4.5
   six-month survivorship exception,
      129.4.2
definition, statutory, 129.3.2
disqualification, 129.3
   generally, 129.2.3, 129.3.1
   gift tax, 123.3.2
   gross estate, 129.3.1
   nonterminable vs. terminable interests,
      129.3.1, 129.3.2
   retained powers of appointment,
      123.3.2
   statutory exceptions, 129.4.1
   succeeding interest in donor or other
      donees, 123.3.2

Terminable interests *(cont'd)*
elections against wills, 129.3.3
enjoyment of property by third person,
terminable interest followed by,
129.3.3
other source of third person interest,
129.3.3
entire property passing to surviving
spouse, 129.3.3
executor-acquired interests, 129.3.5
generally, 123.3.1, 129.2.1, 129.3.2
geographical equalization objective,
123.1, 123.3.1
gift tax
charitable remainder trusts with life
estate in donee-spouse, 123.3.3
disqualified interests, 123.3.2
generally, 123.3.1
joint interests, 123.3.2
life estate with power of appointment
in donee spouse, 123.3.3
QTIP transfers, 123.3.3
qualifying interests, 123.3.3
retained powers of appointment,
123.3.2
succeeding interest in donor or other
donees, 123.3.2
terminability per se, 123.3.2
unascertainable donees, 123.3.2
unidentified assets, 123.3.2
joint and mutual wills, 129.3.3
justification for rule governing, 123.3.1
marital deduction, qualification for,
129.3.3
modifications of terminable interest rule,
129.3.1
nonterminable interests vs., 129.3.1,
129.3.2
patents or copyrights, 129.3.2, 129.3.3
pool of assets, interests payable from
partially unidentified, 129.3.4
postmortem elections, 129.3.3
powers to consume, 129.3.3
preceding third person interests, 129.3.3
purchased terminable interest principle,
129.3.5
qualifying
See also: QTIP transfers
charitable remainder trusts with life
estate in donee-spouse, 123.3.3
defined, 129.3.2
gift tax, 123.3.3

gross estate, generally, 129.3.1, 129.3.3,
129.4
life estate with power of appointment
in donee spouse, 123.3.3
QTIP transfers, 123.3.3, 129.4.5
sales of all other interests in underlying
property, 129.3.3
single vs. multiple properties, 129.3.3
spousal life estate with remainder to
children, 129.3.3
terminable interest rule
common law, effect on, 129.3.1
generally, 123.3.1
modifications, 129.3.1
unidentified assets, interests payable
from, 129.3.4
widow's allowance, 129.3.3

Terminations of trusts
See also: Taxable terminations,
generation-skipping transfers
generation-skipping transfers, 120.2.3,
133.1, 133.2.6

Third parties
community property gifts to, 123.2.1,
123.2.2

Third-party powers
gift transfers, incomplete, 122.5
lifetime transfers subject to retained
powers over transferee enjoyment,
126.5.5

Timber
valuation, 135.6.2

Time value of money
marital deduction, effect on, 129.6.3

Tort claims
claims against estate, 131.4.3
donative intent, gift tax, 121.4.4
gross estate, 125.6
wrongful death recoveries, 125.6, 127.2,
128.2.1

Totten trusts
gift transfers
relinquished power of revocation,
122.3.4
revocable, 122.3.4

Trademarks and trade names
valuation, 135.4.5

Trade secrets
valuation, 135.4.5

Trading With the Enemy Act, 125.7

INDEX

Transfers, gift
See also: Split-gift election; Wealth, transfers of
alteration, transfers subject to, 122.4, 122.5
amendment, transfers subject to, 122.4, 122.5
beneficial powers to revoke vs. nonbeneficial powers to amend or modify, 122.4.1
death benefits, 121.2
debt discharge, 121.2
defective
  acceptance by donee, 122.2
  common law rules, 122.2
  delivery, 122.2
  donative intent, 122.2
  generally, 122.1
  gifts causa mortis, 122.2
  by incompetent donors, 122.2
  by minors, 122.2
  state law, 122.2
defined, 121.2
  gross estate inclusion, for purposes of, 126.3.2
double inclusion, 132.1
eligible transfers, 121.2
generally, 120.1.1, 120.2.1, 120.3, 121.2
incomplete, 122.1, 122.4, 122.5
jointly held powers
  alteration or amendment, powers of, 122.5
  nonadverse interests, 122.5
  revocation, powers of, 122.5
  substantial adverse interests, 122.5
  third-party powers vs., 122.5
lapse of valuable rights as, 121.2
nonbeneficial powers reserved
  alteration, powers of, 122.4.1
  amendment, powers of, 122.4.1
  beneficial powers to revoke distinguished, 122.4.1
  completion of gift vs., 122.4.1
  dominion and control retained, 122.4.1
  enforceable external standard, effect of, 122.4.2
  fixed or ascertainable standard, exception, 122.4.2
  generally, 122.1, 122.4.1
  gross estate inclusion and, 122.4.1
  manner or time of enjoyment exception, 122.4.1

parallelism rationale, 122.4.1
surrender of, 122.4.1
powers of appointment. *See*: Powers of appointment
property. *See*: Property, gift
reorganization diminishing stock value as, 121.2
revocable
  bank account trusts, 122.3.4
  further action by transferor, transfers dependent on, 122.3.5
  generally, 122.1, 122.3.1
  gifts causa mortis, 122.3.1
  interim distributions, 122.3.1
  joint bank accounts, 122.3.2
  joint tenancies, 122.3.3
  life insurance, 122.3.6
  partially, 122.3.1
  tax liability, 122.3.1
  Totten trusts, 122.3.4
  trusts, 122.3.1
statute of limitations on debt enforcement, lapse of, 121.2
tax liens, 137.6.3
third-party powers
  alteration or amendment, powers of, 122.5
  complete power of third party, 122.5
  discretional trusts, 122.5
  fixed or ascertainable standard, 122.5
  joint powers vs., 122.5
  removal power reserved by donor, 122.5
  revocation, powers of, 122.5

Transfers subject to power to revoke, alter, amend, or terminate transferee's enjoyment
"alter," defined, 126.5.2
"amend," defined, 126.5.2
amounts includable, 126.5.1, 126.5.2
changes in transferee's enjoyment, 126.5.1, 126.5.2
contingency, powers dependent on, 126.5.4
custodianships for minors, 126.5.1
fiduciary powers, 126.5.1, 126.5.2
  judicial supervision, 126.5.3
generally, 126.2, 126.3.3, 126.5.1
gross estate, generally, 126.5.1
history, 126.2, 126.5.1
joint powers, 126.5.5

Transfers subject to power to revoke, alter, amend, *(cont'd)*
joint powers *(cont'd)*
termination of trust by unanimous consent, 126.5.5
judicially enforceable external standards, 126.5.3
discretionary powers, 126.5.3
external standard doctrine, 126.5.3
fiduciary powers, 126.5.3
untrammeled power vs. enforceable right of enjoyment, 126.5.3
lapse of time, powers dependent on, 126.5.4
life insurance, 127.6
nonbeneficial powers, 126.5.1, 126.5.2
notice, powers dependent on, 126.5.4
pre-1937 transfers, 126.5.6
releases within three years of death, 126.3.5, 126.5.7
revocable trusts, 126.5.1
"revoke," defined, 126.5.2
scope of "alter, amend, revoke, or terminate," 126.5.2
definitions, 126.5.2
slight or trivial changes, 126.5.2
sources of power, 126.5.1
state law, effect of, 126.5.1
statutory provisions, 126.1, 126.2
substantial vs. insubstantial powers, 126.5.1, 126.5.2
tainted powers, 126.3.5
decedent authority to exercise, 126.5.4
release within three years of death, 126.3.5, 126.5.7
"terminate," defined, 126.5.2
termination of trust, 126.5.5
third party powers
agency, 126.5.5
third-party powers, 126.5.5
transfers covered, types, 126.5.1
trustee removal, 126.5.5
trustee-shopping, 126.5.5
unexercised powers, 126.5.1

Transfers subject to retained reversionary interests
amounts includable in gross estate, 126.7.1, 126.7.5
generally, 126.2, 126.7.1
gross estate, generally, 126.2, 126.7.1, 126.7.5

history, 126.2, 126.7.1
judicial and administrative rulings, 126.7.1
pre-1950 transfers, 126.7.1
life insurance, 127.6
pre-1950 transfers, 126.7.7
release of reversionary interest, 126.7.6
within three years of death, 126.7.6
reversionary interest, 126.7.3
defined, 126.7.3
discretionary trustee powers, 126.7.3
nontechnical meaning, 126.7.3
operation by law, arising by, 126.7.3
release of, 126.7.6
valuation of, 126.7.4
statutory provisions, 126.1, 126.2
survivorship condition, 126.7.2
alternative events, 126.7.2
implied condition, 126.7.2
transition rules, 126.7.1
valuation of reversionary interests, 126.7.4
actuarial computations, 126.7.4
beneficial vs. nonbeneficial interests, 126.7.4
5 percent rule, 126.7.4
life expectancies, based on, 126.7.4

Transfers subject to retained right to receive income or designate income beneficiary
alimony trusts, 126.6.2
annuities, 126.6.2
community income from separate property, 126.6.2
contingent rights, 126.6.4
controlled corporation, retained right to vote stock of, 126.6.5
custodianships for minors, 126.6.2
decedent's debts, payment of, 126.6.2
discretion vs. external standards, 126.6.4
dual vs. sole jurisdiction, 126.6.7
generally, 126.1, 126.2, 126.6.1
gross estate, generally, 126.1, 126.6.1
installment sales, 126.6.2
life insurance, 127.6
life or equivalent period, retention for, 126.6.6
minors, gifts to, 126.6.2
pre-1933 transfers, 126.6.8
reclassified transactions, 126.6.2
retained life estate, 126.6.1, 126.6.2

INDEX

retention of rights, 126.6.2
  informal vs. formal arrangements,
    126.6.2
  residence, transfer of, 126.6.2
  right to designate income beneficiary,
    126.6.3
  broad vs. narrow powers, 126.6.3
  discretionary powers, 126.6.4
  external standards, 126.6.4
  release during life of, 126.6.9
  right to receive income, 126.6.1, 126.6.2
  release during life of, 126.6.9
  right to vote stock of controlled
    corporation, 126.6.5
  sole vs. dual jurisdiction, 126.6.7
  statutory provisions, 126.1, 126.2, 126.6.1
    overlap between Code Sections 2036
      and 2038, 126.6.7
  support of dependents, 126.6.2
  time periods, 126.6.1, 126.6.2, 126.6.6
    life, 126.6.6
    life minus, 126.6.6
    life plus, 126.6.6
    prospective vs. retrospective points of
      view, 126.6.6
  underlying property, value of, 126.6.1

Treaties. *See*: Tax treaties

Trustees
  lifetime transfers subject to retained
    power over transferee enjoyment,
    126.5.5
  statutory trusts for minors, 124.4.2

Trusts
  See also: Charitable trusts; Demand
    trusts; Grantor trusts; Revocable
    trusts
  annual per-donee exclusion, 124.2
  bank account, 122.3.4
  charitable bequests, qualified
    beneficiaries of, 130.2
  estate freezes, 136.4
    See also: Estate freezes—trust,
      transfers in
  estate trusts, 129.4.1, 129.4.7
  generation-skipping transfers, 120.2.3,
    133.1, 133.2.12
  trust as skip person, 132.2.4
  gifts through, making of, 121.1
  gift tax liability, 121.1
  life insurance incidents of ownership,
    127.4.8

  marital deduction. *See*: Life estates with
    power of appointment in surviving
    spouse; Marital deduction trusts
  minors, statutory trusts for, 124.4.2
  nonresident aliens, beneficial interests
    of, 134.2.3
  personal residence trusts, estate freeze
    rules for, 135.4.6
  qualified personal residence trust
    (QPRT), 135.4.6
  special use election, 135.6.8
  spendthrift, 122.5, 124.3.1, 124.3.2
  statutory trusts for minors, 124.4.2
  Totten trusts, 122.3.4
  transfers to
    estate freeze rules for, 136.4
    incomplete transfers, 136.4.5

U

Uncompensated services
  gift property, 121.3.6

Underpayment of tax
  valuation misstatement, penalty for,
    135.5.3]

Understatement of tax
  estate tax, accuracy-related penalty on
    substantial valuation
    understatement, 137.9
  gift tax, accuracy-related penalty on
    substantial valuation
    understatement, 137.9

Unified credit
  estate tax computation, 132.3
  expatriates, tax-motivated, 134.4
  generally, 120.1.1, 126.3.6, 126.4.1
  gift tax computation, 132.2.1, 132.2.2
  marital deduction, 129.1, 129.6.2
  nonresident aliens, 134.2.2, 134.2.5
  phase-out of, 132.1
  split-gift elections, 123.5.1
  survivorship or common disaster
    provision, effect of, 129.4.2
  U.S. possessions, 134.3

Unified wealth transfer tax system
  credits for state and foreign death taxes,
    132.1
  defined, 132.1
  double inclusion of transfers, 132.1
  generally, 120.1.1, 122.4.1, 126.3.6,
    126.4.1, 132.1

[References are to paragraphs (¶).]

Unified wealth transfer tax system *(cont'd)*
gift tax exclusion, 132.1
history, 120.1.1, 126.4.1, 132.1
nonresident aliens, 134.2.2, 134.2.5
phase-out of lower marginal rates and
    unified credit, 132.1
split-gift election, 132.1
tax-inclusive vs. tax-exclusive, 132.1

Uniform Gifts to Minors Act
annual per-donee exclusion, 124.4.3
generation-skipping transfers, 133.2.12
powers of appointment, 128.2.1
retained life estates, 126.6.2

Uniform Partnership Act, 125.8, 135.2.3

Unincorporated business interests
valuation, 135.4.4

United States Constitution. *See:*
    Constitutional issues

United States possessions
estate tax, 134.1, 134.3
generation-skipping transfer (GST) tax,
    134.1, 134.3
gift tax, 134.1, 134.3
U.S. citizens resident in, taxation of,
    134.1, 134.3

United States savings bonds
valuation, 135.4.6

Unitrust interests
estate freeze rules for qualified interests,
    136.4.3

Unitrusts, charitable, 130.5.1, 130.5.2,
    133.2.8
defined, 130.5.2
estate freeze valuation rules, 136.4.7
generation-skipping transfers, 133.2.8

V

Valuation
See also: Fair market value
actuarial tables, 135.4.10, 135.7.4
annuity contracts, 126.8.1, 126.8.3,
    135.4.9, 135.4.10
antiques, 135.4.8
appraisers, role of, 135.5.1
art works
    blockage discount, 135.3.3
    estate freezes, 136.1
    generally, 135.4.8
    gross estate inclusion purposes, 125.7
barter equation method, 135.2.5

basic techniques, 135.2
burden of proof, 135.1.1
business assets, 135.4.5
    intangible, 135.4.5
    tangible, 135.4.5
buy-sell agreements, effect of, 135.3.10
capitalization of income method, 135.2.3
    capitalization (discount) rate, 135.2.3
    estimated future earnings, 135.2.3
    interest rate on bank loans, 135.2.3
    limitations on use of, 135.2.3
    real property, 135.4.1
    salvage value, 135.2.3
charitable bequest deduction, 130.5.3,
    130.5.6, 135.1.2, 135.4.10
charitable contributions, 135.1.2
comparable sales method, 135.2.2
    closely held corporation stock, 135.2.2
    real property, 135.2.2, 135.4.1
concept of value, 135.1.1
contracts
    employment, 135.4.5
    noncompetition, 135.4.5
control premiums and minority
    discounts, 135.3.4
    aggregation, control by, 135.3.4
    amount of premium or discount,
        135.3.4
    bargaining premium, 135.3.4
    computation, 135.3.4
    disaggregation, decontrol by, 135.3.4
    disappearing values, 135.3.4
    property other than voting stock,
        135.3.4
    self-dealing, 135.3.4
    unrecognized values, 135.3.4
    voting control, 135.3.4
copyrights, 135.4.5
court proceedings involving, 135.5.2
covenants not to compete, 135.4.5
date. *See*: Valuation date
debt instruments
    bonds, 135.4.2, 135.4.6, 137.4.2
    flower bonds, 135.4.6
    generally, 135.4.6
    notes, 135.4.6
    not traded in securities markets,
        135.4.6
    traded in securities markets, 135.4.2
    U.S. Treasury obligations, 135.4.6
defined, 135.1.1
discounts and premiums, 135.3

INDEX

[References are to paragraphs (¶).]

blockage, 135.3.3
buy-sell agreements, 135.3.10
control premiums, 135.3.4
encumbrances, 135.3.9
generally, 135.3.1
governmental restrictions, 135.3.7
lack of diversification, 135.3.6
lack of marketability, 135.3.2
loss of key person, 135.3.5
minority discounts, 135.3.4
mortgages, 135.3.9
options, 135.3.10
private restrictions, 135.3.9
taxes, consideration of, 135.3.8
"willing-buyer, willing-seller" standard,
    modifications to, 135.3.1
employment contracts, 135.4.5
errors in valuation, penalty for, 135.5.3,
    137.9
estate freezes
See also: Estate freezes
buy-sell agreements, 135.3.10, 136.3.3
corporations, interests in, 136.2
generally, 136.1
lapsing rights, 136.3
lookback rule, 136.2.7, 136.2.9
options, 135.3.10, 136.3.3
partnerships, interests in, 136.2
qualified payments, corporate and
    partnership interests and, 136.2.1,
    136.2.4–136.2.7
restrictions, 136.3
statutes of limitations, 136.2.11,
    136.4.8
trust, transfers in, 136.4
estate tax
alternate valuation date, 135.7
business real property, special use
    valuation, 135.6
claims against estate, 131.4.2
farms, special use valuation, 135.6
generally, 135.1.1
gifts made in contemplation of death,
    126.4.4
joint interests, 125.11.1, 125.11.4
property owned by decedent at death,
    125.1, 125.5, 125.7
transferred property, 132.6.3
expert witnesses, role of, 135.5.1
films, 135.4.8
franchises, 135.4.5
generally, 135.1.1

generation-skipping transfer (GST) tax
    applicable rate, computation of,
        133.3.4
gift tax, 121.3.2, 121.3.3, 123.5.1, 123.6.2,
    135.1.1
    errors in valuation, 132.2.2
going concern value, 135.4.5
goodwill, 125.7, 135.4.4, 135.4.5
governing standard, 135.1.2
    arm's length bargaining, 135.1.2,
        135.2.1
    cash sale value, 135.1.2
    fair market value, defined, 135.1.2
    "fair value" vs. "fair market value,"
        135.1.2
    forced sales, 135.1.2
    freedom from compulsion, 135.1.2
    hindsight, 135.1.2
    hypothetical parties, 135.1.2
    knowledge of facts, 135.1.2
    nature of market, 135.1.2
    relevant facts, consideration of, 135.1.2
    retail price principle, 135.1.2
    selling expenses, 135.1.2
    "willing buyer, willing seller" formula,
        135.1.2
    willing parties, 135.1.2
heirlooms, 135.1.2
historical cost, 135.2.1
income tax purposes, generally, 135.1.1
intangible assets, 135.4.5
    formula method, 135.4.5
    residual method, 135.4.5
inventories, 135.4.5
life estates, 135.1.2, 135.4.10
life insurance, 127.7, 135.4.9
    incidents of ownership, 127.4.8
    reversionary interests, 127.4.4
literary works, 135.4.8
litigation, role of, 135.5.1, 135.5.2
manuscripts, 135.4.8
marital deduction, 129.1, 129.5
    See also: Marital deduction—valuation
market data method, 135.2.2
memorabilia, 135.4.8
motion pictures, 135.4.8
music manuscripts, 135.4.8
mutual funds, 135.4.2
noncompetition contracts, 135.4.5
options, 135.3.10, 135.4.7
patents, 135.4.5
penalty for errors in, 135.5.3, 137.9

Valuation *(cont'd)*
procedural matters, 135.5
property, specific types, 135.4
real property. *See*: Real property
  valuation
remainder interests, 135.1.2, 135.4.10
replacement or reproduction cost,
  135.2.4
retained reversionary interests, 126.7.4
salvage value, 135.2.3
securities
  See also: Stock—valuation
  generally, 135.1.2, 135.2.2, 135.3
  over-the-counter market, 135.4.2
  stock exchange trading, 135.4.2
special use. *See*: Real property valuation
  —special use election
specific types of property, 135.4
split-gift elections, 123.5.1
split interests in property, 135.4.10
  actual life expectancy, 135.4.10
  events other than death, probability of,
    135.4.10
  interest factor, 135.4.10
  marketability, 135.4.10
stock
  See also: Securities—valuation; Stock
    —valuation
  closely held corporations, 135.4.3
  generally, 135.1.2, 135.2.2, 135.3
survivorship annuities, 126.8.3
Tax Court, role of, 135.5.2
techniques, generally, 135.2
trademarks and trade names, 135.4.5
trade secrets, 135.4.5
trial court, role of, 135.5.2
unincorporated business interests,
  135.4.4
"willing buyer, willing seller" standard,
  135.1.2
  modifications to, 135.3.1
witnesses, expert, 135.5.1
zoned property, 135.3.7

Valuation date
alternate date for estate tax purposes,
  135.7
  binding contract for sale of property,
    135.7.3
  changes in value due to time lapse,
    135.7.4
  charitable deduction, 135.7.5
  collateral effects of election, 135.7.5
  consistent value, 135.7.5
  disposition of property within six
    months of death, 135.7.3
  double deductions, denial of, 135.7.5
  election procedures, 135.7.6
  estate tax return, filing on, 135.7.6
  excluded property, 135.7.2
  generally, 135.7.1
  included property, 135.7.2
  marital deduction, 135.7.5
  mere lapse of time, changes in value
    due to, 135.7.4
date of death, 120.3, 125.7, 125.11.3,
  129.5.1, 131.4.2, 135.7, 137.3
filing requirement, 137.3
mutual funds, 135.4.2
options, 135.4.7
securities, 135.4.2
transactions on date, 135.2.1
transactions prior to date, 135.2.1

Veterans' administration
funeral expense payments by, effect on
  deduction of, 131.2

Veterans' organizations
charitable bequests, qualified
  beneficiaries of, 130.2
nonresident aliens, contributions by,
  134.2.4
contributions to, gift tax deductions for,
  121.8

Voting rights
defined, 136.3.2
estate freeze valuation, 136.1, 136.2.2
lapse of rights, 136.3.1, 136.3.2

W

War Revenue Act of 1898, 120.1.2

Wealth, transfer of
See also: Estate freezes; Estate planning;
  Estates, decedents'; Estate tax;
  Generation-skipping transfer (GST)
  tax; Generation-skipping transfers;
  Generation-skipping trusts; Gifts
  made within three years of death;
  Gift tax; Income in respect of
  decedents (IRD); Life insurance,
  gross estate inclusion; Powers of
  appointment; Property owned by
  decedent at death, gross estate

INDEX

[References are to paragraphs (¶).]

inclusion; Transfers, gift; Transfers subject to power to revoke, alter, amend, or terminate transferee's enjoyment; Transfers subject to retained reversionary interests; Transfers subject to retained right to receive income or designate income beneficiary

Direct Tax Clause of Constitution, 120.1.2

estate tax, generally, 120.1.1, 120.1.2, 120.2.2

generation-skipping transfer tax, generally, 120.1.1, 120.2.3

gift tax, generally, 120.1.1, 120.2.1

state authority to regulate transfers at death, 120.1.2

taxation, generally, 120.1
  basic structure of federal taxes, 120.2
  constitutionality, 120.1.2
  grandparent rules adopted to regulate, 120.1.2
  history, 120.1.1

unified system of taxation, 120.1.1

unified wealth transfer tax system, 132.1

Widow's allowance
claims against estate, nondeductibility as, 131.4.1
terminable interests, 129.3.3

Widow's election wills, 126.3.4

Will contests
charitable bequests, settlements involving, 130.3.2
legal expenses, 131.3.2
marital deduction
  property passing from decedent, 129.2.3
  settlements, 129.2.3

Wills
See also: Will contests; Wills, elections against

apportionment of estate tax, provisions affecting, 137.8

equalization provisions, marital deduction and, 129.6.3

joint and mutual, terminable interests, 129.3.3

Wills, elections against
charitable bequests, 130.3.2
gross estate, 125.5, 125.9, 126.3.4
marital deduction
  acceptance, 129.3.3
  apportionment of estate tax, 129.5.2
  disqualified interests under will vs., 129.2.3, 129.3.3
  generally, 129.2.3
  postmortem elections, 129.3.3
  state law, 129.2.3
taxable estate, 125.9
terminable interests, 129.3.3

Witnesses
valuation issues, 135.5.1

Workers' compensation
occupational disease, awards for death from, 125.6

Works of art. *See*: Art, works of

Wrongful death or injury award
gross estate, 125.6, 127.2
life insurance payments distinguished, 127.2
powers of appointment, 125.6, 128.2.1
state statute based on England's Lord Campbell's Act, 125.6
survival statutes, 125.6

Z

Zero-tax bequests, 129.6.2

Zoned property
valuation, 135.3.7